Our Journey Through the Broken Path

Finding Hope Amidst Adversity

APRIL KEY

OUR JOURNEY THROUGH THE BROKEN PATH:
Finding Hope Amidst Adversity

ISBN:
Hardbound - 979-8-9915546-6-4
Softbound/Paperback - 979-8-9915546-9-5
MOBI/KINDLE - 979-8-9915546-8-8
Audiobook - 979-8-9915546-7-1

Writer
April Key

Editor and Layout Artist
Issabel Miraflor

Book Cover Design
Mary Bern Cabo

Life is a journey, full of lessons.
Life is a challenge, full of mystery.
But through our journey, we learned our lessons.
We learned that challenges make us stronger.

- April Key

AUTHOR'S NOTE

We all go through a broken path at some point in our lives. The journey can be bumpy and hard to traverse, especially if it starts at a very young age. For me and my sister, going through these broken paths in our journey made us creative, brave, confident, and resilient in facing all the adversities that we face in our lives. These mold us into who we choose to become as human beings.

Navigating this challenging path is not a barrier to a successful life; it should inspire us to work hard and make righteous choices throughout our journey.

The objective of this book is to inspire the youth to persistently forge ahead, regardless of the difficulties they may encounter in life.

MAIN CHARACTERS

April - the author and the older daughter

Juhan - the intelligent younger sister

Monica - the brave mother of the two girls

Dan - the father of the two girls

Cortes and Priego Families
Aureo Priego - their maternal grandfather on their mother's side
Nimrod - the youngest son of Monica
Justin - the paternal grandfather of the two girls
Nancy - their paternal grandmother
Nicole - Juhan's favorite aunt
Lucy - the fourth older sister of their father, the girls' aunt
Riley - their aunt and another older sister of their father
Genevie - their cousin and the oldest daughter of Riley
Denise - the youngest daughter of Riley
Marydel - the older sister of their father
Eden - their father's sister and youngest daughter in the family

Relatives
Tinang - the sister of their grandfather Justin
Metring - the brother of their grandfather, who took them in
Ceiling - the kind wife of Metring
Sandra - a cousin of their father
Emma - another cousin of their father
Lily - another cousin of their father
Netnet - the cousin of their father, who took them in
Eddie - their first cousin on their father's side

Aurea - their cousin on the Priego side

Marybeth - the daughter of their cousin on the Priego side

Nanay Dina and Tatay Daniel - the kind married couple from Damulog, Bukidnon, whom their mother met at a public market in Lutopan, and let them live with them together with their seven children

Letecia - their cousin on the Priego side, the wife of George, who stood as their guardian and took care of their newborn brother

George - the kind husband of their cousin Tata

Other Characters

Nathan - the father of April's two wonderful kids

Lola Penny - the old lady in Lutopan who helped Monica

Press - an old lady who helped and sheltered April's family

Chloe - the niece of Lola Press who lived in the compound

Samantha - a neighbor friend who was like a big sister to them

Tatay Demy and Nanay Belen - the owners of the rental place they rented in Naga

Lola Tonya and family - the owner of the house they used to live in Naga

Tita Thalia and Nathalie - the owner of the house they rented in Naga and who became their family not by blood but by heart

Tita Shayne - Monica's co-worker and the owner of the house they rented in Banawa

Ate June - the young high school girl who helped April and Juhan; their facilitator in YFC

Ate Jing-Jing and Kuya Jong-Jong - the brother and sister they met and became their older siblings or relatives

Jez - a kind friend who helped April in any way she could

Elien - April's college friend with whom they went to work at the airport

Haze - April's closest friend who stayed with them for a while after her father's death

Jen - April's closest friend whom she met after she borrowed money from her to buy a composition book

Miss Christine - Juhan's co-worker who became close to the two sisters

Director Esperanza - the director at DFA

Miss Arlene - the 3rd ranking officer in DFA and the head of the Finance Department

Miss Del - supervisor of April in a sales company

Miss Lenny - April's co-worker who had a similar body figure as hers

Tatay Felimon - Juhan's co-worker who became close to the two sisters

Chris - the father of Nimrod, the two sisters' younger brother

Brennan - April's partner for Mr. Valentines

Leo - April's classmate who consistently took the lead in causing disruptive incidents at their school

Faye - April's classmate in 5th grade who was a bully

Miss Jenny - April's teacher-adviser in 5th grade

Xhyrstnn, Josh, Rex, and Neslie - April's college classmates who were in her thesis writing group

SETTINGS IN THE STORY

Tagasa Beach - the birthplace of their father and where the story originated

Tabogon - the main town and the youngest municipality in Cebu Province

Guiwanon Spring - a natural spring where the locals enjoy swimming and washing their clothes

Toledo - where their parents used to live and where their father used to work

Cagayan De Oro - where they moved and lived with their cousin and family

Titay's - a popular delicacy store in Cebu and their favorite stop every time they travel to their father's place

Asturias - where they used to live with their mother and experienced the civil war during President Aquino's term

Balamban - the next town where the older sister was hospitalized

Cebu - one of the provinces in the Philippines

Cebu City - called the "Queen City of the South" and is the second largest city in the Philippines

Naga - a town in Cebu where they lived after they arrived in Mindanao; this was where they both continued their elementary schooling and attended high school

USJR - where April graduated with her Bachelor of Science in Hospitality and Tourism Management

FOREWORD

Childhood trauma can have a profound impact on a person's life, shaping their future and influencing their decisions. Trauma can be experienced through physical, sexual, emotional, or spiritual abuse. Neglect, natural disasters, accidents, injury, and war can also cause traumatic experiences. In this book, we follow the journey of two sisters who experienced childhood trauma but found hope and healing through the kindness of people who crossed their paths and through their faith in God.

Through their experiences, you will see how the power of love, support, and faith helped these sisters to stick together and guide each other to safety. With unstable housing and always moving out of fear, these sisters had to always keep their guard up. Two sisters, and two children, who could not count on anyone but themselves and the kindness of those who crossed their paths. You will see how these sisters have found strength, resilience, and hope in the face of adversity and how they kept themselves as safe as they could.

This book is a testament to the human spirit and the power of kindness, love, and faith in God. The resilience of these two sisters and the power they hold to create their future despite the way they grew up can serve as a guide for those who are struggling with the effects of childhood trauma, and a source of inspiration for those who are looking to help others in their healing journey. It includes many therapeutic approaches, journal prompts, and tools that can be put into practice as a guide to healing. Above all, it is a reminder that no matter what challenges we face in life, we can always find hope and healing through the love of others and our faith in God.

As a Licensed Professional Counselor, I think this book can provide great insight into ways and tools of healing and therapy approaches. I have experienced childhood trauma myself. Every day is a day towards healing the wounds of my past.

And if not for those kind souls who crossed my path, there is no doubt my life would be different. Growing and healing is a daily journey that is strengthened through my awareness of my feelings in my body, and then being able to regulate them.

I hope that this book will serve as a source of encouragement and inspiration for anyone who has experienced childhood trauma or who knows someone who has. May it remind us that no matter how dark our circumstances may seem, there is always hope for a brighter future. May it encourage us to be positive people in the lives of those around us - offering love, support, and hope to those who need it most.

- Tayla Gatson, LPC

PREFACE

This book is written with the belief that the author's life journey can instill hope in children, particularly those who are facing struggles and still navigating their path to self-discovery.

As the two sisters reflect on their challenging years, they attribute their resilience to the kind and positive adults they encountered along the way. These individuals gave them hope, guided their focus, and maintained a positive outlook on life.

The narrative sheds light on some of the sister's life struggles, showcasing instances where others positively influenced their journey. These encounters served as anchors, keeping the sisters on track and contributing to their overall well-being.

 The primary aim is to inspire individuals in their generation to emulate the positive qualities of the supportive adults they encountered amid their struggles, thereby enriching their life journeys.

Moreover, the book serves as a platform to raise awareness and educate readers about mental health. It emphasizes how adult behavior can significantly impact young children, providing insights into appropriate reactions in challenging situations. The ultimate goal is to minimize the adverse effects on children's mental health.

TABLE OF CONTENTS

INTRODUCTION

April and Juhan are the daughters of the only son of a former Barangay Captain and a Tagasa-based businessman. Their father came from a family of seven siblings and used to be a College Varsity Basketball player and an Electrical Engineer. Unfortunately, he faced deteriorating mental health triggered by substance abuse after the birth of his children.

Their mother, originally from another part of the country, crossed paths with their father during her visit to his town for the town fiesta celebration. Armed with a Bachelor of Science in Agriculture, she pursued a career as an Agriculturist in Cebu.

At an early age, the two sisters found themselves escaping their grandparent's residence with their mother, marking a pivotal moment that altered the course of their lives. Constantly relocating to ensure safety from their troubled father, they navigated a transient existence during their formative years due to the nature of their mother's work. They forged new connections in each new locale, all while being raised by a single parent.

Their circumstances seemed poised for improvement when their mother secured a stable job in her field at the city office. However, fate took an unexpected turn when their mother became pregnant by a co-worker. The ensuing journey led them to their mother's family in a distant part of the country, far from their paternal relatives. They all hoped life would be easier there, only to find that reality is more cruel than they anticipated.

Despite the myriad challenges they faced, the siblings exhibited resilience, both successfully earning degrees. The elder daughter graduated with a Bachelor of Science in Hospitality and Tourism Management, while the younger one, attained honors, and obtained a Bachelor of Science in Secondary Education majoring in Physics and Chemistry. Both daughters are now living in the United States and have two children, each of their own.

Family is about caring, loving, supporting one another, and being there for each other regardless of blood relations.

April Key

Close family ties are one of the family traditions in the Philippines.

CHAPTER 1

A Dream

Living in our grandparent's house with Papa at a young age meant living abundantly. There were no worries about having food on our table, as there were plenty of vegetables around the house and in the farmland. If we wanted meat, it was easily accessible in the backyard, including chicken and turkey. The seashore was within walking distance across the street, and our grandfather frequently went fishing there every night with the local fishermen.

I formed a close friendship with a girl who lived across the street from the seashore. Tragically, we received news one day that she had drowned and was found dead on the spot where we used to play. The community, including myself, was deeply saddened by the news. I pleaded with my grandmother to allow me to get closer to her, but due to the cramped space in their small bahay-kubo, I was only permitted to observe from their balcony. Tearfully, I watched as everyone, especially her parents, embraced her.

In the province and during those times, quick burials were customary. Unfortunately, due to my illness, my grandmother did not permit me to accompany them. It was a superstitious belief that being near a deceased body could worsen my sickness. Though I didn't believe in such superstitions, my prolonged illness remained, leading to a journey with my grandmother to another town to seek a traditional medicine cure, which proved ineffective.

My bond with my grandmother was strong, and I accompanied her wherever she went. I learned both the bad and the good at a young age. She smokes tobacco leaves and drinks lambanog (a Filipino alcoholic drink made from coconut), which I learned to drink with her at the age of three! We often returned home late at night, with me tightly hugging her as she held me.

My grandmother's specialty was cooking grated cassava roots, known as "puto balanghoy" in Filipino, one of my favorite snacks. One day, she cooked it, and I excitedly shared it with my father. To my surprise, he became angry, leading to a chaotic evening. Misunderstandings arose. My aunt Nicole, in frustration, placed me in a sack of rice near a lamp's smoke, wrongly assuming I had spoken ill of them to my father.

For the first time, Mama managed to move us out of our grandparent's house when I was three and my sister was two years old. We lived with an old lady, Lola Penny, near Papa's workplace. Lola Penny graciously allowed us to stay in her small house, which also served as a sari-sari store.

While living with Lola Penny, Mama started a pedicure and manicure business in the area. She went from house to house, trying to make ends meet and saving money to return to her hometown. One night, I had a distressing dream about Papa committing suicide. Distraught, I convinced Mama and my sister to dress up and visit Papa, preventing a potential tragedy.

After a three-hour journey, we found a crowd in our grandparent's backyard pleading with Papa not to commit suicide. Running towards them, I begged him to reconsider, and thankfully, he listened. We stayed with Papa for a while before returning to Lutopan, where Mama found a friend from her hometown. Living with them, we were treated kindly, as if we were part of their family.

During Mama's busy schedule offering pedicures and manicures, my sister and I stayed with Nanay Dina. She occasionally took us to the church for "Flores de Mayo" and waited for Tatay Daniel to finish work. It was a joyous time, especially when Mama had time to sing for us. The first song she taught us was "Greatest Love of All," creating cherished memories that helped us navigate our journey.

Greatest Love of All

by Whitney Houston

I believe the children are our future
Teach them well and let them lead the way
Show them all the beauty they possess inside
Give them a sense of pride to make it easier.
Let the children's laughter remind us how we used to be

People need someone to look up to
I never found anyone who fulfills my needs
A lonely place to be
And so I learned to depend on me

I decided long ago.
Never to walk in anyone's shadows
If I fail if I succeed.
At least I'll live as I believe
No matter what they take from me
They can't take away my dignity.

Because the greatest love of all
Is happening to me
I found the greatest love of all inside of me
The greatest love of all, it's easy to achieve
Learning to love yourself
Is the greatest love of all

I believe the children are our future
Teach them well and let them lead the way
Show them all the beauty they possess inside
Give them a sense of pride to make it easier
Let the children's laughter remind us how we used to be

I decided long ago
Never to walk in anyone's shadows
If I fail, if I succeed
At least I'll live as I believe
No matter what they take from me
They can't take away my dignity

Because the greatest love of all
Is happening to me
I found the greatest love of all inside of me

The greatest love of all
It's easy to achieve
Learning to love yourself
Is the greatest love of all

And if, by chance, that special place
What you've been dreaming of
Leads you to a lonely place
Find your strength in love

REFLECTION

Reflecting on the first chapter and the early years of my childhood, I now understand why I am prone to illness and have a weak immune system. It's remarkable how I managed to endure such pain at such a tender age, but I console myself, saying, "You made it!"

Imparting a powerful song to our children at a young age, one that can resonate throughout their lives is among the best things a parent or guardian can do. The song Mama taught us when we were three and two years old remains embedded in our hearts and its lyrics are firmly rooted in our minds.

Growing up in chaos and facing a traumatic and abusive environment is disheartening, especially for a child. I wouldn't wish such an experience on any child. It emphasizes the importance of adults treating their kids with kindness and respect from an early stage in their lives. Despite the prevailing notion that children know nothing, many survivors who share similar journeys with us have shown a keen awareness of their surroundings and the actions of the adults in their lives. While we may be confused and seeking answers, the impact of those tragic events will forever linger.

I am grateful for the gift that God has bestowed upon me and for the wisdom to heed and follow the revealed truths. I consider them the greatest blessings in my life.

In 1 Peter 4:10, we are reminded to use our gifts to serve others as faithful stewards of God's grace, emphasizing that these gifts are not given for our sole benefit.

PSYCHOLOGICAL ANALYSIS

"I formed a close friendship with a girl who lived across the street near the seashore. Tragically, we received news one day that she had drowned and was found dead in the spot where we used to play. The community, including myself, was deeply saddened by the news. I pleaded with my grandmother to allow me to get closer to her, but due to the cramped space in their small bahay-kubo, I was only permitted to observe from their balcony. Tearfully, I watched as everyone, especially her parents, embraced her."

The psychological process that individuals undergo when they experience the loss of someone or something is known as grief. Death, being an inevitable aspect of human existence, proves challenging to assimilate when a loved one departs.

Children may experience grief differently from adults, as their understanding of death varies depending on their age. The assimilation of the death process is often complex, not only because the person is no longer present but also due to the lack of societal emphasis on comprehending death as a natural human process.

In an attempt to shield children from the pain of loss, parents or other adults may employ disenfranchised grief, disguising their grief. However, this approach is misguided, as children can intuitively recognize the absence of someone they care for.

When faced with loss, it becomes crucial to explain the situation to the child, particularly if they exhibit signs such as looking for what was lost, crying, or displaying tantrums.

Providing children with a foundational understanding of death from an early age increases the likelihood that they will navigate future losses more adeptly. Without this foundation, a child may develop prolonged grief disorder, characterized by difficulty moving forward and accepting the loss, impacting their daily life. Hillary I. Lebow, as mentioned on psychcentral.com, refers to this condition as complicated grief.

Other causes of grief

- losing a pet
- losing someone from violent situations, sudden deaths, accidents, suicide, or miscarriage
- changing schools
- transferring or moving to a different place
- separation or divorce
- relationship breakups whether intimate or pure friendship

Children of varying ages have distinct levels of comprehension when it comes to grieving. Those under three years old may not fully grasp the concept of loss but can sense a change, particularly if it involves someone they care about. Children over five years old have better understanding and memory but may struggle to articulate their feelings about the loss. Teenagers, although more mature, present unique challenges for parents and adults as each child copes differently, influenced by factors like the relationship with the deceased.

Recognizing signs that a child is struggling with grief is essential. These signs include increased anxiety, unexplained anger, heightened neediness, nightmares or sleep disturbances, regression, withdrawal from previously enjoyed activities linked to the lost person, substance use, heightened isolation, appetite loss, prolonged depression, refusal to return to school, and even suicidal thoughts.

Adults in a child's life must be compassionate, understanding, and patient, providing a safe space for grieving. It is important to create an environment where children feel comfortable opening up when they are ready. With teenagers, it may take longer for them to express their grief, and adults need to be prepared and allow them the necessary time. Forcing them to discuss their feelings prematurely can be counterproductive.

How to assist young children and teens in coping with grief

- Facilitate playdates with their close friends and/or peers.
- Maintain their regular routines or establish new ones to provide comfort.
- In conversations (Joseph and Strain, 2003), parents and teachers should help introduce emotional vocabulary to children, emphasizing that various emotions are valid. It is crucial to teach them how to manage and express these emotions appropriately.
- Demonstrate and emphasize the importance of self-care to children, illustrating that it is acceptable to prioritize one's well-being and engage in activities that bring happiness despite the loss.
- If necessary, seek professional help and explain to the children the reasons behind seeking assistance, highlighting the potential benefits.
- Cognitive Behavioral Therapy (CBT) is an effective method for treating prolonged grief disorder; further details can be found in Chapter 4 of this book.

JOURNAL

- Write about the things you loved and enjoyed doing with the person you've lost.
- Write about the place, activities, and favorite hangouts from your previous residence or home.
- Share a personal experience of grief and outline what strategies helped you to overcome it.

As we fly high and reach our dreams remember those who help us climb the ladder.

April Key

The Philippine Eagle is a massive bird of prey that can carry humans. Due to native claims that it only ate monkeys, this raptor was only originally known by the name "Monkey-eating Eagle"

CHAPTER 2

Escape

One fine day, my younger sister and I were joyfully playing at my aunt Lucy's house—a typical day for children aged 3 and 4. We were running, chasing each other around the yard, and having fun with our cousins. Our play was interrupted when our aunt called us over to see our mother.

Mama continued staying at Aunt Lucy's house instead of our grandparents' house; my sister and I wondered why this was so. We had plans to inform Papa about Mama's presence, but whenever we tried, Mama would run or hide. Confused and curious, we persistently questioned Mama, and her response was always, "It can happen, and it will be hard."

One late afternoon, our plan to have Papa and Mama meet came to fruition. Mama, trying to avoid Papa's attention, walked ahead of us as we passed by the big house. However, my sister and I had devised a mischievous plan. Spotting Papa in the front yard, we called out happily, "Papa, Papa, come here! That's Mama! Get her!" Papa approached, patted Mama's shoulder, and despite her attempts to feign ignorance, hugged her tightly. Despite our initial excitement, Papa didn't allow us to return to Aunt Lucy's house and ushered us all inside.

We thought this marked the beginning of a happy family reunion. However, our joy was short-lived, as Mama's first night with us unfolded into another chapter of her sorrowful life. Every night, Mama endured pain, choking, and abuse from Papa. Though I couldn't physically intervene, I could hear her cries while lying in bed, feeling helpless.

Despite being a silent child, I grew more observant of my surroundings. I realized that as long as I or my sister stayed close to Mama, Papa wouldn't harm her. I decided not to play outside with cousins and friends, aiming to protect Mama. Meanwhile, my younger sister, unaware of the situation, continued playing freely.

Sometimes, I would join my sister early in the morning, along with my grandmother, as we waited for my grandfather and the other fishermen to arrive at the seashore and display the fish they had caught during the night. While waiting, we enjoyed chasing small crabs, attempting to catch them before they could retreat into their holes. Simultaneously, we played in the shallow water during low tide by stomping our feet. Growing up near the ocean, these activities became cherished memories.

My grandparent's house was a Spanish-style residence with exterior stairs leading to the second floor. This architectural detail sometimes made me fail to look after my mother.

There were moments when I caught Papa starting to harm Mama, prompting me to grab a broom and warn him not to mess with Mama. Surprisingly, my gigantic father always obeyed me and refrained from hurting Mama when I was around.

However, I couldn't bear to hear about Mama's nightly ordeals. I felt compelled to help her escape from my grandparents' house. Often, we were caught because my sister played near the ocean, making it easy for Papa to locate us. One time, I planned an escape during a barangay fiesta or town festival, hoping the crowd would notice and assist Mama. Unfortunately, Papa easily caught up with her, leading to another failed attempt.

He stands at a height of 5 feet and 11 inches and was once a basketball player. In contrast, my mother is only 4 feet and 11 inches tall—a significant difference! Papa grabbed Mama and carried her back into the house, while bystanders merely stared without offering assistance. On the other hand, I slowly ascended the stairs back to my grandparents' house, feeling saddened and confused as to why I was the sole individual recognizing the urgency for my mother to escape and seek help. It marked another unsuccessful attempt.

In a final attempt to escape, my sister and I found ourselves near a giant water tank at the back of my grandparents' house, wearing our favorite camouflage dresses and playing happily. We spotted Mama wearing my aunt's white dressy top with a blue flower print skirt, sprinting toward us. At that moment, I realized it was time to escape. Before Mama could utter the word "run," my sister and I had abandoned our play and followed her into the woods. Mama raced as fast as she could, and though my sister and I lagged, we still managed to keep track of her direction. Navigating through the woods was challenging due to twigs, tall weeds, and rocky terrain, especially for my sister, who was not accustomed to it. I waited for her, ensuring we held hands to run faster together. It took us 15 to 30 minutes.

Once in the woods, we discovered a small bamboo and nipa hut. An elderly couple invited us inside, revealing that Mama had arrived before us. Both my sister and I hurried to the Bahay Kubo. Upon opening the door, we found Mama sitting on the bamboo floor, her legs crossed with knees drawn to her chin and arms wrapped around her legs. She was shaking, and she looked scared, but also relieved to see that my sister and I had made it.

The elderly couple courageously assisted us in our escape. However, a few hours later, we heard Papa's voice, asking if they had noticed us. Through the bamboo floor, we could see his foot and the large bolo he held in his hands. Mama, unable to contain her fear, began sobbing loudly. I got my sister's attention, whispered instructions to her, and guided her on how to handle Mama while I played my part.

As Papa roamed around the bahay kubo, I followed him while staying inside and facing his direction. I prayed silently, "Mama Mary, please help us." Meanwhile, my sister placed her tiny hands over our mother's mouth, ensuring her cries were muffled, and directed Mama's movements as Papa moved.

I instructed my sister to position herself on the opposite side of Papa to ensure their safe exit if he attempted to break in. Fortunately, it didn't happen. We stayed in the Bahay Kubo for a total of seven days, with Papa stopping by occasionally but being polite and obedient to the elderly couple. He refrained from attempting to breach the small Kubo's window, answering our prayers. After a week, at dusk, we relocated to my aunt's nearby house, as it seemed Papa did not care to search in the area.

We lived there for a couple of months before Mama got pregnant after our 40-day stay with Papa. Due to her medical condition, Mama was forced to abort the baby. My mother, accompanied by two of my aunts, went away for a few days for this procedure. Upon their return, my sister Juhan and I observed the change in my mother's belly size and questioned why it was smaller than when they had left. She simply replied that the baby was no longer there.

Papa occasionally visited his sister's place. We always hid Mama whenever he was around, relieved when we successfully avoided detection. However, one day, we almost faced exposure when Mama was in an outdoor bathroom. If she tried to escape, there was no way she could make it. During this close call, my aunt confronted Papa, insisting that none of us, especially my mother, were inside or anywhere near her house. It took Papa some time to thoroughly search the premises. Following this incident, we concluded that it was unsafe for Mama to remain at my aunt's house, and a decision was made to leave as soon as possible.

The following day, we moved to Lola Tenang's house, the sister of my grandfather, who resided in my great-grandparents' house. I was grateful that she welcomed us to live with her. Mama secured a job at the municipality as an agriculturist, utilizing her bachelor's degree in agriculture. It brought me joy to see her restarting her career and earning a living to support herself, my sister, and me.

Lola Tenang proved to be a wonderful grandmother to my sister and me. Though strict, she remained calm and fair in her disciplinary actions. Occasionally, she would join us on the beach behind the house or accompany us to the farm, as they owned extensive farmlands in the vicinity. She appeared content with her single life, staying busy every day.

We relished playing with our second cousins near Lola Tenang's house and befriended three little girls our age, along with our cousins Kuya Eddie and his elder brother across the street.

One afternoon, after lunch, Lola Tenang asked Juhan and me to stay indoors while she went to the beach to wash pans and pots. However, we decided to play outside. Initially, we played tag, laughing and circling a tree. Eventually, my sister decided to climb the tree, becoming frustrated when she couldn't reach a particular branch. Foolishly, I offered to help her climb, but our victory was short-lived when she wanted to come down. Despite assuring her safety, the situation took a turn for the worse.

Being just a year older, an inch taller, and thinner than my sister, I missed catching her as she jumped, causing her forehead to collide with a large rock under the tree. Desperate to stop the bleeding, we attempted to address the situation. However, all our nice dresses lay scattered and stained in Lola Tenang's living room. With no dresses left for me to wear, I wiped the blood off my sister, fearing for her safety. Terrified of losing her, I called for Lola as blood continued to pour from the cut.

Lola Tenang promptly left her dishes on the seashore, rushing with me to assist my sister. Shocked at the sight of blood filling the entire living room, she quickly retrieved a chromoleana odorata leaf or siam weed, diced it, and applied it to my sister's forehead cut. While I sat anxiously on the stairs, Lola Tenang treated my sister, and thankfully, the bleeding finally stopped. I then helped her clean the living room, relieved that she did not scold me for helping my sister climb that tree.

Although I was relieved that my sister was safe, I couldn't shake off the sadness of losing all my nice dresses soaked in blood. However, Mama assured us that she would buy another set of dresses. Following this incident and with Lola Tenang's house being close to my grandparents' house, Mama decided to move into the town near the municipality.

REFLECTION

As John Maxwell aptly states, "Maturity is not about age but about a deeper understanding of a person." He illustrates this by sharing an example of a thirteen-year-old possessing wisdom and maturity surpassing that of a fifty-six-year-old. Reflecting on this aspect of our journey, I am thankful for God's gift of knowledge and wisdom. Both my sister and I understood the situation, responding appropriately to navigate the circumstances, while our mother, frozen with fear, grappled with indecision.

Even at the tender ages of three and four, I am amazed at how prayerful I was back then. It's remarkable for a young child to exhibit such strong faith in God during challenging circumstances. This chapter shows that nothing is impossible with God, as He never forsakes His children when they cling to Him. My intelligent sister, seemingly unaware of our parents' struggles and our mother's daily challenges, followed instructions diligently, playing a crucial role in our successful escape. Her persistence and ability to instruct and remind our mother not to cry were instrumental in ensuring our survival.

In moments of trauma and when children behave unexpectedly, maintaining a calm demeanor instead of resorting to shouting is crucial. Such calmness reassures children and fosters appreciation for the love and care provided by adults.

Lastly, seeking guidance from God is paramount, as He accompanies us every step of the way. He is a living God who loves all His children.

"The basic needs of our children are simple: a simple greeting and inquiry about their well-being, daily hugs and kisses, and the comfort of a safe home where they feel loved and valued. Often, adults tend to overcomplicate these basic needs."

- April Key

"I will not leave you as orphans; I will come to you."

- John 14:18

PSYCHOLOGICAL ANALYSIS

"We spotted Mama wearing my aunt's white dressy top with a
blue flower print skirt, sprinting toward us. At that moment, I realized
it was time to escape. Before Mama could utter the word
'RUN,' my sister and I had abandoned our play and followed her
into the woods."

Domestic violence encompasses various forms of abuse and mistreatment that occur in different settings. This can manifest physically, verbally, emotionally, psychologically, technologically, and financially. Studies indicate that women are more prone to experiencing such abuse, with factors like control, power dynamics, the nature of the bond with the abuser, and limited resources making it challenging for them to break free.

Not all victims of domestic violence can escape, but those who do often do so deliberately, seizing an opportune moment. Children raised in such environments may come to perceive these violent situations as normal, potentially perpetuating these patterns in their own lives over the years.

Domestic violence manifests through various signs, including:

- Blaming the other person when something goes wrong
- Using derogatory names when referring to the other person
- Exerting control over every aspect of the other person's life, such as monitoring their finances, dictating their social interactions, and deciding who they associate with
- Threatening the other person with violence, often using alarming language like "I'm going to kill you"
- Making threats against pets, with statements like "I will hurt/ kill your pets"
- Coercing the other person into unwanted activities, including non-consensual sexual relations
- Displaying violent behavior while under the influence of drugs or alcohol

Physical abuse ———————————— is characterized by one person intentionally causing harm or injury to another through the use of their body.

The abuser may engage in the following actions:

- Physically harm you by pulling your hair, punching, slapping, kicking, biting, choking, or smothering
- Prohibit or hinder you from eating or sleeping
- Utilize weapons, including firearms, knives, bats, or mace, against you
- Restrict your access to emergency services, including medical attention or law enforcement
- Inflict harm on your children or pets
- Drive recklessly or abandon you in unfamiliar places
- Coerce you into using drugs or alcohol, especially if you have a history of substance abuse
- Confine you in your home or prevent you from leaving.
- Throw objects at you
- Prevent you from taking prescribed medication or deny you necessary medical treatment

Emotional/Verbal abuse ———————————— is a form of continual emotional mistreatment, sometimes referred to as psychological abuse. It involves the following: harassing, scaring, humiliating, ridiculing, intimidating, threatening, name-calling, claiming a victim is crazy, asserting that you can't live without the abuser, bullying, gaslighting, coercing, infantilizing, controlling, silencing, blaming the victim for infidelity, expressing jealousy even with family members, and isolating or ignoring the victim for extended periods. This type of abuse is initially hard to detect but can have lasting physical and mental effects. Seeking help promptly is crucial once identified.

Sexual coercion ———————— falls on the continuum of sexually aggressive behavior, ranging from persuasion to forced sexual contact. It may involve verbal and emotional tactics such as pressure, guilt, or shame. Even if you are not forcing unwanted sexual acts, making someone feel obligated is a form of coercion. No relationship, regardless of arrangement, implies intimate acts.

People in **same-sex, bisexual, or transgender relationships** can experience domestic violence. Concealing one's sexual orientation or gender identity may lead to threats of exposure. The abuser may justify this by questioning the victim's orientation and instilling fear that nobody will believe them due to their identity.

Reproductive coercion ———————— involves the abuser manipulating the victim into pregnancy early in the relationship.

Immigrants or those new to a country may face additional challenges. Government programs, shelters, medical care, and free legal services are available in many countries, including the United States. Do not isolate yourself or allow the language barrier to stop you from getting the help you need and deserve.

Nobody should suffer from violence, so it is crucial to get away from the situation after identifying the signs.

If you suspect domestic violence, take these actions:

- Call hotlines in your country or town (refer to the book's Appendix for hotline numbers).
- Contact the police or helpline before situations escalate.
- Confide in a trusted person.
- Erase online traces and personal information to prevent tracking.
- Check phone bills and messages for privacy.
- Plan an escape route, communicate with others involved, and pack essentials.
- Collect important documents in a safe place.
- Keep cash for initial survival.
- Take precautions to review anything that might reveal your location and ensure it is eliminated to prevent your abuser from tracking you, especially in life-threatening situations.
- Inform your trusted family and friends of your plan so they can offer support when needed.
- Stock up on noodles, canned foods, and essential personal necessities for challenging days while you navigate your next steps.
- Accumulate gift cards from your preferred stores or versatile cards that can be used anywhere.
- After enduring the ups and downs, remember that you deserve moments of joy and relaxation. Include gift cards to your favorite eateries or hangout spots for you and your friends, spouse, or children to enjoy.
- Seek support from church or government personnel.

JOURNAL

Have you ever been a victim of domestic violence? If so, how did you handle the situation? Alternatively, do you know someone who has experienced domestic violence, and if yes, what was their experience?

What challenging situations have you encountered in your life that required you to make an escape?

CHAPTER 3

Moving Into Town

moved to town and stayed with a distant relative who shared my
ther's family name. They treated us as part of their family, and we
ckly settled into a routine, developing strong bonds with the adults and
der children in the household.

he younger children's favorite activity was walking to the beach with the
two sisters, Abeth and Goyang. We enjoyed watching the sunset,
collecting seashells, and swimming in the ocean. Every day, Abeth and
Goyang would read stories to the younger children, including Kuya
Marsden, Kuya Julius, Juhan, and myself. We would all gather at the dining
table to listen. My all-time favorite storybooks were "Hansel and Gretel"
and "Goldilocks and the Three Bears."

At times, the four younger kids would stroll to the crossing to request
snacks from their grandparents, Lolo Seno and his wife. We also visited
Mama Pon in the high school building. She was a teacher there and the
mother of the two younger boys in the family.

Being close in age, the four of us formed a tight-knit group. The two older
brothers acted as big brothers to my sister and me, with Kuya Marsden
always there to care for and protect us in the absence of adults.

Mama would often take us to her office at the municipal hall. Occasionally,
my sister and I would walk with my grandpa, the Chief Police Officer at the
time, who was a distant relative of my grandfather on my father's side. He
showed us the people currently in prison, explaining the reasons for their
incarceration. This experience served as a lesson for us to always obey the
law and avoid engaging in wrongful activities, lest we end up like those
prisoners.

If Mama and Lolo, the Chief Police Officer, were occupied, my sister and I
would dash into the church to visit Father Borces since it was conveniently

The greatest g[ift] child can offer t[o] parents and elder[s] to respect and hon[or] them all the days o[f] their lives.

April Key

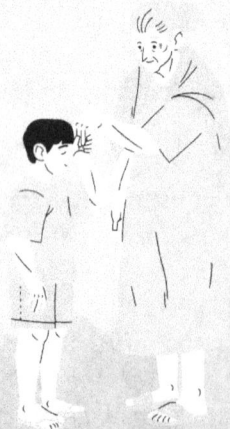

"Mano po" is a respectful gesture of the younger to their elders and asking for the blessing of the elder. The usage of the word "Po & Opo" is a salutation of respect and honoring a person who is older than you.

located beside the municipal hall. We cherished our time with him, as he was always kind and made an effort to bring us laughter.

The church, situated next to the sea, provided an opportunity for us to explore the rocks at the back. It became our bonding ritual, and looking back, I recall Father Borces as a father figure to me and Juhan. Our younger selves found joy in visiting the church, a place we loved besides going to the beach or grabbing snacks from Lolo Seno's store at the street corner.

During the summer month of May, Ate Abeth ensured that we attended "Flores de Mayo" at the church. My sister and I eagerly anticipated the event, taking naps and waking up just in time to prepare for church. We relished learning about God, angels, and Mama Mary. My favorite part was witnessing all the kids adorned in white dresses and angel wings. The post-mass snacks were a bonus we appreciated.

A significant change occurred when one of my aunts arrived in Cebu and relocated her family to the city. We frequently visited their spacious rented house and played with our two cousins, Ate Genevie and Denise. It was a delight to watch fish swim in the tanks placed by my uncle, Papa Kris, right in front of the garage before the main entrance.

We were all around the same age—Ate Genevie was six, I was five, Juhan was four, and Denise was three. Remarkably, the four of us never fought during our playtime.

I cherished special moments from that time, especially Ate Genevie's piano practice and her play sessions with the blue hula hoop. Attempting to copy her hula hoop moves proved challenging for my sister and me; our stiff bodies made the hoop slip easily from our waists to the ground. Despite the difficulty, we all had fun every time.

The four of us delighted in sneaking out to play in a large building filled with old, unused items. Jumping and playing catch inside the building became one of our favorite pastimes.

Several months later, my aunts, Mama Del, and Aunt Eden, arrived in Cebu for Aunt Eden's wedding. We enjoyed chasing our two-year-old cousin Mary around the house and into the yard. Fortunately, Juhan and I had become accustomed to simple English, allowing us to communicate effectively with our English-speaking cousins.

Our aunt, Mama Del, gifted all of us with watches. I particularly loved my Mickey Mouse watch with Mickey's hands showing the time—I spent moments watching those hands move. Juhan received a pink duckling watch. Everyone adored their cute watches, all proudly made in the USA.

We returned to the province as Mama had to work. She requested Aunt Riley to drop off the wedding invitation at Lolo Seno's sarisari store. When Mama went to retrieve it, Aunt Lucy arrived and confronted her, exclaiming, "What did you do and say to my sister to make your daughter join the entourage as a flower girl?"

I was taken aback by witnessing this event as I had never seen my Aunt Lucy behave this way towards my mother before. While observing my mother's facial expression, I couldn't understand why my aunt acted in such a manner. I knew my mother hadn't done anything, especially considering I wasn't even part of the wedding. Mama chose not to engage and simply walked away.

The wedding day finally, arrived and my aunt Eden looked stunning alongside her handsome American husband, as did the entire entourage. My younger sister looked beautiful in her white and gold dress, standing there with my Dutch cousins.

After the wedding, we returned to Aunt Riley's house and slept beside my cousins. Curious, I asked Mama why it was only Juhan who was part of the entourage while my other two cousins and I were not included, despite also being Aunt Eden's nieces. Mama simply replied, "It's okay, that's your aunt's decision about her entourage," and then went to sleep.

One late afternoon, Papa visited the house of Lolo Seno, where we lived. I was relieved that the house was gated and protected by many dogs. Papa couldn't enter easily, but he inquired whether we indeed lived there. Despite his pleas for us to come out and join him, they had to lie for the sake of our safety.

The four of us were frightened, but Kuya Marsden hid us at the top of the bahay kubo. Straining to listen carefully to what would happen next, I could discern the concerned expressions on the adults' faces, particularly as Papa was still strong and youthful at the time. It was another scary incident for us, and since Papa now knew where to find us, we had to move again.

We moved to another house closer to the church and municipal hall where Mama worked. However, after a few months, it became unsafe for us to stay nearby. Mama found a place in the next barangay, renting a one-bedroom gated apartment for the three of us. Mama felt more secure because other trustworthy families could look after Juhan and me when she wasn't around.

At times, we accompanied Mama on trips to mountainous areas, with the military ensuring her safety while conducting her work as an agriculturist. Unfortunately, one of our military neighbors passed away and the other had a change in assignments. Consequently, the Office of Agriculture in Tabogon opted to transfer Mama to the next town as there was an opening for an agriculturist.

REFLECTION

Reflecting on these childhood memories, it's remarkable how we used to love attending church at a young age and learning about God, Jesus, and Mama Mary.

In conflicts, it takes two to fight, and sometimes the best course of action is to refrain from engagement, especially when young children are present. Listening to what they have to say and walking away calmly can prevent the situation from escalating.

Jealousy can be challenging to navigate, yet it's essential not to let children feel disregarded. It is the responsibility of parents to guide their children with a correct and positive attitude, discouraging the development of jealous behavior towards others.

Being a single parent, especially a mother of small children, is no easy feat, particularly when work involves frequent travel to dangerous mountainous areas in the province to hold classes and educate farmers about their livelihood. The children often have no choice but to accompany their mother on these work trips, as there was no one else to stay home with them. On a side note, the two learned the value of hard work through their mother's example.

"Parents are the children's first teachers on how to work with integrity."

- April Key

"Parents have the power to teach their children about the importance of conducting their profession with integrity."

- April Key

"The Lord your God is supreme over all gods and over all powers. He is great and mighty, and he is to be obeyed. He does not show partiality, and he does not accept bribes. He makes sure that orphans and widows are treated fairly; he loves the foreigners who live with our people and gives them food and clothes. so then, show love for those foreigners, because you were once foreigners in Egypt."

- Deuteronomy 10:17-19

"He is near to those who call to him, who call to him with sincerity. He supplies the needs of those who honor him; he hears their cries and saves them."

- Psalm 145:18-19

PSYCHOLOGICAL ANALYSIS

"It was another scary incident for us, and since Papa now knew where to find us, we had to move again."

Escaping from domestic violence doesn't necessarily grant a person complete liberation, as this form of violence, leaves both physical and emotional scars. Even when the victim manages to find safety, there is a lingering sense of unease, hindering their ability to achieve peace of mind and leading to high levels of stress and anxiety.

Beyond the fear of potential pursuit, victims often grapple with a range of emotions linked to grief, with pain and loss being predominant. Feelings of abandonment and betrayal emerge, severely impacting the victim's self-esteem.

Recovery after escaping domestic violence is a gradual process, particularly when the victim is also a parent, responsible for the well-being of affected children. Coping becomes even more challenging for a parent who has fled an abusive relationship.

While healing is attainable, it requires seeking help, as escaping physical violence doesn't automatically remove the emotional damage. Victims may endure serious repercussions, including depression, anxiety, trust issues, sleep disturbances, and other symptoms affecting their emotional health.

There are instances where victims, having successfully escaped, may contemplate returning, falsely believing that the abuse was their fault. The psychological toll is significant and often exacerbated by manipulative attempts from the abuser, reassuring them that the abuse won't recur.

Escaping domestic violence involves not just physically breaking free from the abuser but also recognizing one's victimhood, understanding it's not their fault, and acknowledging that future relationships need not be characterized by the same harmful intentions.

In the healing process, it is crucial to seek information about domestic violence, explore support groups, and consider therapy as an essential component of recovery.

Steps in Healing Oneself from Abuse and Traumatic Experiences

Safety First

- Stabilized environment
- Boundaries and the ability to say no
- Self-care and self-love
- Building a strong support system

Remembrance and Mourning

- Process one's emotions
- Share and talk about the experience
- Regain control of one's emotions; positive thinking

Reconnection and Integration

- Taking action
- Healing
- Investing in oneself and taking back one's identity
- Mentoring
- Socializing

In therapy, individuals embark on a journey to heal from the adverse experiences they have encountered by using various strategies. They learn to fortify their self-esteem and nurture their personality. For a comprehensive exploration of these strategies and techniques, please refer to the Psychological Analysis section in Chapter 4 of this book.

JOURNAL

What are the factors that contributed to your healing process? Have you encountered someone undergoing recovery from a traumatic situation? How did you support them in coping with their past trauma and difficult experiences?

Virtues are our supernatural gifts from God that helps us in being different.

April Key

Reyna Elena

Santa Cruzan of Sagala depicts how
St. Helena found the Cross of Jesus.
In the Philippines, women wear grand
Filipiniana attire with a male escort
while making processions on the street.

CHAPTER 4

God Sent an Angel

Finally, we were out of my father's hometown, three towns away to be specific. We rented a simple bahay kubo made of nipa with bamboo wooden floors. It had a kitchen area and a small elevated space for sleeping. The gated compound mostly housed relatives. Mama felt secure there as it was right across from our school, making it convenient for us to cross the street when going to and from our classes.

Mama was new to her job and didn't know anyone in town. She worked as a temporary government employee and their salaries were often delayed. This made it challenging for her to pay the monthly rent.

One day, while Mama was trying to fetch water from the well, the owner of the house confronted her for not paying the rent. Despite Mama's honest assurance that she would pay once she received her salary, the owner remained unconvinced. Mama had committed to a specific payment date, aligning with her promised payday, but unfortunately, it didn't materialize. Consequently, the owner decided to evict us from the rental property.

It was already dark and Mama had just returned from work when the eviction took place. Inside the house, my sister and I sat on the bamboo floor, overhearing the tense conversation and worried about our uncertain future in an unfamiliar area. With my hands on my knees, I prayed to God and Mama Mary for guidance. As we went to bed, we wondered what the next day would bring.

The following day, an old lady named Lola Press from the neighboring house came to our rescue. Her sister-in-law had been shouting at us and Lola Press intervened, defending Mama. She invited us to live with her, an unexpected act of kindness that felt like a heaven-sent miracle.

Lola Press, a retired teacher and the sister of the house owner's husband, became a strict yet kind and fair grandmother figure to us. She consistently protected us from the townsfolk and even from her own family, standing up for us when needed. We gathered our belongings, swiftly followed her, and moved to her house. This house featured two bedrooms, a hardwood floor, an upstairs balcony leading to the living room, a dining area, and a kitchen with an unfinished floor—the ground was still plain soil. It was a humble abode, but we were grateful for the refuge it provided.

Lola Press allowed us to use her spare room where we stored our belongings and slept. Occasionally, when Mama wasn't around and we wanted to be with her, she graciously let us sleep in her room.

Living with Lola Press was a unique experience as she was already in her late 60s when she cared for me and my sister. We were only five and six years old at the time. Recognizing the challenges, Mama and Lola hired a house helper to assist with household chores and taking care of us.

Despite having a helper, Lola emphasized to me and my sister the importance of us helping with household chores. She made sure we learned how to manage tasks around the house.

Our Friday nights with Lola Press were a highlight for my sister and me. We eagerly anticipated watching movies at our neighbor's house, the abode of Lola Press' niece and nephew who happened to be the only ones showing films in the area. To secure seats, we had to arrive early before the venue filled up.

During basketball league season, Lola Press would take us to watch the games, helping us remember who the best players in town were. We always stayed to finish the games. One night, a basketball player approached Lola Press, jokingly asking if we were still awake as he patted our heads. We smiled with fake sleepy expressions, confirming that we were wide awake. When he inquired about our parents, Lola explained that our father was a skilled basketball player, which was why my sister and I enjoyed watching the games very much. Lola's kindness in engaging with us while Mama was away meant a lot to both of us.

Once a month, Lola Press treated us to a chiffon cake that she baked using the charcoal-fired oven that was popular in older times. She often reminded us that being good would result in this sweet reward, using it as an incentive for us to complete our chores diligently.

She also taught us how to earn a little money. My sister and I happily collected empty bottles and cans from our neighbors or within the compound, selling them for a small amount of money. At that time, receiving two pesos made us happy and content. Mama arranged with a neighbor who owned a sari-sari store to allow my sister and me to purchase snacks during snack time, with Mama settling the bill when she received her salary. That's why we never had to worry about our daily snacks, as we could easily choose what we wanted from the store. Our favorites were ice candy and Bahug-Bahug, a kind of sweet bread with a reddish filling.

One time, Mama lost her money, certain that she had kept it safely inside the house. Lola Press was furious, warning us that the hands and fingers of whoever took the money would become irregular in size. Though we weren't the culprits, Lola's words left us scared.

Because of this, we had this crazy idea of simply accepting the blame. Juhan, proficient in math, calculated the prices of our favorite snacks until the total reached 200 pesos. Every day during recess, we thought of ways we could have used the money. Rushing to the stores, we compiled a list of possible purchases. As Juhan grew tired of making the list, we remained unable to match the amount Mama had lost. In a smart yet silly move, Juhan claimed we used the money to buy a whole gallon of ice cream, conveniently matching the stolen amount. Of course, Mama saw through our lies.

One time, our house helper took us to the market and we saw her buy a nice wallet worth 50 pesos, among other things. My sister and I were clueless about her actions and scheming. Eventually, Mama caught her when she attempted to pretend that the money had fallen from the top of the dresser. Mama knew it was her because my sister and I were not around at the time and the dresser was too high for us to reach. Fortunately, our helper returned the money, understanding its importance to Mama.

When I fell ill again, I experienced convulsions and my fever soared so high that Mama had to take me to the next town since there was no hospital where we lived. Despite lacking the funds to cover the hospital bill, we were fortunate that the doctor recognized us, being from my father's town and acquainted with our family. Mama conveyed a message through him, asking him to inform my aunts about our situation and the urgent need for assistance in paying the hospital bills and purchasing my medicine.

We waited anxiously, hoping for the arrival of one of my aunts, but as the days passed, we became increasingly disappointed. Mama had to remove my dextrose, urging me to pray fervently as help seemed elusive. Fortunately, my fever subsided after a few days, and Mama, desperate to discharge us, pleaded with the doctor to allow us to go home, promising to settle the hospital expenses later.

Following this ordeal, Mama began taking us to work, traversing mountains and crossing rivers to reach far-flung barangays where the farmers that she needed to teach and collect samples from live. Due to Mama's job, we rarely saw her, as she was assigned to visit remote barangays. Some areas were perilous due to the rebels who were active during Cory Aquino's regime. Many soldiers were dying and it became normal for the town's residents to see an army truck full of dead bodies.

On occasions, we had to wade through deep water, holding onto each other to avoid being carried away by the strong current. As a single parent with two children to feed, Mama had no choice but to undertake tasks that her co-workers avoided, just to secure her job.

One morning, a man knocked on Lola Press' door inquiring about Mama's work. He cautioned that Mama needed to be careful, as she might be the next target. In response, Lola Press defended her, emphasizing Mama's role as an agriculturist with young daughters and pleading for her safety.

The rebellion in the area intensified, resulting in numerous casualties. Many barangay leaders and officials perished, and the town witnessed trucks delivering bodies of soldiers, arranged next to one another like so much fish in a sardine can, waiting for families to identify them.

There were moments when Lola Press, my sister, and I went to look at bodies, fearing one might be our mother. There were also occasions when we accompanied Mama to identify officials or friends who might have died that day. It was a harrowing experience for Mama, and especially for us, as we lived in constant fear of losing her. Despite the rebels' strength during that period, God protected Mama, and their plan to harm her did not happen. I vividly recall seeing President Cory Aquino stepping out of a helicopter to visit our area. I watched her walk from the vacant lot towards the Municipal Hall.

My sister and I formed strong friendships in this town, facing no problems in school. Juhan also excelled academically. During this time, she made a promise to herself to pursue every medal and award offered at the end of each school year. Juhan told me, "Ate, every year I'll surely work hard for this."

Smiling, I looked at her and said, "Okay, if that's your dream. I, on the other hand, just dream about not getting sick." I was exhausted from having a fever every single month.

During Christmas, we both enjoyed collecting coconut twigs and crafting them into a Christmas tree. Dreaming of having a bigger tree one day, we envisioned decorating it with colorful ornaments and hoped to hang chocolates from the branches. Mama also hung two large Christmas stockings and discreetly placed coins in them every night. Of course, Juhan was suspicious about this and made sure to keep a watchful eye during the night, eventually catching Mama in the act!

When the school year ended, Mama decided to move us to Consolacion City, where my father's cousins lived. This move was to ensure that they could take care of Juhan and me while she was away for work. Yes, we had to move again.

REFLECTION

It can be challenging for children to understand situations, especially when they don't know where to go and live. The threats that their mother received from the rebels were part of the difficult experiences the children faced. Despite everything, the two girls turned out to have the best life, thanks to Lola Press, whom God sent to take them in and help their mother. Lola Press was an incredibly kind person who protected them from everyone, including her own family.

"It's good to have an angel that can be physically present and be there for you when necessary."

- April Key

"We may face difficult and dangerous paths in life, but there's one thing we have to remind ourselves: God is in control."

- April Key

PSYCHOLOGICAL ANALYSIS

"The rebellion in the area intensified, resulting in numerous casualties. Many barangay leaders and officials perished, and the town witnessed trucks delivering bodies of soldiers, arranged next to one another like so much fish in a sardine can, waiting for families to identify them. There were moments when Lola Press, my sister, and I went to look at bodies, fearing one might be our mother."

Not only do soldiers typically develop a series of symptoms affecting their mental health, but also individuals living in places where such events occur. Wars leave behind destruction and physical death, along with a range of emotional problems, making it challenging for many to overcome those traumatic events.

Living through war can lead to chronic anxiety, characterized by uncertainty about what might happen at any moment, difficulty falling asleep, concentration problems, and prolonged states of depression, among other issues. These symptoms are commonly observed in individuals who develop post-traumatic stress, a disorder diagnosed in those who have been in war zones. It is not uncommon for people to develop post-traumatic stress, a mental illness that emerges after individuals have lived through or experienced traumatic events.

The symptoms experienced by a person with post-traumatic stress include:

- avoidance of thoughts related to the traumatic event
- avoidance of places associated with the traumatic event
- flashbacks - memories related to the traumatic event
- nightmares

Being witness to others experiencing traumatic situations can lead to post-traumatic stress. Treatment for post-traumatic stress aims to help individuals regain control of their lives. This treatment involves a series of strategies and processes that allow the individual to gain insights into themselves, understand their thoughts about the traumatic event, and learn effective coping mechanisms.

Treatments and coping mechanisms for managing PTSD

1. Psychotherapy. A clinician guides individuals through negative thoughts, emotions, and behaviors using talk therapy. Seventy-five percent of clients report benefiting from this technique. It is believed to be effective for various mental conditions, including depression, addiction, stress, anxiety, insomnia, bipolar disorder, personality disorders, and more.

2. Cognitive Behavioral Therapy (CBT). This therapy aids individuals with PTSD and addresses various mental health issues such as phobias, anxiety, depression, addiction, eating disorders, anger, panic attacks, personality disorders, and bipolar disorder. CBT techniques also assist in coping with grief and loss, relationship problems, divorce or break-ups, stress management, low self-esteem, insomnia, and chronic pain.

Techniques within CBT include:

Diaphragmatic breathing, also known as belly breathing, it maximizes breathing efficiency to 100% capacity, reducing oxygen demand, slowing breathing rates, and strengthening the diaphragm.

Progressive Muscle Relaxation (PMR), developed in the 1930s, PMR involves systematically relaxing major muscle groups, helping alleviate anxiety, neck pain, lower back pain, migraines, muscle tension, and high blood pressure.

Self-monitoring involves journaling or maintaining a diary of daily life, documenting thoughts, decision-making, and actions. This helps both individuals and therapists assess and track behavioral patterns to inform recovery and treatment.

Behavioral activation, targets changing negative behavioral patterns, such as oversleeping. Identifying consequences, like missing meals and lack of exercise helps create a positive action plan. Scheduling and completing tasks contribute to effective treatment.

3. Compassion Focused Therapy (CFT). This form of psychotherapy is known to be beneficial, focusing on high self-criticism and shame. CFT can aid in treating panic disorders, anxiety disorders, mood disorders, personality disorders, hoarding disorders, eating disorders, and psychosis. Developed by Dr. Paul Gilbert, CFT specifically helps individuals who have experienced abuse, bullying, neglect, and trauma.

Three types and functions of CFT

The Threat System. This triggers a fight or flight response, keeping anxiety levels high as victims or survivors manage threats, seek protection, and navigate survival.

The Drive System. Here, survivors strive to survive and thrive within their circumstances. They set goals, plan actions, and delegate tasks to achieve their objectives.

The Soothing System. Clinicians predominantly focus on this system to help clients achieve a balanced approach between the threat and drive systems. Emphasizing caring for oneself and others, soothing, resting, and digesting, this system acknowledges that safety has already been achieved, encouraging clients to slow down and embrace a healthy approach to their healing journey.

4. Dialectical Behavioral Therapy (DBT). Developed by Marsha Linehan in the late 1980s, DBT is a type of cognitive-behavioral therapy primarily designed to treat individuals with borderline personality disorder (BPD). Combining mindfulness, acceptance, and change-based strategies, DBT aims to assist individuals in regulating emotions, improving interpersonal relationships, and managing stressful thoughts and behaviors. The goal of DBT is to enable individuals to:

- understand and accept challenging emotions,
- acquire methods to regulate these emotions, and
- make positive changes in their lives.

Dialectical Behavioral Therapy delves into understanding how two opposing things can both be true. For example, DBT emphasizes that it is feasible for individuals to simultaneously love themselves and change their behavior.

Very emotional people, such as those with borderline personality disorder (BPD), bipolar illness, or post-traumatic stress disorder, may benefit from dialectical behavior therapy (DBT).

DBT incorporates a variety of strategies, some of which are as follows:

- Practicing awareness and acceptance
- Developing one's social skills
- Figuring out how to deal with and withstand stress
- Emotional regulation training

Dialectical behavior therapy is another name for this approach. When you put these DBT skills into practice, you will first learn to recognize the negative behaviors that bring you pain, discomfort, or an inability to function in relationships and your day-to-day life. Then you will learn how to modify those behaviors.

Methods used in DBT

DBT stands out from other forms of therapy due to the unique methods employed throughout the process. Even though there are a great many methods that might be utilized, there are only a few that are consistently applied. Distress tolerance, interpersonal effectiveness, mindfulness training, and emotional regulation are the four primary components of dialectical behavior therapy (DBT).

1. Acquiring the skill of practicing mindfulness
The practice of mindfulness can be beneficial in a wide variety of facets of one's life. You can improve your ability to be fully present in the here and now by concentrating on fundamental mindfulness skills as a DBT component. This skill in dialectical behavior therapy helps you stop living in

the past or the future. Mindfulness practice is often considered the cornerstone of DBT. When practicing mindfulness, you learn to:

- Notice and examine your thoughts, feelings, emotions, and surroundings non-judgmentally
- Explain your situation in a way that is easy for others (and yourself) to comprehend
- Participate effectively in value-based and goal-directed actions

2. Educating oneself on how to be productive in interpersonal relationships
Core mindfulness is the foundation for effective interpersonal communication. It focuses on how you will engage positively with the people that are a part of your life. You will learn how to manage the severe issues you may face in the future and how to deal with your relationships in your personal life. You'll concentrate on the following skills:

- Clearly expressing yourself
- Letting go of grudges
- Developing the ability to say "no"
- Figuring out how to ask for your requirements without feeling you've lost your self-respect

3. Acquiring the ability to control and tolerate stress
You are practicing the art of being able to adapt to change when you learn how to tolerate discomfort (radical acceptance). If you pay attention to them, there are a few strategies that can teach you how to handle better and deal with any crisis you encounter. They can include:

- Concentrating on making stressful circumstances less stressful
- Learning how to self-soothe
- Finding ways to divert oneself
- Weighing the benefits and drawbacks of a particular situation

4. Acquiring the ability to control one's feelings
Emotional control is typically the last DBT skill taught during therapy sessions. One of the most valuable abilities developed through DBT is the capacity to manage one's feelings. Learning to manage and control your

emotions be exceedingly difficult if you are intense, but it is not impossible. Improving your skills in emotion regulation can help you do things:

- Safer and more secure
- Try to rein in strong feelings before they take over
- Gain self-assurance in your capacity to manage your emotions
- Learn the warnings

Learning to control your emotions might help you succeed. If you feel overloaded, angry, depressed, nervous, or frustrated.

Which disorders might benefit from DBT treatment?

Depression, suicidal ideation, and self-injury are just some mental health issues that DBT has been demonstrated to help with. DBT is more likely to be successful for you if you meet the following criteria:

- You are committed to making positive changes in yourself
- You are ready to work hard in therapy and do homework assignments
- You're ready to stop dwelling on the past and start making plans for the future. You're confident enough to participate in group sessions.

What happens during DBT sessions?

Pre-treatment, individual therapy, group skills training, phone coaching, and consultation team meetings are often the components of DBT sessions.

1. DBT pre-treatment
Your DBT therapist may start with an evaluation or a pre-treatment phase. The therapist will assess your situation at this stage to see if DBT is a good fit. They may provide you with several sessions in which you will obtain information regarding the DBT model. After that, if you determine that the treatment is appropriate for you, they will ask you to commit to the course of treatment.

2. Individual counseling or therapy

Together, the client and the therapist strive to design a treatment plan considering the client's unique objectives and concerns. The therapist may employ a variety of treatments, including:

- Validating and problem-solving techniques
- Helping the client learn how to manage their feelings and emotions better, improving their interpersonal relationships
- Learning how to manage upsetting thoughts and actions better

3. Group skills training

These sessions typically last six months and involve learning mindfulness, distress tolerance, emotion regulation, and interpersonal effectiveness skills. You will be taught to observe and describe your thoughts and emotions without judgment, develop coping strategies for managing distressing situations, regulate emotions, and communicate effectively with others. You may be assigned homework assignments to practice the skills you have learned in the group sessions.

4. Phone coaching

A crisis coach may support your daily life over the phone if you participate in DBT. This indicates that you are free to call your therapist for support in the time that passes between appointments. For instance, such times include when you are experiencing:

- an acute emotional state (such as suicidal thoughts or the want to self-harm)
- attempting to implement DBT skills but would need some guidance
- when your therapeutic alliance requires repair

These are just a few examples of when you might want additional support. However, you should anticipate that your therapist will establish clear boundaries. For instance:

- Calls are typically brief and should only occur between the hours you agree with them
- They may ask you to wait twenty-four hours before calling them in certain situations

5. Acceptance techniques

Techniques of acceptance focus on understanding who you are and determining why you might engage in certain behaviors, such as inflicting harm on yourself or abusing substances. Acceptance can be difficult to grasp, but it is essential to healing. For instance, a therapist trained in DBT may suggest that this has been your only method of coping with intense feelings throughout your life. Your behavior makes perfect sense, even though it is counterproductive in the long run and may cause concern in other people.

6. Changing methods

The purpose of changing methods is to help you swap harmful routines for more productive ones. This may mean your therapist will:

- Question negative assumptions you've made
- It motivates you to experiment with new coping mechanisms when feeling down

Advantages of engaging in DBT

Every type of therapeutic environment has its individualized structure and objectives. These are the six primary tenets of DBT:

- Understanding and embracing change. You will learn to accept and tolerate your life's circumstances, feelings, and yourself. In addition, you will acquire skills that will enable you to bring about positive changes in how you behave and interact with others.

- Behavioral. You will learn to identify and break unhealthy or unproductive habits and replace them with more positive and productive ones.

- Changes to your thoughts and beliefs that aren't productive or helpful will be the primary focus of this aspect of therapy.

- You will improve your ability to communicate clearly and become more adept at working cooperatively with others (therapist, group therapist, psychiatrist).

- You will acquire new skill sets that will significantly improve your capabilities.

- You'll receive support and encouragement to identify your positive strengths and attributes and develop and use those strengths and attributes.

Is it possible to carry out DBT all by yourself?

Because of its complexity, DBT is typically something individuals can only perform with a trained therapist's supervision.

Yet, you can take steps to improve your coping mechanisms. These options are there whenever you feel the urge to experiment. Skills like mindfulness, breathing exercises, and gradual muscle relaxation can all help you increase your pain threshold.

Remember that none of this is meant to replace the expertise of medical professionals. If you are struggling with an illness that impacts your mental health, getting help from a trained expert as soon as possible is in your best interest.

5. Emotionally Focused Therapy (EFT). In EFT, the therapist helps patients recognize their feelings' impact on their daily lives and the people around them. EFT was developed by Sue Johnson and Les Greenberg in the 1980s and is primarily used to help couples and families improve their relationships.

In EFT, the therapist works with individuals or couples to identify and understand their emotional experiences and explore the underlying attachment needs that drive those experiences.

What EFT can help with

Couples who are having trouble communicating with one another, dealing with conflict, or experiencing distress may benefit from EFT. It is most frequently applied in the context of couple's therapy; however, it is equally helpful in individual therapy and family therapy. This strategy can help assist individuals in improving issues that are related to their emotions. Also, it can assist members of the family in developing stronger ties with one another.

It has been demonstrated that EFT effectively treats various relationship issues. The following are some instances of problems that can be helped with EFT:

1. **Marital distress.** EFT is effective in improving marital satisfaction and reducing marital distress.
2. **Depression.** EFT is effective in reducing symptoms of depression in couples.
3. **Anxiety.** EFT is effective in reducing anxiety symptoms in couples.
4. **Post-traumatic Stress Disorder (PTSD).** EFT is effective in reducing symptoms of PTSD in couples.
5. **Parent-child relationships.** EFT has improved parent-child relationships, particularly in families with children with emotional or behavioral problems.
6. **Attachment injuries.** EFT effectively treats attachment injuries, which are experiences that cause a significant rupture in the emotional bond between partners.

Techniques of EFT

EFT uses various techniques to help individuals and couples identify and understand their emotional experiences and develop more secure and satisfying relationships. Here are some standard techniques used in EFT:

1. Identifying negative cycles. EFT therapists help clients identify negative cycles in their relationships that perpetuate feelings of disconnection and distress. The therapist helps the clients explore how their behaviors and emotions contribute to the cycle and develop new ways of relating that promote emotional safety and security.

2. Heightening emotional awareness. EFT therapists help clients identify and express their emotions more effectively. Clients are encouraged to identify and explore their primary emotions, such as sadness, fear, and anger, and to express them to their partner to promote understanding and closeness.

3. Encouraging vulnerability. EFT therapists help clients to become more vulnerable with their partners and to express their needs and desires in a way that promotes emotional safety and security. This helps clients identify the underlying attachment needs that drive their emotions and communicate these needs to their partner in a way that promotes understanding and connection.

4. Promoting acceptance and validation. It helps them to feel accepted and validated in their emotional experiences. The therapist validates their emotions and helps them to understand that their emotions are normal and understandable given their past experiences and current situation.

5. Enhancing communication. It helps you to communicate more effectively with your partners. You are taught to listen actively and respond in a way that promotes understanding and connection. The therapist may use role-playing exercises to help you practice practical communication skills.

6. Building positive interactions. EFT therapists help you to develop positive interactions with your partner. Clients are encouraged to engage in activities that promote emotional connection, such as sharing intimate thoughts and feelings or engaging in enjoyable activities together.

Benefits of EFT

EFT has many opportunities for growth and improvement for married couples and families. Some examples of this are as follows:

- EFT gives a language for healthy dependency between partners and examines important actions and events that constitute an adult love relationship. This results in better emotional functioning. The model's principal objective is to expand and reorganize the pair's emotional responses.

- EFT is founded on attachment therapy, which claims that attachments between individuals often provide a haven—a retreat from the world and a method to acquire comfort, security, and a buffer against the effects of stress. This idea is central to EFT, which aims to strengthen relationships between people.

- EFT helps people become more aware of the needs of their spouse, which contributes to improved interpersonal understanding. They can listen and discuss difficulties from a position of empathy due to this awareness rather than from a place of defensiveness or wrath.

- Emotionally oriented treatment can undo habitual, counterproductive responses that endanger interpersonal connections.

Things that should be considered

It can be challenging to engage in emotionally oriented therapy because one of its central tenets is to investigate the unfavorable feelings and behavior patterns that are factors in relational friction. The treatment process may provoke challenging or overwhelming feelings in a patient.

Participation from each person is essential to the accomplishment of this task. If one person is more enthusiastic about participating in EFT, the process as a whole may be less effective.

Because of problems with safe attachment, we tend to view it as threatening any sense of distance or separation in the close connections we maintain.

Our series of safety is jeopardized whenever we lose the connection to someone we care about.

As a result, people resort to methods of self-preservation and rely on the activities they engage in as children to "survive" or cope with the stresses they face. This is why people, as adults, are triggered into repeating destructive behaviors from their formative years when they are involved in love relationships. Even though the procedure can be challenging at times, EFT's primary purpose is to assist in changing these patterns so that they are replaced with more beneficial ones.

6. What exactly is meant by the term "psychodynamic psychotherapy"?—
Talk therapy has many forms, including psychodynamic therapy. It is predicated on the notion that talking to a trained professional about the challenges one encounters will assist in locating relief and finding answers to those challenges.

When engaging with a psychodynamic therapist, people can better understand the thoughts, feelings, and conflicts that contribute to their actions. This understanding allows them to manage those behaviors better. This method of psychotherapy helps you better understand some of the unconscious reasons that sometimes impact how you think, feel, and act. Another benefit of this approach is the potential to learn self-control over your emotions.

This method of psychotherapy might help cope with mental or emotional anguish as it takes a more holistic approach. It can potentially encourage introspection, insight, and the development of one's feelings.

A deeper understanding of your emotional patterns and their triggers will help you deal with challenges more effectively and develop long-term coping mechanisms.

The objectives of psychodynamic treatment

The primary objectives of psychodynamic therapy are to improve the client's self-awareness and foster an understanding of the client's thoughts, feelings, and beliefs concerning the client's previous experiences, particularly the client's experiences as a child.

Both of these objectives are intended to be accomplished through the client's participation in the therapy.

This is performed by the therapist assisting the client in analyzing key occurrences and conflicts from the client's past that still need to be satisfactorily addressed.

In psychodynamic therapy, it is often assumed that the source of recurrent issues is in the client's unconscious mind and that these issues need to be brought to light for catharsis to occur. Hence, for the client to be able to deal with these patterns of thought, they need to have the self-awareness to uncover these unconscious thought patterns and the understanding of how these patterns came to be.

Types of psychodynamic therapy

1. Brief psychodynamic therapy. The fact that brief psychodynamic treatment is shorter in duration than other forms of psychodynamic therapy is the primary characteristic that differentiates it from other psychodynamic therapies. This particular form of treatment typically consists of only a handful of sessions, and in some instances, it may even be limited to a single session. There are instances when a person having difficulty with a specific issue needs to do nothing more than make a few significant connections to solve that issue. For instance, if a client suffers from acute anxiety with no recognized source, it is possible to identify an incident or scenario that contributed to developing this worry and develop a strategy for coping with it in a single session. While it's unrealistic to hope that a single treatment session can fix all of a patient's issues, there are times when pinpointing and fixing a specific problem is possible. This is especially true for those patients who seek treatment for mental health issues.

Brief psychodynamic therapy has been applied to situations such as the following:

- accident (traffic, physical injury, etc.)
- rape
- an act of terrorism
- acute psychological disturbances (such as anxiety or depression)
- traumatic family events (discovery of a secret, divorce, etc.)

2. Counseling for families based on psychodynamic theory. It doesn't matter if the family in question is made up of two adults in a romantic relationship, a parent and child(ren), siblings, grandparents and grandchildren, a traditional nuclear family, or any combination of these types of family members; this type of psychodynamic therapy is conducted within the context of the family.

Like other psychodynamic therapies, this approach emphasizes the client's unconscious processes and unresolved conflicts but does it through the lens of the client's familial relationships. The therapist will guide the family members through an investigation of the family's history, paying particular attention to any traumatic family experiences.

This type of therapy frequently emphasizes the significance of the adult members of the family resolving any disputes they have with their parents as a means of gaining a deeper comprehension of the issues they have with their partner(s) and child(ren).

A better and happier family dynamic can be achieved through psychodynamic family therapy, which can assist families in identifying and resolving the underlying issues that are the root cause of difficulties within the family.

3. Art and music therapy with a psychodynamic orientation. Expressing one's sentiments and emotions via art or music is at the heart of this non-traditional approach to psychodynamic therapy.

This style of psychodynamic treatment is non-directive and nonstructured, allowing the client to take the reins of the session. It is similar to other varieties of psychodynamic therapy. Clients don't need artistic or musical talent or expertise; all that is required is that they can express themselves via music or art.

The client may also choose to create art or music during the session. The work of art or music doesn't need to be of "high" quality; instead, it merely needs to express the ideas or emotions of the customers in a manner that is understandable to them.

The therapeutic relationship between therapist and client can be strengthened significantly by using art or music as a medium for communication. Communicating deeply through art and music is more effective than talking.

Clients experiencing crippling anxiety or fear, which can be helped to soothe by music or art, may find that this therapy is particularly well suited to them. Those who are shy or otherwise find it challenging to talk may also find this therapy particularly well suited to them.

Instruments and methods of psychodynamic analysis

1. The freedom to associate. In this method, the client is encouraged to speak their mind freely and not restrict the content of their statements. This makes it easier for the therapist to recognize patterns and recurring themes that may have therapeutic significance.

2. Analyzing a dream. This can provide insight into the workings of one's subconscious, and this is a common interpretation of dreams. Clients undergoing psychodynamic therapy may be asked to keep a dream journal and discuss the meanings of their dreams during therapy sessions.

3. Transference and countertransference involve the following. Transference is when a client unknowingly projects their emotions for other significant individuals in their lives onto the therapist they see for therapy. The therapist's thoughts, emotions, and responses to the client are referred to as countertransference.

4. Interpretation. Psychodynamic therapists may offer interpretations of the client's thoughts and feelings, helping the client gain insight into unconscious patterns and conflicts. These occurrences can provide vital insights into the client's relationships and past experiences.

5. Working through. This entails exploring and processing challenging emotions and experiences to settle disputes and move toward emotional recovery. Working through requires exploring and processing difficult emotions and experiences.

Crucial aspects of psychodynamic psychotherapy to consider

The following are some essential components of psychodynamic treatment:

1. **Recognizing patterns.** Psychodynamic treatment can assist you in becoming more aware of patterns in your conduct and the dynamics of your relationships. It's common to develop automatic responses whenever you're stressed, even if you aren't always aware that you're doing so. Yet, gaining the ability to recognize them can assist you in developing novel responses to the challenges you face.
2. **Exploring and comprehending one's feelings.** It has been demonstrated through research that psychodynamic therapy is an effective method for doing both things. You will be better able to detect patterns in your life that have contributed to dysfunction and then more easily be able to make changes if you acquire insight into the emotional experiences that you have had.
3. **Enhancing one's relationships** is one of the primary goals of psychodynamic therapy, which strongly emphasizes interpersonal connections. Working with a therapist enables one to understand how one typically reacts to the actions and words of others.

Applications of psychodynamic psychotherapy

Like other forms of treatment, this approach can be used to deal with various mental health problems.

- anxiety disorders
- depression disorders
- eating disorders
- interpersonal problems
- personality disorders
- psychological distress
- post-traumatic stress disorder
- social anxiety disorders
- substance use disorders

7. Eye Movement Desensitization and Reprocessing (EMDR). This treatment procedure is widely accepted and used in clinical settings. Shapiro has developed this procedure to alleviate posttraumatic stress disorder (PTSD) effectively. But now, it is used in various situations like phobias, test anxiety, dermatological disorders, and pain management.

Why is this treatment used?

EMDR therapy does not require the patient to discuss the traumatic event in great detail. Altering the feelings, thoughts, or behaviors that are a direct outcome of a traumatic event is the primary focus of EMDR therapy rather than resolving the traumatic event itself (trauma). This makes it possible for your brain to resume its natural repair process. Although "mind" and "brain" are sometimes used interchangeably, they do not refer to the same thing. One of the organs in your body is called the brain. Your thoughts, memories, beliefs, and experiences have all contributed to the formation of who you are, and they are all stored in your mind.

Your mental processes are directly related to the physical makeup of your brain. This structure is made up of networks of brain cells that can communicate with one another and span a variety of different regions. This is especially true for the parts of the chapter that involve your memories and senses. Networking allows those sectors to work together more quickly and with less difficulty. Because of this, the things that stimulate your senses—sights, sounds, smells, tastes, and feelings—can awaken vivid memories.

1. Processing of information that is adaptive
The EMDR treatment is predicated on a paradigm called the Adaptive Information Processing (AIP) model, which is a theory about how your brain remembers memories. This idea, conceived by Francine Shapiro, PhD, who developed the concept of eye movement desensitization and reprocessing (EMDR), acknowledges that your brain stores everyday and traumatic memories differently.

Your brain can store memories efficiently during everyday occurrences. In addition, it networks them so that other things you remember become connected to them. When uncomfortable or upsetting occurrences occur, proper networking does not occur. There is a discrepancy between what is experienced (felt, heard, seen) and what is remembered (via language) in the brain. The brain can be "offline", and there is a separation between the two.

2. Triggers

These wrongly stored memories will be "triggered" when the individual is exposed to sights, sounds, or odors that have a relationship or are comparable to the traumatic incident.

These memories, unlike others, have the potential to bring on overpowering emotions such as fear, anxiety, rage, or panic.

A flashback is a symptom of post-traumatic stress disorder (PTSD). It occurs when your mind accesses specific memories uncontrolled, distorted, and overwhelmingly because incorrect storage and networking have caused it to do so. Because of this, many who have experienced flashbacks in the past have described feeling as though they were reliving a traumatic occurrence. The present is transformed into the past.

3. Reprocessing and repair

When you go through the process of EMDR, your memories of a traumatic experience are brought up in very particular ways. Accessing those memories, in conjunction with eye movements and being led through specific instructions, can assist you in reprocessing what you remember from the upsetting experience.

The mental damage caused by that memory can be "repaired" with the help of reprocessing. You will no longer feel as though remembering what occurred to you is the same as reliving it, and the associated sensations will be much easier to manage.

Can illnesses and issues be remedied with EMDR therapy?

Treating post-traumatic stress disorder is the most common and extensive application of EMDR (PTSD). It is also utilized by professionals in the field of mental healthcare in the treatment of the following conditions:

Anxiety disorders. It ranges from generalized anxiety disorder and panic disorder to specific phobias and social anxiety.

Depression. Major depressive disorder (MDD), persistent depressive disorder (PDD), and illness-related depression are all types of depression.

Dissociative disorders. Amnesia/dissociative identity disorder and depersonalization/derealization disorder are dissociative disorders.

Eating disorders. This can be broken down into three primary classifications: binge eating, bulimia nervosa, and anorexia nervosa.

Obsessive-compulsive disorders. Hoarding disorder, OCD, and body dysmorphic disorder are all examples of obsessive-compulsive disorders.

Personality disorders can range from mild to severe, with the most common types including borderline, avoidant, and antisocial.

Disorders associated with trauma include acute stress, posttraumatic stress, and adjustment.

What exactly is involved in EMDR therapy?

Eight different phases make up EMDR therapy. These phases occur throughout numerous sessions, with some phases' components appearing in a single session. One illustration of this would be that stages 1 and 2 often only occur in the initial sessions, but phases 3 through 8 typically occur over numerous sessions later.

In most cases, the required sessions are between three and six. This is the case even for a single upsetting experience or memory. It may take eight to twelve sessions to treat traumas that are more complex or have lasted longer (or sometimes more). Classes often last anywhere from 60 minutes to an hour and a half. The following are the eight stages:

1. Gathering information about the patient and their history ─────────
Your healthcare professional will collect information about you and your medical history throughout the process. This assists them in determining whether or not EMDR is likely to be beneficial to you. In addition, you will be questioned about memories and occurrences from your past that you want to be the primary focus of your therapy and the objectives you have established for this particular treatment.

2. Education and preparation ─────────

At this phase, your healthcare professional will talk to you about what to anticipate throughout EMDR sessions and what you may expect to happen during those sessions. In addition, they will talk to you about things to concentrate on that will help you feel more secure and comfortable when attending sessions. They will provide you with strategies to assist you in controlling your feelings to serve you better.

3. Assessment phase

Your healthcare practitioner will assist you in identifying general topics and particular memories you might wish to focus on while reprocessing your experience. They will help you determine how the traumatic experience has altered your beliefs about yourself and how you would prefer to think about yourself in the future.

4. Desensitization and reprocessing

In this step, your healthcare professional will work with you to jog your memory by prompting you to recall a terrible experience. This prepares you for the next phase, desensitization and reprocessing. Throughout the reprocessing, they will assist you in becoming more aware of how you are feeling and any new ideas or insights you have on what you are going through.

5. Installation

At this step, your healthcare practitioner will have you focus on the optimistic belief that you want to put in as you process a memory. This will be done in preparation for the next phase, which is activation. This constructive belief may be expressed in phase 3 or something fresh that comes to mind during step 4.

6. Body scan

Your healthcare provider will have you concentrate on how you feel in your body, paying close attention to any symptoms that arise as you think about or relive the traumatic experience. This is called a body scan. During this phase, you will help to determine how far along you are in the EMDR treatment process overall. As you progress through the sessions, you should experience a reduction in your symptoms until you no longer have any (or as close to none as possible). Your reprocessing will be over when you are no longer experiencing any symptoms.

7. Closure and stabilization

This phase acts as a bridge between subsequent sessions and focuses on closure and stabilization. During this stage, your healthcare practitioner will discuss with you what you can reasonably anticipate happening between sessions. They will also talk to you about ways to steady yourself, which is particularly important if you have negative thoughts or feelings during sessions when you are supposed to be doing well. After you have gained a greater sense of comfort and safety in your surroundings, will they only end the session? They may also ask you to write down any new thoughts regarding the upsetting event(s) so you can discuss them during your subsequent session. This is done so you can bring them up during your subsequent session.

8. Reevaluation and continued care

Your healthcare practitioner will review and assess your progress as part of the final phase of EMDR therapy. This can help determine whether you require further sessions or how to modify your goals and expectations for the therapy that you are receiving. They will also assist you in exploring what you may experience in the future and how you would like to approach things at that time, given what you know now about yourself and the traumatic event that has occurred in the past.

8. What is Interpersonal Psychotherapy (IPT). IPT aims to improve a person's quality of life by helping them interact more effectively with others. It focuses more on adult concerns and relationships than it does on topics relating to children or development. A therapist is proactive, does not take a neutral stance, is encouraging, and offers possibilities for change.

IPT has the following characteristics:

- It is structured.
- It has a time limit (the active phase of the treatment typically lasts between 12 and 16 weeks).
- It focuses on interpersonal relationships and communication focuses on here-and-now relationships.
- It aims to improve interpersonal functioning and social support.

- It is intensive.
- IPT can be given in a one-on-one setting or a group setting.

How does it work?

The idea that psychological symptoms can be seen as a response to existing challenges in daily connections with other people is one of the fundamental tenets of interpersonal psychotherapy.

IPT focuses on four areas:

- Relational conflict is a cause of tension and discomfort
- Life changes, such as the birth of a child or the loss of a job, impact people's feelings about themselves and others
- Loss and mourning
- Difficulty in beginning or maintaining relationships

Your symptoms will typically begin to improve once you have learned valuable methods for coping with the difficulties in your relationships.

Structure of IPT

During the initial sessions (1-3). The primary focus will be gathering information and determining the direction the therapy will go. Your therapist will assist you in compiling a list of the most critical relationships in your life (interpersonal inventory). The four primary aspects of the problem have been utilized to categorize these interactions.

In the middle sessions (4-14). In these sessions, you concentrate on trying to improve the chosen problem area or areas with the help of the therapist. You work with your therapist to identify potential answers to the issues, and in between sessions, you try to put these potential solutions into action.

During the last sessions (15-16). The primary focus will be on resolving any feelings of grief connected with the conclusion of therapy, as well as evaluating the problems found in the interpersonal assessment and the steps taken to address those problems.

Who might benefit from engaging in IPT?

IPT is utilized during the acute phase of major depression, the majority of the time, however, it may also be administered as a maintenance treatment to assist in the prevention of relapse and recurrence of the condition. Moreover, it treats anxiety, bulimia nervosa, chronic tiredness, and mood disorders such as bipolar disorder and dysthymic disorder.

IPT is currently suitable for treating patients of every age, ranging from adolescents to old people. It is beneficial to use both alone and with other therapies, such as medication, to achieve the best results.

9. Therapeutic Exposure. A form of cognitive-behavioral therapy known as exposure therapy is employed in the treatment of anxiety disorders, post-traumatic stress disorder (PTSD), and other problems that are closely connected to PTSD. The client will learn that the fear reaction is not essential and can be handled by confronting the feared item or circumstance in a controlled and safe manner throughout the therapy. This will allow the individual to understand that the fear response can be regulated.

Theoretical mechanisms of exposure therapy

There are four primary ways that exposure therapy may help:

1. Fear extinction. It is the process by which the brain learns to disassociate a previously feared stimulus from a negative outcome or response. During exposure therapy, repeated exposure to the feared stimulus without any negative consequences can decrease the fear response over time as the brain learns that the stimulus is not dangerous. This process is mediated by the amygdala and prefrontal cortex changes involved in fear processing and regulation.

2. Habituation. It refers to the process through which the brain becomes desensitized after repeatedly being exposed to stimuli. As the individual is repeatedly exposed to the feared stimulus, their initial fear response may decrease due to the brain habituating to the stimulus. This process is thought to be mediated by changes in the locus coeruleus-norepinephrine system, which is involved in arousal and attention regulation.

3. Emotional processing. Exposure therapy can also change the individual's emotional processing of feared stimuli. By confronting the feared stimulus and staying with the resulting negative emotions, individuals may learn to process and regulate their emotions more adaptively. This process is mediated by changes in the hippocampus and prefrontal cortex, which are involved in emotional memory and regulation.

4. Cognitive restructuring. Exposure therapy can also be combined with cognitive restructuring techniques to help individuals change their negative thoughts and beliefs about feared stimuli. By challenging and replacing these thoughts with more realistic and adaptive ones, the individual may experience a decrease in their fear response. This process is mediated by changes in the prefrontal cortex and anterior cingulate cortex, which is involved in cognitive control and regulation.

What is the goal of Exposure Therapy?

By gradually exposing patients to the things that cause them to feel nervous or fearful, exposure therapy assists them in confronting and overcoming their phobias. This is done for the following reason—when a person is scared of something, their natural reaction is to try to escape whatever they are afraid of; but this leads to repercussions, further feeding the person's anxiety.

A person who suffers from anxiety may, for instance, be terrified of being among other people, which may lead them to shun human interaction altogether and, consequently, not have any friends. This scenario demonstrates how problematic it can be to avoid confronting one's anxieties. According to the principles of exposure therapy, to live happy, healthy lives, we must face and conquer our anxieties rather than run away from them.

Exposure therapy typically involves three stages:

1. Preparation stage. The therapist and individual work together to identify the feared object or situation, develop a treatment plan, and learn to cope skills to manage anxiety and stress.

2. Exposure stage. During this stage, the person is exposed to their dreaded stimulus safely and progressively. The exposure may be in vivo (real-life exposures) or imaginary (imagining the feared situation), and it may be gradual or intense, depending on the individual's needs and preferences.

Throughout the exposure, the therapist guides the individual to confront the fear and manage their anxiety using the coping skills they have learned. The goal is to help the individual learn that the fear response is not necessary and can be managed to reduce their overall anxiety and distress. After the exposure, the therapist and individual debrief the experience, discussing what was learned and any remaining anxiety or stress.

3. The post-exposure stage. This is an opportunity to review progress and identify any further work that may need to be done.

How does exposure therapy work?

The approaches a therapist utilizes during exposure therapy are determined by the condition that is the primary focus of the treatment. What follows is a description of possible occurrences.

- Your therapist or psychologist will begin treating your fear or anxiety once the root reason has been discovered. This will involve gradually exposing you to the stimuli that cause you the most concern.

- They commonly take a step-by-step strategy, beginning with gradually increasing the intensity of the feared stimuli or starting with a less intense replica of the original stimulus.

- Throughout therapy, your therapist will gradually introduce you to increasingly frightening stimuli in a controlled setting.

- Your level of improvement will determine the total number of sessions required and the total amount of time spent receiving therapy.

For instance, if you have a phobia of mice, the therapist may present you with photographs of mice during the first session with them. They may bring a live mouse confined in a cage to the subsequent meeting. You can be asked to control a mouse in the third and final session.

Which conditions can be helped by exposure therapy?

Exposure treatment is often utilized to treat anxiety disorders like phobias, panic disorder, post-traumatic stress disorder, generalized anxiety disorder, obsessive-compulsive disorder (OCD), social anxiety disorder

The therapy helps individuals confront their fears and learn to manage their anxiety, ultimately reducing their overall distress and improving their quality of life.

10. What is Cognitive Behavioral Therapy? Cognitive therapy is predicated on the idea that our thoughts, feelings, and actions are intertwined, which means that our mental processes affect our feelings. This therapy, also known as CBT, aims to improve patients' awareness of how faulty thinking affects their actions or behavior. CBT requires you to work with your therapist to build skills to examine and adjust your thinking, beliefs, and responses.

What is the theory behind CBT?

A central tenet of CBT is that our mental representation of events can directly impact our feelings and actions in response to those events. For instance, if you perceive a particular circumstance pessimistically, you can find that you have pessimistic feelings. And those negative emotions may cause you to act in a particular manner.

Cognitive therapy sessions typically last between 45 to 60 minutes and occur once a week for three to six months. Cognitive therapists may employ the following strategies to treat patients suffering from psychiatric illness or behavioral problems, depending on the patient's condition.

Examples of cognitive therapy in action

Organizing one's activities. Depression is characterized by a lack of interest in activities that were once sources of pleasure for the individual. This loss of interest is one of the acute symptoms of depression. A cognitive therapist might put together a schedule of things their patient used to enjoy, such as going on long walks or meditating, and encourage them to give those hobbies another shot. The patient may find these activities pleasurable as part of their treatment and experience improved feelings while participating.

Observational exercises with grading. Those who suffer from anxiety disorders can benefit from another method of cognitive therapy, which involves giving them graded exposure assignments. One form of CBT is called exposure, and it involves gradually exposing a person to whatever causes them to feel afraid or anxious. This was already discussed in previous pages.

Mindfulness and skills training. A person who has lost hope in overcoming new difficulties may benefit from cognitive therapy. For illustration's sake, let's say someone believes they are doomed to fail in anything they put their mind to because they have experienced failure in the past. Because of this erroneous assumption, they may be prevented from advancing in life, which only serves to aggravate their depression and disappoint them further.

This person may benefit from seeing a cognitive therapist to better understand what is wrong with their thinking and how to change their thought pattern.

A cognitive therapist can assist their patient in living in the present by employing skills training and mindfulness practices instead of dwelling on events from the patient's past. The practice of mindfulness is a method for learning to pay attention in the here and now instead of constantly replaying mental chatter from the past or future.

The person can improve abilities such as problem-solving by using a training strategy for skills. To accomplish this goal, the therapist may provide the individual with personalized tasks and encourage them to do them.

10 core values that guide CBT

1. The therapy relationship must be strong for CBT to be effective. ────

It is critical to earn a patient's confidence and build a solid rapport with them before beginning treatment. Changing your tone of voice and body language to express a sense of warmth and concern is a necessary step in this process. In addition, you should present them with your treatment plan and solicit their input after each appointment.

2. CBT is both goal-oriented and problem-focused. ────

The issues a patient brings up during the initial consultation will be the basis for developing goals. For instance, if a depressed patient tells you they are disorganized, you can direct them towards making a goal, such as, "Keep to a daily regimen." This would help them feel more in control of their life. During the route, you will also assist the patient in identifying any barriers that hinder them from accomplishing their objectives.

3. The patient is encouraged to learn how to become their therapist as part of the CBT approach. ────

Patients are assigned 'homework' to complete in between their scheduled therapy appointments. This comprises completing CBT worksheets at home so that they can understand the triggers that cause them to experience negative thoughts and practice coping techniques to overcome them. This action will continue to be beneficial to the patient for many months or even years down the road.

4. The goal of CBT is to have a time limit. ────

Patients suffering from anxiety and depression typically participate in the treatment for a shorter period, with sessions ranging from 6 to 14. It's important to remember that not every patient improves at the same rate. This is one reason some patients may require further sessions, particularly those who have struggled with dysfunctional beliefs for a considerable time.

5. Collaboration and active engagement are encouraged throughout CBT. ─

Although therapists typically take a more active role in the treatment process at the beginning of a therapy partnership, patients should still be included in the decision-making process for their care. This will become increasingly apparent as people continue to report improved symptoms. Put decision-making power in their hands by asking them to select the issues they want to discuss throughout the session.

6. CBT employs a wide range of methods to effect changes in thinking, mood, and behavior.
Since patients' struggles, intellectual levels, backgrounds, and motivation to change differ, CBT can include strategies from other types of therapy. For instance, a therapist can employ Socratic questioning to change a person's negative thinking pattern, encouraging the individual to think analytically. "Can you give an illustration that shows what you have just stated?" "Is there another point of view that could be considered?" "What are the repercussions of this over the longer term?"

7. CBT sessions are organized.
At the beginning of each treatment session, the therapist will assess the patient's mood and then decide on a specific objective for that session. During the middle portion of the appointment, you will review the patient's past homework assignments and give them their new assignments. You and the patient will conclude the session by reviewing everything covered during the session.

8. Clients who participate in CBT learn how to recognize, assess, and react to their dysfunctional thoughts and beliefs.
The patient is taught, with the assistance of a therapist, how to assess their thoughts to improve not only their moods and behaviors but also their overall quality of life. In CBT, one method is termed "behavioral experiments". It can be used to examine a patient's preconceptions.

9. CBT is predicated on an ever-evolving articulation of patient issues and an individualized cognitive conceptualization of each patient.
When you first meet a patient, you will base your understanding of them on the information they disclose at the beginning of the session. On the other hand, you continue to hone this knowledge when they reveal further facts about themselves during their therapy sessions.

10. At the beginning stages, CBT emphasizes the present.
This indicates that cognitive therapy focuses on issues that are occurring in

the "now and now" rather than issues that occurred in the past. On the other hand, therapists can bring up a patient's history if the patient expresses a wish to do so or if it is essential to bring up the patient's past because the patient is having difficulty overcoming their cognitive distortion.

What conditions is cognitive therapy used for?

This treatment has been studied extensively and found to be beneficial for a wide range of psychiatric conditions, including but not limited to the following: depression, anxiety, ADHD, eating disorders, substance misuse, personality disorders, bipolar disorder, schizophrenia, anger problems, drug or alcohol problems, hoarding, phobias, psychosis, self-harm, stress, sleep problems, obsessive-compulsive disorder (OCD), perinatal mental health problems, post-traumatic stress disorder (PTSD), and schizoaffective disorder.

In addition, it has been demonstrated that cognitive therapy is a successful treatment for people who suffer from non-psychiatric disorders such as irritable bowel syndrome, as well as for people who suffer from depression and anxious chronic fatigue syndrome, fibromyalgia, insomnia, and migraines.

Medications. It is crucial to have a thorough evaluation by a qualified healthcare professional before beginning treatment with any medication to determine the treatment strategy that is going to be the most effective. Here are some examples of conservative and holistic approaches to consider before using medication in conjunction with talk therapy.

1. Conservative approaches

Modifications to one's lifestyle, including alterations to one's eating habits, exercise routine, and sleeping patterns, can affect one's mental health. Adaptations to one's lifestyle, such as increases in physical activity and alterations to one's nutrition, may help alleviate the symptoms of depression, as suggested by a synthesis of research published in the Journal of Clinical Psychiatry.

Talk therapy, such as cognitive-behavioral therapy (CBT), can effectively treat various mental health conditions. CBT is one example of talk therapy. CBT has been demonstrated to help treat mental health conditions such as depression, PTSD, and anxiety, as stated by the American Psychological Association.

Psychoeducation refers to gaining knowledge about the signs and causes of a mental health disorder to manage such illness better. Psychoeducation may be an effective strategy for reducing the symptoms of anxiety and depression, according to a new review of the relevant studies published in the Journal of Affective Disorders.

Support from others. A robust social support network can be good when managing mental health disorders. According to research recently presented in the Journal of Health and Social Behavior, it is possible to lessen the negative impact of stress on an individual's mental health.

Meditation on mindfulness means concentrating on the here and now and allowing oneself to experience one's thoughts and emotions without attaching any value judgments to them.

According to the findings of a meta-analysis that was just recently published in the Journal of Psychiatric Research, mindfulness-based therapies have the potential to reduce anxiety and depression symptoms.

2. Holistic approaches

Mind-body therapies focus on the connection between the mind and the body, such as yoga, meditation, and tai chi. These have shown promise in alleviating the symptoms of anxiety and depression. Mind-body therapies were shown to help treat anxiety disorders, according to a review of previous research published in the Journal of Clinical Psychology.

Art therapy can be beneficial in expressing feelings and lowering symptoms of anxiety and depression. Art therapy can also help people who have difficulty expressing themselves verbally. An analysis of previous research published in the Journal of the American Art Therapy Association suggests that engaging in art therapy may help alleviate anxiety, depression, and PTSD.

Animal-assisted therapy, including therapy for dogs, may help alleviate some symptoms of depression and anxiety. An analysis of previous research published in the Journal of Psychiatric Research suggests that animal-assisted therapy may be beneficial in treating the symptoms associated with mental health problems like anxiety and depression.

Regular exercise has been demonstrated to be good for both physical and mental health. Regular exercise may be a helpful method to lessen the symptoms of depression, according to the results of a meta-analysis recently published in the American Journal of Preventive Medicine.

A healthy diet is recommended since it has been shown that eating foods rich in omega-3 fatty acids, B vitamins, and antioxidants will improve mental health. According to the findings of a study compiled and published in the Journal of Clinical Psychiatry, dietary treatments can help treat depressive symptoms.

Yoga asanas (yoga postures), pranayama (breathing exercises), and Meditation are all components of yoga. Yoga helps lower symptoms of anxiety and depression, according to the findings of a meta-analysis published in the Journal of Psychiatric Research.

Acupuncture is a form of complementary medicine that involves the insertion of needles into specific body sites. According to the findings of a study compiled and published in the journal Current Opinion in Psychiatry, acupuncture may be an effective therapy option for patients suffering from depression.

3. Spiritual approach

By exploring a person's specific belief systems and utilizing that person's faith in a higher power, spiritual therapy is a type of psychotherapy that aims to treat a person's soul in addition to their mind and body. Spiritual therapists accomplish this. Individuals who have faith in a benevolent higher power may discover that spiritual counseling assists them in developing a more intimate relationship with that force. A person who is suffering from depression may discover, via the process of spiritual treatment, that there is a moral conflict existing in some aspect of their life.

When a person unintentionally engages in self-sabotage, they may experience anxiety. Some people may find that spiritual counseling is a helpful model for identifying and resolving conflict areas and probable mental health difficulties that may occur throughout their lives. Nevertheless, this is simply one way among many others that can be used to do so.

Generally speaking, pairing medication with a spiritual or faith-based approach to mental health care is a personal choice that should be discussed with a healthcare provider. Some forms of "spiritual approach" may concentrate entirely on ways that do not involve the use of medication, while others may opt to make the use of medication a component of their treatment strategy.

Prayer is sometimes part of faith-based and spiritual methods for treating mental health issues. It can help people feel more connected to something, whether that be a higher power, their values, or even to other people. Additionally, prayer can reduce feelings of isolation, anxiety, and fear. On the other hand, these practices should not be depended upon as the only form of treatment for mental health disorders; instead, they should be utilized in conjunction with treatments.

JOURNAL

What situations have you experienced that have generated high stress and anxiety levels?

Let's all be positive adults to every child we stumble so they may grow up compassionate, kind, emphatic, generous, and thoughtful to others. Our kindness will be multiplied a million times.

April Key

Filipinos are known for their close ties
with family and friends.

CHAPTER 5

Living With Papa's Uncle

We lived in Consolacion, Cebu, with my father's uncle during the summer. He, the brother of my paternal grandfather, and his wives were good to us. We enjoyed living with them.

My sister and I had a favorite morning ritual of waking up early to ask Lola Ceiling for some Filipino crackers called dunggan-dunggan and bahug-bahug. These crackers were commonly found in sari-sari stores. Dunggan-dunggan resembled an ear, with a dark pink line spiraling around it. Bahug-bahug is a red sweet bread. Thankfully, Lola Ceiling and Lolo Metring willingly shared them with us, making mornings something to look forward to.

My father's cousins treated us well, ensuring we had enough to eat. However, mealtime was challenging for me as I struggled to finish my food, often being the last at the table. Auntie Sandra was a good disciplinarian and insisted that I eat everything on my plate. Tearfully, I complied, as I was not particularly fond of eating then. I only liked dried fish and rice, which caused my relatives to raise concerns about my health as I also got sick quite easily.

My sister and I posed a challenge to my aunts, who still lived with their parents. We loved sneaking out during noon, evading their attempts to make us take naps. Instead, we would wait until they had left or were napping themselves and we would run to the neighbors to play Jackstone—it's one of those sneaky things kids like to do.

When it was time for me to enroll in first grade and my sister in kindergarten, we moved to stay with my father's two cousins. The second sister cared for our needs, accompanying us to school as it was a bit of a long walk. She prepared our meals and made sure we had our snacks for recess, including cold Tang juice, chips, sandwich bread, and 20 pesos each for Juhan and me, in case we needed to buy something.

During this period, I struggled because of one of my aunt's abusive behaviors. She would hurt me during meals and sometimes physically harm me on our way to school if we were late. My aversion to meat, preferring fish, only aggravated the situation. Maybe it was because I ate fish at my grandpa's house where it was available fresh daily. This aunt's forceful attempts to make me eat were painful, diverting my focus from finishing my food to enduring the pain.

One night, Mama took me to watch a movie, along with a male companion. This was followed by dining out and shopping for my sister and me. Mama then sent us home as she stayed with the man. Her early return the next morning angered me, leading to a confrontation with my aunts. When I revealed Mama's whereabouts and the company she kept, they dismissed it as a lie. They told my mother about what I said, and I couldn't understand why they all got very angry and why my mother beat me up for an entire day so I would tell the truth. After a year, we moved back to Lola Press when I was in second grade.

REFLECTION

From a young age, individuals often have a clear sense of their preferences in clothing, food, and activities. Unfortunately, it appears that adults sometimes overlook a child's taste, particularly when it comes to food. Rather than addressing the issue and creating a comfortable eating environment for the child, mealtime becomes a source of trauma.

While children may occasionally fabricate stories, they generally remain honest about their observations, especially when they find situations confusing. This is particularly true in the case of their parents, as children tend to harbor unconditional love for them, regardless of how they are treated at times. Adults must avoid introducing or exposing children to additional adult figures in their lives without providing adequate explanations first. Such actions can leave the child feeling upset and bewildered about their guardian's behavior.

Finding solace in the company of an extended family that genuinely cares and treats them as part of their own is a positive experience. This is especially comforting for troubled children grappling with confusion about their family life, those questioning why their family structure differs from others.

"No matter the challenges within a child's home, the kindness shown by others becomes a positive influence in their lives."

- April Key

PSYCHOLOGICAL ANALYSIS

""During this period, I struggled because of one of my aunt's abusive behaviors. She would hurt me during meals and sometimes physically harm me on our way to school if we were late."

Abuse is treating a person with violence. It is acting aggressively both physically and emotionally. Many people often think of abuse as just showing physical abuse to another person, but it is also called abuse when offensive words or other actions are used to hurt another.

The person who receives the abuse is not guilty of it; no one should be blamed for being abused. The abused may think that it is normal and that he or she deserves it. A person who grew up in an environment of violence may believe that this is a common practice, which may lead them to repeat similar violent behaviors in the future.

Some of the behaviors that denote abuse are:

- Mistreatment through blows, kicks, burns, bites, hanging, spitting, or hair-pulling
- Humiliation, using words that can hurt one's self-esteem, such as "No one loves you," or hurling insults and blame or accusing or manipulating another

Parents should keenly observe their children, exercise caution in choosing caretakers, and foster trust to encourage open communication in any situation. To identify signs of potential abuse, pay attention to changes in the child's behavior, speech, or actions around others. Examine their body for physical indications of abuse and ask the child directly if they have experienced any behaviors indicative of mistreatment.

JOURNAL

How would you handle a situation in which you or a family member has been a victim of abuse?

If we have patience and we learn to understand others, we will have a kinder world to live in.

April Key

Santo Niño de Cebu is the oldest artifact in the Philippines. It's a gift of Magellan to Rajah Humabon.

CHAPTER 6

A Whisper

We were back at Lola Press' house in Asturias. Mama had a hard time visiting us, as Consolacion, Cebu, was quite far for her to travel. The transition for my sister and me was not difficult because we were familiar with the kids here whom we knew from our previous time living here. Lola Press remains the same person we knew before.

The civil unrest in the area persisted, but we continued accompanying Mama on visits to the farmers' fish ponds when we weren't in school.

One afternoon, I went to the sari-sari store to buy something, and a man asked the sales lady, who was also the owner of the store, about my Mama's residence. Fortunately, he didn't notice me, and the lady didn't reveal anything. I quickly fetched my sister, and we hid at our neighbor's house near the highway, keeping an eye on the man.

Another man disembarked from a bus, also searching for Mama. It frightened Juhan and me. Why were two men arriving on the same day at the same time, looking for our mother? We observed the men like mice from inside our neighbor's house.

After a few hours, Mama got off the bus after work, and the two men approached her. As they both waited there, they were unaware that they were looking for the same person. I wasn't sure how Mama handled the situation. Fortunately, their conversation was brief, and then both men left. I was relieved that the men didn't resort to fighting, either with each other or with Mama. I feared they might be connected to the death threats against her.

One evening, as we were playing outside, a miracle occurred. My sister noticed the clouds resembling the Virgin Mary. She urgently called for me to join her, but by the time I arrived, the cloud formation had disappeared. That was the first time Mama Mary appeared to Juhan. She was convinced it was a miraculous sign, but I had missed it.

Many mistook my sister and me for twins. Mama took care to dress us alike, with only variations in color to prevent any disagreements. Juhan consistently excelled academically, finishing each school year at the top of her class, while I struggled with health issues. Despite my academic shortcomings, Mama ensured we both received new outfits, shoes, and accessories that matched, making us presentable on stage for our end-of-year school presentations. She maintained fairness between us, despite the academic disparity.

One morning, a bird perched on Lola Press' roof, and her nephew falsely told his kids that my sister and I had stolen it. We clarified the truth to Lola Press, who just let it go. However, one afternoon, as Juhan and I stood outside the school gate's waiting shed, our friends approached with their father. We called them excitedly, and although they initially looked enthusiastic, their father told them something that made them stop interacting with us.

I told Juhan, "I know what happened. Uncle told them not to play with us because we're thieves." I could tell that was what he said just by watching the way his mouth moved. I told Lola Press and thereafter, we avoided entering their property and stopped watching movies at their place. Lola Press also refrained from speaking to them, instructing us to stay away.

Eventually, Ate Samantha's mom, Lola Press's niece, gathered the courage to call Uncle's family. She inquired about the rift and why Lola Press no longer talked with them. Lola told her the story I related to her.

Auntie Chloe questioned Ate Samantha, who confirmed what her father said. I was glad she told the truth. Auntie Chloe's husband also admitted to the truth when she called him to ask him about it, sparing us from potential trouble. I was shaking and praying, "Please, Mama Mary, let the truth come out."

I was relieved that everything got settled before our return to the city. Knowing Lola Press needed her family's support as she was alone in her house. I was glad that harmony was restored between us and Lola Press's family.

REFLECTION

Juhan and I were fortunate to have Lola Press by our side. Despite the early traumas we faced and the limited time we spent with our mother, having someone who listened to us and defended us felt like hitting the jackpot. Lola Press was the first person to teach us that doing the right thing is more crucial than blindly supporting blood relatives, especially when they are in the wrong. Lola Press and Tita Chloe handled the conflict admirably, demonstrating respect by allowing the other to speak first as the other person listened. Acknowledging mistakes and taking responsibility resolved issues, fostering forgiveness, and allowing everyone to move forward. I only wished Tita Chloe had approached Lola Press sooner, rather than waiting a year to initiate the conversation. Nevertheless, the situation was handled gracefully without resorting to verbal abuse.

"If people took the time to listen without immediate judgment, conflicts could be resolved faster."

- April Key

"There's nothing wrong with pointing out faults, as long as it is done in the right manner."

- April Key

"People with great minds welcome constructive feedback to improve, while those with small minds refuse to listen, perceiving it as an attack."

- April Key

"If everyone refrained from verbal abuse during conflicts, forgiveness and a return to normalcy would be more achievable."

- April Key

"Conflicts serve as catalysts for change and personal growth."

- April Key

PSYCHOLOGICAL ANALYSIS

"Despite my academic shortcomings, Mama ensured we both received new outfits, shoes, and accessories that matched, making us presentable on stage for our end-of-year school presentations. She maintained fairness between us, despite the academic disparity."

While each child is unique, these differences should not be a basis for a parent to favor one child over another. Every child has their personality, interests, and needs, and parents must recognize and appreciate these distinctions, avoiding comparisons or favoritism that may harm one child's feelings.

Certain situations may justify favoritism, such as when a child is a newborn or when one is unwell, requiring additional care and attention. However, parents must communicate openly with their children, explaining the reasons behind unequal attention and assuring them that it doesn't reflect lesser love or neglect.

Parents may unknowingly show preference when making comparisons between siblings. Phrases like "You should be more like your brother" or "Why aren't you as studious as your brother?" can create feelings of insecurity and low self-confidence in the child.

One common reason for parental favoritism is the perception that one child is more accommodating than the other. Parents may favor the child who consistently obeys, excels in school, and appears less problematic. However, this favoritism can lead to negative consequences for both the favored and unfavored children, affecting the family dynamics.

JOURNAL

Have you experienced favoritism? How did it make you feel?

The coolest thing to do is to live a life of kindness and compassion to others.

April Key

Sorbetes or often called 'dirty ice cream' is one of the delightful refreshments for kids. It is not dirty but the name was coined because it is usually prepared and sold on the streets.

CHAPTER 7

Spill the Lies

Now, we found ourselves in a new school, surrounded by unfamiliar faces and a different environment. This change meant we had to make an effort to adapt once again and establish new friendships. Our residence was within the compound of one of Mama's bosses, Mommy Monette, who owned a gated rental property. This arrangement provided a sense of security, and we were warmly welcomed and well-cared for, especially when Mama had to travel within the province. Although Mama sometimes did fieldwork, she primarily worked in the office, which allowed us more time together.

At times, my sister and I joined Mama in her work, helping with tasks such as preparing and planting seeds, occasionally on weekends. This was a preferable alternative to the challenging journeys involving river crossings and long hikes under the scorching sun.

Within the neighborhood, my sister and I made friends, most of whom were in section A, attending school in the morning and returning home after lunch. Every afternoon around 3:00 pm, after settling down from school or napping, the children in the neighborhood formed two teams and played soccer on the spacious vacant lot. This became one of my cherished childhood memories.

Juhan often visited our neighbor's house upon returning from school, while I had to head home to handle chores. I occasionally had a difficult time locating Juhan to ensure her safe arrival, knocking on every neighbor's door just to make sure she was okay.

Sometimes, when I was too unwell to walk home, my sister had to run home to fetch our house helper for assistance. I was taller than my sister and had a heavy backpack, so the helper struggled to carry me and our two backpacks.

There were times when going home became difficult because of the two boys in my class who always tried to bully me. They both made sure that I had a hard time going home. It was so bad that I begged my teacher to accompany me when I saw her, saying that I did not feel safe going home alone. Unfortunately, she didn't take me seriously. I was just glad I was a good runner. I always managed to get home safely but I had to spend one to two hours roaming around the area before arriving safely at home.

The time came when I couldn't take it anymore and I told my sister about it. From then on, she started to wait for me to finish school so we could go home together. It wasn't an easy journey for us, but we're glad we always made it home safely. I didn't tell my mother about this as our relationship was beginning to falter. She had been physically hurting me whenever I tried to get her attention or ask her to spend more time with me and my sister. She was so occupied with her love life that she forgot to ask how my sister and I were doing.

Mama's boyfriend sometimes slept at our apartment, and I caught them being intimate with each other. I saw them kissing one morning. Sometimes, Mama would physically hurt me whenever I would try to stop her from going with him. There was a time when I caught her boyfriend trying to get my sister to ride with him on his motorbike. I didn't let him do it without me. I bravely and stubbornly said, "No, you can't bring her anywhere without me!" I asked him where they were going. I was shocked to find out that Mama was waiting in a cafeteria so they could all eat together without me.

We seldom visited my mother's boyfriend's apartment. Neither of them admitted to Juhan or me that they were in a relationship. They pretended they were just friends. Whenever Mama would see her other friends from work, this guy was always with us no matter how late it was.

It was Mama's birthday and my sister was waiting for her patiently so she could sing to her and wish her happy birthday. But Mama didn't arrive, and it was so late in the evening so we just went to bed without her. In the middle of the night, she came in walking quietly. I was happy to see her and just as I was about to wake my sister up so both of us could greet her, she got angry and told me to go back to sleep. She went out again and left my sister and me alone in the house.

We stayed with Ate Abeth when Mama was busy with fieldwork, which meant she had to travel around Cebu for a few days. Ate Abeth would sometimes bring us with her to her younger sister Goyang if Ate Abeth was also busy. We would stay there for a few days.

Ate Goyang was such a caring elder to my sister and especially to me. Even though they lived near a dumpsite in Cebu, she always managed to keep my food and water very clean. She made sure that all my dishes, utensils, drinking glasses, and drinking water were boiled for a couple of hours so they were all sterilized.

As far as my memory serves me, I never fell ill under her watchful eye. She consistently ensured that I refrained from playing with other children in the neighborhood amidst piles of trash. Given my reluctance to play outdoors at a young age, complying with this rule was effortless for me. However, my younger sister, Juhan, yearned to engage with the local kids. Ate Goyang diligently maintained her cleanliness to prevent me from falling ill.

Ate Abeth would occasionally take us back to the province to visit relatives at Lolo Seno's house. Our time with the Priego family was enjoyable, and we played with friends in the town, alongside our big brothers, Kuya Marsden and Kuya Julius.

During our return trips, Ate Abeth often found herself in a predicament, especially when my Aunt Riley's bus was in front of us and my sister would plead to board it, knowing her favorite Aunt Nicole was on board. Ate Abeth and I concurred with Juhan, recognizing the opportunity to save on bus fares and enjoy complimentary snacks, courtesy of our aunt's pit stop at Titay's for our favorite treats.

Whenever Juhan spotted Aunt Nicole, she clung to her, expressing a strong preference for her over Mama and me. However, I never allowed Juhan to go alone; I always accompanied her. Meanwhile, Ate Abeth would return empty-handed, telling Mama, "The kids are not with me anymore."

Our aunts often took Juhan and me when Aunt Riley, the owner of the bus and spouse to a French businessman, relocated to a new house in another subdivision. This made it challenging for Mama to track us down, especially in the absence of cell phones. Mama would walk into that affluent subdivision just to see my sister and me.

We relished our time with our French-Filipino cousins and savored the French cuisine crafted by our uncle. Despite the delectable dishes, I deliberately limited my intake. Although they occasionally kept us for weeks, Mama would inevitably be notified or contacted at work when my fever resurfaced. They were worried whenever I got sick.

The time came when they all decided to have Juhan and me live in my grandparents' house. They understood that it would be challenging for Mama to travel and retrieve us, especially with Papa living with us. Consequently, we spent that summer with our grandparents. During that period, Papa spoke to me, disclosing his illness and entrusting me with the responsibility of safeguarding my sister and our family. As the eldest, I had to summon courage. I was only nine when he shared this with me. From that moment onward, I always remembered his words, diligently watching over my sister as he had requested.

However, there came a day when my father was not in his right mind. He was chopping wood in the backyard when I noticed him laughing to himself. I heard him mention me and my sister's names. Fortunately, Mama arrived on time, and I promptly told her this. She was hiding in one of our aunt's houses, a short distance from my grandparents' residence. Despite my warnings to everyone about an imminent threat, only Mama believed me. I had to prepare and watch Papa's actions.

On a late afternoon, we were playing in the backyard with our older cousins. While they were occupied with chores, Juhan and I joyfully played around them. Papa emerged from the house, calling, "April, come here." I signaled to my sister not to approach. He summoned our two cousins, but they did not come. Finally, he called Juhan, and she willingly went to him. Suddenly, he lifted her by her neck and dropped her onto a large rock. Fortunately, she sustained no major injuries, though the fall did hurt her ribs.

My grandfather was furious. He instructed my father to put my sister down. He brought all of us inside the house, including the ladder so Papa couldn't climb it. Papa circled the house a few times before settling in the bahay kubo in the backyard. Following that incident, the family decided to return Juhan and me to my mother.

I finally obtained a large fish-shaped figurine in which I could save the money received from my grandmother. Grandpa proudly displayed it in the living room downstairs, and I had been asking for it for years. Delighted to finally have it, I happily returned to the city with my mother and sister.

We woke up early, boarded the bus at dawn, and on our way to the city, I noticed a big boat passing under the bridge. That area was known for paranormal activities. I informed Mama about the large boat passing in front of us. Although scared and about to shout, Mama advised me to simply close my eyes as she couldn't see anything. Opening my eyes, I was relieved that nothing bad had happened while crossing the bridge.

Back in the city, we resumed our normal routine. I started my "yema balls" business, learning to cook them myself and selling them to neighbors, friends, and classmates. I also joined my neighbor friends in caroling during the Christmas season to earn some extra money.

My goal with this business was to fill my fish piggy bank. However, one day, upon returning from school, I discovered that my nearly full fish piggy bank was almost empty. My cunning sister had ingeniously used a spoon, fork, and knife to extract the coins from the small hole. While I was confused about how she did it, she effortlessly figured it out. Despite being upset and angry that my hard work seemed for naught, her sweet demeanor made it challenging to express my frustration. I let it go, cautioning her not to repeat it. Nevertheless, we occasionally ended up doing it together when Mama refused to give us money for snacks. Juhan always led in such silly activities, but they were among the crazy, fun things we enjoyed growing up!

We rarely visited Mama's office, but when we did, her co-workers would always inquire about my younger sister. "Where is your younger daughter, the pretty and smart one?" they'd ask. Mama would respond, "April is sick again, so I had to bring her with me while Juhan is in school." Mama never made me feel like she favored one of us over the other, based on our beauty or strengths. I admired her for that.

One day, Mama encountered one of my grandparent's farmland workers who informed her that my father's family had decided to take my sister and me, with no intention of returning us to our mother. Mama shared this distressing news with us and sought our opinion. I suggested that Mama hide from them and take us to her family in Mindanao, making it difficult for Papa's sisters to retrieve us. All three of us agreed, choosing to be with Mama's family.

As the school year neared its end, Juhan's teacher called Mama, requesting her to sign an agreement. The teacher wanted Juhan to agree to be second in academic standings, even though she was one point ahead of her classmate, who happened to be the principal's daughter and a friend of Juhan's. The teacher justified this arrangement by labeling Juhan as a "transferee."

Mama discussed the situation with Juhan, saying, "It's just an honor, not that important. Since the school cares about it so much, let your classmate have first place." My sister simply nodded in agreement.

Following our recognition ceremony at school, Mama deemed it the right time to take us to her family in Mindanao. Her boyfriend assisted us with our luggage as we boarded the boat. We spent one night on the journey to Cagayan de Oro City and then endured a five-hour bus ride to reach Damulog, Bukidnon.

We safely arrived at Mama's older sister's house, the one who had taken care of Mama in her youth and supported her education. Mama stayed for a couple of days and then unexpectedly left us to return to Cebu without informing us.

She left our school cards inside our favorite biscuit tin, and then I knew it was final. I was very sad, crying so hard when I couldn't find Mama anywhere in the house upon waking up. My aunt informed me that Mama had already left and gone back to Cebu. After shedding tears, I wiped my eyes and went with Ate Mary Ann and my sister to the market to buy some groceries.

Passing by my grandpa's house, I saw Lolo Aureo wearing a black shirt standing right in front of the upstairs window. He appeared angry and sad, thinking that Mama and his nephew's family might have been in an accident at dawn. He shouted angrily, urging everyone to bring Mama's dead body home. Mama hadn't said goodbye to him before leaving for Cebu.

The news he heard on the radio reported that a private jeep had fallen into a deep cliff. The vehicle owner, a doctor, and his wife, also a doctor, were in the vehicle with their sons, nephew, and cousin.

The situation left my grandpa and others confused because multiple vehicles crashed that day, and numerous people died from early morning until the afternoon. However, only the jeep with the doctor couple fit the description of our family who had left early in the morning.

I worried again upon learning the news, realizing we might never get a chance to see Mama and Papa again after this accident. However, I felt happy and relieved when they confirmed that our family members had all survived the crash, and no one died in that private vehicle.

It became known that Mama was pregnant because the doctor who took care of her mentioned she was two to three months pregnant during the accident. Everyone was surprised that she had never told anyone about her pregnancy.

Living with Mama's older sister was not a great experience for us. She was controlled by her husband, and they didn't care for me and Ate Mary Ann, who was one of my cousin's daughters. At that time, she was fifteen years old and lived with my aunt Nanay Merly, Mama's sister, as a working student. Ate Mary Ann helped my aunt take care of the house and other needs, while my aunt helped her with her education.

The packages Mama sent from Cebu containing our favorite snacks and food were not given to us; instead, they offered moldy bread that my sister and I refused to eat.

Juhan had a better life here as our aunt and uncle adored and treated her as their child. Sometimes, she went on vacation with them, leaving Ate Mary Ann and me alone in the house. However, we enjoyed it because we could call Lolo Aureo and have him sleep over. But my aunt later enforced a rule not to let Lolo Aureo into her house. She became angry when she found out we let him in, possibly disliking the idea that Lolo knew how she treated me and Ate Mary Ann.

The day came when Ate Mary Ann couldn't bear it anymore and wanted to escape. I strategized and planned the escape. Although we told Lolo about our plan, he disagreed, fearing my aunt's anger. Nonetheless, we pursued our plan and Ate Mary Ann managed to escape safely.

When it was our turn, I ran to Lolo's house and informed him that Ate Mary Ann was already gone, insisting that he let Juhan and me in. He hesitated as Mama left us with my aunt, not with him. He was already 92 years old at that time. It took me a long time to persuade him, and my aunt noticed my absence. She went to Lolo's house and tried to give me a beating. Lolo Aureo defended me, bearing the brunt of the beating. He was too old to protect me, and so his blood pressure skyrocketed, causing an attack. My aunts who lived with him decided to keep me away from Lolo.

I returned to my aunt crying and begging, expressing our unwillingness to live with her. I pleaded for her to hand us over to Lolo, but she refused. Instead, she gave us to my grandfather's brother, claiming we needed to pay the debt of my mother's medical expenses, and my sister and I had to work there. Another nightmare! However, Mama later confirmed that she didn't owe anything to Daddy, as she had Medicare and health insurance to cover all her needs.

Because of Lolo's high blood pressure and our aunts who didn't seem to care, we were left with no choice. We packed our belongings and moved to a nice, spacious house—one of the nicest in their town.

Mama sent another package containing our school belongings, as she always did – brand-new backpacks, pencil cases, pencils, erasers, papers, and more. Despite Mama giving us money, only 20 pesos made it to our hands. I used the money to purchase a whole pack of candy from a wholesale store, intending to sell it to my classmates and friends in school to turn a profit.

I was grateful that my grandmother Nelly had taught me how to earn money before leaving Cebu. It proved beneficial for my sister and me, providing us with cash when we needed it. I grew our initial 20 pesos by selling various snacks in school, like candies and junk food.

Juhan and I cried together when we were in the mood to talk instead of fight. We would hold hands and sing "Bawal na Gamot," reassuring ourselves that we were stronger than Papa and that we could overcome challenges together. Together, we found the strength and courage to face new obstacles without our parents by our side.

In our new environment, we had to wake up between 3:00 and 4:00 a.m. to light a fire, a lifestyle unfamiliar to us coming from the city. While living in my aunt's house on my mother's side, we never learned how to build a fire using wood, as it was Ate Mary Ann's responsibility to cook for us. Frustration and misery set in, but we were grateful that Daddy woke up before 5:00 a.m. to help us light a fire so we could cook the food that we would bring to school. Every day, we had corn grits and dried fish. Although I loved dried fish, the type we had caused me to feel miserable and develop a fever for a couple of weeks.

Juhan and I resorted to snatching some food occasionally. My two older cousins who used to live there locked away the eggs, sausages, milk, sugar, and other food items in the kitchen cabinets. My sister proved to be the bravest in this matter. We were sometimes successful at stealing some eggs.

The experience became comical, resembling a game of hide and seek. We would check where all the adults were, then run to the kitchen to grab some food—we were like mice. Juhan excelled at it, which fit her very well as she was small and cute.

Thankfully, God had angels in school. Some teachers noticed the kind of food we brought, and every day, they made sure that Juhan and I had some of their food. They would exchange our dried fish for the lunch they had packed, perhaps they have learned to bring extra to ensure enough for themselves and both of us.

After my sister and I won our Student Council candidacy in school, and my sister emerged victorious in the Math Quiz B competition across the entire district, making history as the first student from Old Damulog Elementary to defeat Central Elementary School, the principal began to take notice of us.

Since we had to walk 3 kilometers from Damulog to Old Damulog, he noticed us walking to school and generously allowed us to ride his motorbike. We were grateful; otherwise, we would always be late for class as we were still adjusting to this new lifestyle.

My sister and I slept beside Daddy, and I observed that he began to kiss my sister in a way that made me uncomfortable. I disliked it, so I asked Juhan to switch places with me. From that point on, I couldn't sleep at night and had to kick him to make him move away. I felt relief when one of my cousins, who worked on and took care of Daddy's farmland, would occasionally take my sister and me to be with him. In their company, I could relax, breathe, and play with his younger kids.

Once, I had a fever for many weeks that wouldn't subside. No one in the house bothered to give me medicine. I told my sister that we needed to stand at the gate and try to get the attention of my two cousins across the street. My prayers were answered, and they called us over, noticing my high fever. They promptly gave me medicine.

Prayers were fully answered when Mama returned home. We were overjoyed to see her, especially because we were struggling at the hands of her family. All the teachers at our school pleaded with her to transfer us and bring us with her, as they could sense we were not being treated well. I am grateful she listened and brought us to Cagayan. However, despite my happiness that Mama arrived to take us away, I felt frustrated with her. She never mentioned that she was pregnant, and I noticed her growing tummy, even though she tried to hide it by wearing a tummy control shapewear.

In my frustration, I would cry loudly and kick her just to provoke a reaction.

I think I didn't know how to express my feelings to her, as well as the things that were happening with me and my sister under her family's care.

Fortunately, she brought us with her, freeing us from the miserable life under her uncle and auntie's care.

REFLECTION

This is the most challenging year of our life as kids. It was tough to get away from the place we were used to, the familiar people we were used to seeing and communicating with. The daily lifestyle was different and we were not used to how my aunt treated my grandfather, Mary Ann, and me.

The adult should straightforwardly talk to the kids about the situation, instead of waiting for the child to notice the changes and start looking for answers. It's frustrating and confusing for the kids.

Looking back, it's essential to teach our children to follow their instincts so they can protect themselves. This situation clearly showed us that not everyone has the same talents and gifts. Fortunately, I noticed what Daddy was trying to do before it was too late for my sister. It put pressure on me as an older sister trying to protect both of us. I couldn't sleep at night trying to be vigilant, kicking him whenever he moved. Fortunately, we were not there for too long as I didn't know how long I could manage to keep us safe. I didn't know what he was trying to do at that time and didn't even realize it was part of sexual abuse. Our children need to be educated about sexual abuse so they can protect themselves and others.

I'm glad that I learned how to earn money in simple ways as we were able to get some cash on hand.

"Give them fish and you feed them for a day; teach them how to fish and you feed them for a lifetime."

- Lao Tzu

"The earlier we educate our children about inappropriate touching, the safer they will be."

- April Key

"We should instill in them the importance of trusting their instincts; if something doesn't feel right, they should know how to respond appropriately."

- April Key

"Not everyone possesses strong instincts, and it's not related to intelligence; it's about a gut feeling that signals when something is amiss."

- April Key

PSYCHOLOGICAL ANALYSIS

"She had been physically hurting me whenever I tried to get her attention or ask her to spend more time with me and my sister. She was so occupied with her love life that she forgot to ask how my sister and I were doing."

Parents have the right to rebuild their lives after a separation, but this does not entail neglecting their children as certain behaviors can adversely impact them.

Returning to the dating scene and even starting new families is only natural. Single parents seek to explore new connections and possibilities. Following a separation and a period of mourning, the father or mother often feels ready to meet new people. When children are involved, parents must consider how dating might influence their relationship with their children.

As a parent begins to date, several factors need consideration: the qualities sought in a potential partner, arrangements for the children's care when the parent is out, the appropriate time to introduce children, and the overall impact of dating on their health and well-being. These considerations ensure that the process of meeting others is carried out in the healthiest manner possible.

Before venturing into new relationships, parents must be clear about the nature of the relationship. If it is deemed non-serious, introducing different people to the children at specific periods may not be in their best interest. Once the parent defines the relationship, sharing this information with the children should be done gradually.

JOURNAL

Does separation hurt more due to the pain children experience witnessing their parents part ways, or is it a result of how the situation is handled? What are your thoughts on this matter?

Our home is our haven. We must strive to love one another and pray for our family that we will live in harmony, love, and peace.

April Key

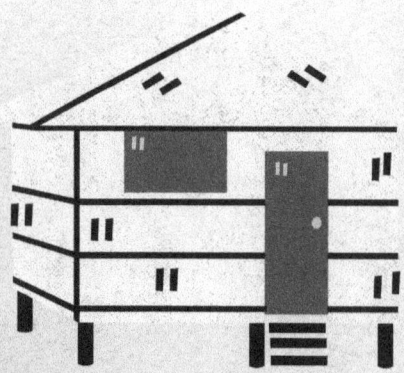

Bahay Kubo is a traditional home in the Philippines. It is made of Nipa and Bamboo.

CHAPTER 8

Living with Our Cousin

My sister and I were happy, thinking we had finally found a stable place to stay where we could relax for a while. Unfortunately, our expectations were not met.

Our cousin appeared indifferent and constant conflicts arose with our nieces, who were slightly older and around our age. Fortunately, my cousin's husband, Kuya George, was a good man who consistently treated us fairly. Whenever he witnessed his children mistreating my sister and me, he reprimanded them and shielded us from their actions.

Living with them required another adjustment for my sister and me. Unlike the previous homes we had lived in, this one lacked electricity. They relied solely on a lamp for light during the night, a lifestyle we were not accustomed to.

Thankfully, the financial support Mama provided them for taking care of us enabled them to install electricity in their house and start a sari-sari store business.

Juhan and I used to bring snacks and drinks daily, along with 20 pesos each for our pocket money, in case we wanted to buy something we wanted or needed.

Upon our arrival, we discussed our daily school allowance, and one of my nieces overheard, expressing surprise at the amount— 20 pesos. "What, 20 pesos?! Why do you need that much?" This moment signaled to me that we might not be in a good place. Nevertheless, I kept quiet, having just arrived at their house.

Midway through the school year, we transferred to another school. Juhan was in third grade, and I was in fourth grade. Fortunately, the principal permitted and welcomed us.

Juhan, originally slated to compete as the Damulog representative at the Math Quiz Bee provincial level, couldn't pursue it due to our relocation.

Despite my teacher's strict demeanor, I admired her fairness toward every student in the class. She faced challenges as one of my classmates was a gang leader in the area. Our class' Christmas savings were stolen and it was evident that Lord, our classmate, led the group who took the money as he knew exactly where we kept our bamboo piggy bank.

On another note, Juhan, as a transferee, wasn't initially placed in section A as intended. One day, during a discussion about the beat of the Philippine national anthem, my sister disagreed with her teacher's declaration that the anthem has a 3/4 beat, asserting that it was 4/4. The teacher took her to the principal's office, only to realize that she (the teacher) was wrong and that Juhan was indeed a bright student who belonged in section A.

The principal promptly coordinated with the teacher in section A to allow Juhan to take a test with them, enabling her to join the honor class. While her performance wasn't as stellar as in the previous two years, she managed to secure a spot in the top ten.

I, on the other hand, had the opportunity to represent my class as Miss Valentines in our school. During the coronation day, the class Miss Valentines and Mr. Valentines received red-shaped cards with numbers on them.

My partner for this event was Brennan, Lord's best friend. Frankly, I didn't like him due to the misbehavior he and others displayed in class and our school. Because of his popularity and good looks, he was full of himself. I resented him and his group for their disruptive actions.

For some reason, I sensed that we had a chance to win. My neighbor, who also represented her class, stood behind me. I handed her my card. Just as my number was called, she smiled and said, "Go, your number is called, it is yours." I replied, "I don't mind, it's okay, I'll give it to you."

Needless to say, Brennan wasn't pleased. He aspired to be crowned Mr. Valentine and take the stage, but I deliberately thwarted his plans.

This decision had repercussions for both of us throughout the rest of the year. He tried to make my life harder but my skills as a runner proved beneficial.

The card swap remained a secret known only to my neighbor, her older sister, our partners, and my younger sister. It was the best thing I did that year. Despite the hardships of living in that house, my neighbor's gratitude and smile each time she passed by were enough to put a smile on my face, as if to tell her that it was okay.

Our lifestyle in this new place differed significantly from what we were accustomed to in Cebu. Early mornings were dedicated to lighting the firewood to cook food for all of us, a task my sister and I struggled with initially, having never learned it at Daddy's place. Over time, Juhan mastered the skill, making our lives easier.

Given that the circumstances here were a little harder for me, Juhan learned to step up and take on more responsibilities. She accompanied Kuya George to gather seafood from the fishpond. She didn't mind getting dirty in the pond and would join them in the middle of the night to catch frogs for food.

There were times when we needed to collect kangkong leaves to sell to neighbors to ensure we had enough money to buy corn grits for all of us. Juhan took the lead in this venture, as I was prone to illness in dirty environments. I assisted her in segregating and bundling the leaves, selling each bundle for 5 pesos around the neighborhood by pushing our cart through the area.

Additionally, Juhan learned to handle tasks such as carrying and cutting banana trees to feed the pigs. Recognizing my vulnerability to sickness, she took charge of the strenuous work, ensuring our survival in our challenging circumstances.

We learned to fetch drinking water from a neighbor's house, about half a mile from my cousin's residence. At times, we had to walk barefoot, especially when the ground became too wet and muddy for our slippers.

Both of us also learned to sometimes get snacks from their sari-sari store. Occasionally, my cousin would instruct his kids to share some candies with us, even though my nieces were reluctant to part with the 25-cent treats. There were instances when they refused to give us the snacks, even when their parents requested them to do so.

Here, we learned to lie just to get out of the house for a while. We would prepare an empty rice sack and ask either my cousin's eldest daughter, Ate Geraldine, or my cousin Ate Layla to venture into the woods to collect firewood. Fortunately, they often allowed us to go on our own.

Sometimes, Juhan and I would spend hours crying together. We made sure to find a secluded spot so no one would see or hear us. We would sing our song, "Bawal na Gamot," while crying and expressing our wishes for our father's well-being. After releasing our emotions, we would resume gathering coconut twigs and wood, as this was what we told our cousin. We were cautious not to raise any suspicion regarding our activities or the reasons for our prolonged absence.

REFLECTION

It was good for both of us to discover our strengths and help each other during those difficult times, especially in the absence of our parents. I appreciated my sister for taking on the challenging tasks on my behalf.

These experiences taught us how to adapt to a different way of life and overcome difficulties and obstacles. They made us flexible and humble, instilling in us kindness, compassion, and consideration for others.

"We have to navigate the difficult road to build resilience."

- April Key

"Life isn't fair, but those who undergo severe tests often emerge as the toughest people."

- April Key

"Don't simply agree with things you know are wrong; instead, learn to speak up. Those brave enough to speak up are often the ones who can put a stop to wrongdoing and bring about positive change."

- April Key

"Our children don't need to endure abusive living to learn compassion and empathy. Parents can teach these values through example."

- April Key

"Then the King will say to the people on his right, 'Come you that are blessed by my father! Come and possess the kingdom which has been prepared for you ever since the creation of the world. I was hungry and you fed me, thirsty and you gave me a drink; I was a stranger and you received me in your homes, naked and you clothed me; I was sick and you took care of me, in prison and you visited me.' The righteous will then answer him, 'When, Lord, did we ever see you hungry and fed you, or thirsty and gave you a drink? When did we ever see you as a stranger and welcomed you into our homes, or naked and clothed you? When did we ever see you sick or in prison and visited you?' The King will reply, 'I tell you, whenever you did this for one of the least important of these followers of mine, you did it for me!'"

- Matthew 25:34-40

PSYCHOLOGICAL ANALYSIS

"Living with them required another adjustment for my sister and me."

Moving from one place to another poses a challenge for both parents and children, as the reasons behind the move may not always be clear to the latter. It involves more than just relocating physical possessions; it often means leaving behind cherished people and places crucial to personal development. For children, a move entails bidding farewell to a beloved home, school, friends, and a familiar environment where they feel at ease.

Exposing a child to multiple relocations may lead a child to manifest certain things, like oppositional behavior, crying, difficulty falling asleep, aggressive behavior, and confusion and frustration with parents due to a lack of understanding about the necessity to move.

In certain situations, the parents themselves may be reluctant to move, but factors like changing jobs, escaping from an abusive environment, or seeking new opportunities may make a move unavoidable.

To mitigate the adverse effects of moving on children, it is crucial to explain the reasons behind the move. Even though they are young, children as young as three can comprehend many aspects of the situation.

How can the detrimental effects of moving be minimized for the children?

Houses are where memories are made. Inside the home, children learn to smile, laugh, and love. The walls witness their milestones, the floors support their bare feet, closets become venues for games like hide-and-seek, and garages resonate with the sounds of their adolescent bands. Homes are more than physical spaces.

While some children experience their entire childhood in one stable home, letting their roots grow solid, others find themselves having to relocate.

Moving can impact children negatively, leading to anxiety, stress, and academic challenges. Adjusting to new homes and surroundings may take time, but there are strategies to alleviate these adverse effects. Here are some suggestions:

1. Involve children in the moving process. Their active participation, whether in packing their belongings, choosing new furniture, or deciding on decorations for the new home, empowers them and reduces anxiety.

2. Maintain routines. Children thrive on routines, so preserving consistent schedules during and after a move helps them feel secure and less stressed. This involves sticking to regular mealtimes, bedtime routines, and extracurricular activities.

3. Stay positive. The attitudes and behaviors of parents significantly influence how children perceive a move. If parents maintain a positive and enthusiastic outlook, their children are likely to mirror these sentiments.

4. Provide social support. Moving can be isolating, especially for children leaving behind friends and familiar surroundings. Encourage opportunities to make new friends, such as joining sports teams or clubs, to help children adjust.

5. Talk it out and communicate openly. Moving is universally acknowledged as one of the activities that can subject a person to the most mental and physical strain. Encouraging open communication is therefore crucial. If our kids wish to express their concerns, we must listen. If they choose not to share, we can reassure them that we're always available whenever they're ready to talk. Verbalizing issues or admitting and respecting that they are feeling sad is one of the most effective ways for children to process big emotions. For older children who may not enjoy communicating, we can encourage them to talk openly with friends or a counselor. They could also keep a private journal. They must find a healthy outlet so their feelings aren't pent up.

We can further promote our kids' communication by opening up ourselves. If we admit our difficulties with a move, kids will likely feel less alone and discouraged by overwhelming emotions. It's crucial to be upfront by immediately sharing the news and details about a move with our kids.

Hiding or withholding information that they eventually discover might make them feel like relocating is worse than it is—or something to fear. Additionally, sharing the news promptly gives kids more time to face the transition. They need, and deserve, as much time as we do to process their emotions.

6. Be patient and empathize with them. Imagine that your 12-year-old struggled last year with transitioning from elementary to middle school. She was fraught with emotions from puberty and the pressure of making friends. You're relieved when you finally see her find a group of kids she likes and cliques with. Then, one afternoon, after your spouse secures a long-sought-after job, you're forced to break the news to her that the family has to move to the other side of the country by next month.

The news might be unbelievable and devastating. You may hear phrases like, "My life is over" or "How could you do this to me?" It's easy to feel hurt and angry when kids unleash backlash over a relocation—especially when it's outside our control. Rather than fighting fire with fire, we can use patience and empathy to diffuse the battle. This might even help dispel any resentment our kids are harboring toward us.

We can say, "I know how scary this must be for you. Moving is tough. I know you'll miss your friends." Or, "You have a right to feel sad and frustrated."

7. Make the kids' rooms a priority. Last and first—that's how you should think about packing and unpacking your kids' rooms. They should be the last to pack up and the first to unpack. This way, your kids have the most time possible in their old room and they can begin settling into the new house right away.

JOURNAL

What measures would you take to ensure that the moving process does not negatively affect your children or other people living with you?

Our journey in life is not easy but if we have fortified faith and resilience we can make it through all the storms.

April Key

This is a jeepney called Sarao, it is the traditional model of transportation in the Philippines.

CHAPTER 9

The Revelation

One day, my sister and I were at the well washing our clothes. My cousin approached us, looking scared and confused about how to start the conversation. Finally, she told us that our mother would be visiting us soon, bringing along our baby brother. Trying to explain who the father of the child was, I made sure to interrupt her and said, "Chris?" She was shocked to hear me say it and asked how I knew. I replied that I knew because there was no other guy who was always with us and with her all along when we were still in Cebu.

My sister and I did our best not to show our frustrations to our cousin. We pretended that we were fine and continued with the task at hand. After a long wait, they finally revealed the truth. However, it didn't change my feelings toward my mother. I felt betrayed, cheated, and unloved.

I felt that she didn't care for my sister and me all along. After all, we had lied for her, and defended and protected her against my father's family, but she dared lie to our faces to the extent that she would physically hurt me for it.

The day finally came when my mother arrived with my one-month-old baby brother. I honestly couldn't figure out how I felt. Would I be happy or sad? Sure, I was happy to see my mother but had mixed feelings about my brother. I didn't know how to explain the butterflies in my stomach.

I didn't know if it would change my feelings if she had been honest with me from the very beginning. I don't know if it would have made a difference if she explained it to us and let us understand the situation and what she did.

We were already leading a miserable life even without our brother. Now, we had a younger brother to watch, and another sibling to protect!

Being the eldest was never an easy task, especially when your weakness is your sickness. My brother was a challenging baby to take care of and was often sick. Maybe it's a result of all the medicine Mama had to take during her accident while she was pregnant with him.

We were the ones assigned to wash his clothes and cloth diapers. I am glad my sister was so patient with it and always saved me from this chore. She always made a joke about the poop and didn't feel weird when she touched them, and the smell didn't even bother her.

I handled my brother well and helped take care of him more. My sister was good at washing his things. I knew that she was having a hard time processing her emotions toward my brother.

She's always been jealous of me because Mama always had her attention on me due to my sickness, and now she had another competition for our mother's attention.

My sister was the only one who never got sick. If she got sick, she easily got better with simple over-the-counter medication, while my brother and I always ended up going to the doctor's clinic or the hospital.

One day, my teacher had to send me home due to a high fever. I walked a mile or two to get home, but upon arrival, I had to take care of my brother since my cousin decided to go to her in-law's house.

Despite shivering badly due to my high fever, I had to stand up and carry my brother with me to soothe his cries. The younger son, who was about the same age as my brother, grabbed firewood from the kitchen and ran after us. I ran around outside in the heavy rain, hoping the fire would be extinguished soon. My cousin showed no concern and continued talking to her in-law, who lived next door.

My sickness persisted for two months, on and off, even with over-the-counter medication. I usually respond well to antibiotics, but this time it seemed ineffective.

One afternoon, my cousin finally decided to spend time with me and my sister alone. As we talked, we mentioned that I always visit the Senior Sto. Niño Church on my birthday.

At that time, it was the first year I missed visiting my beloved church. After a couple of minutes, a guy passed by trying to sell a Sto. Niño statue and offered a six-month layaway. It meant my cousin would pay a certain amount of money every month for six months. I didn't know why she believed in our religious custom, as they were non-Catholics from another Christian group.

She put it up in their house but continued to attend their church. Miraculously, my fever went away! I didn't know if there was a connection with the Sto. Niño image healing me, but I did feel better.

Finally, I reached 5th grade at the age of 11. I cherished the friendships I formed here, which were among the best during my elementary years. However, life wasn't perfect, as I didn't agree with my teacher.

Miss Jenny was single, pretty, and smart. I initially had no problem with her, but towards the middle of the school year, we noticed something odd about the way she treated the rich bully girl classmate. We noted favoritism and a noticeable unfairness in her actions.

I overlooked it until the time came when the mother of our classmate Faye died. The whole class even went to visit and paid their respects to Faye's family. After a few weeks, we noticed my teacher was already riding on the motorbike owned by Faye's father.

It wasn't appropriate for a teacher to bully and mistreat her other students for incorrect answers while sweet-talking Faye if she failed to give the right answer. The rest of the class experienced yelling and anger if their answers were wrong.

Before the school year ended, I informed my classmates that I would talk to our teacher, and I did. I made sure to arrive early in the morning before anyone could be in class. I said to her, "Miss Jenny, you are so pretty and smart, but you are not setting a good example for your students. If you decide to flirt with the father of our classmate right after her mother died, please don't show it to us. No wonder you are being sweet to Faye; you are seeking her approval for your relationship with her dad."

She didn't reply and told me it was not my problem. However, she made sure to get my cousin's attention and cried to her after the final recognition in school.

Most of my friends were the smart ones in class, but they were also the less privileged ones. We all knew that we would be in the top 10 or at least on our teacher's honor list. We considered going to see the principal and calling the attention of the school head if we were unfairly graded. Luckily, our teacher did give us the award that we truly deserved.

Meanwhile, in the afternoon after our school recognition, my cousin talked to her sister-in-law and loudly stated that if she were the teacher, she would never give an award to a student with a nasty attitude. Without even asking for my side of the story, my cousin decided to shame me in front of her in-laws and let the neighbors hear it.

I decided to let it go as it didn't matter to me anymore. My teacher gave us the award for our hard work throughout the year, and that's all that mattered to me at the time. Plus, I would be leaving for Cebu in the summer anyway.

REFLECTION

Looking back at that moment, it showed how I was able to think ahead and protect my classmates. It was one of the best elementary years, and I love all my friends here. Despite being away from my parents, I made many friends who were like family to me. We were very close, and there was no drama!

"Adults always demand respect from children but don't give respect to the little ones—how rude is that?"

- April Key

PSYCHOLOGICAL ANALYSIS

"I didn't know if it would change my feelings if she had been honest with me from the very beginning. I don't know if it would have made a difference if she explained it to us and let us understand the situation and what she did."

When parents lie or hide things from their children, they breed distrust and disappointment. When children discover that their parents have been hiding something or lying, the child begins to feel more mistrust, and there is a greater chance of developing aggressive behavior.

Often, parents prefer to lie or not talk about a specific situation, thinking that telling the truth may make the child feel sad or upset. However, this creates the opposite effect. When the child discovers the truth, they don't see it as their parents trying to protect them but rather as a lie, generating sadness and anger.

A parent's mission is not to be perfect. In many cases, parents do not want to lie or hide information from their children, but not knowing how to handle sensitive information, they decide to act in a certain way.

JOURNAL

As a parent, what did you do when you discovered that your child lied to you?

Like the tallest mountain, let our faith be as strong and as robust and it can never be shaken by trials.

April Key

Mayon Volcano is a perfect cone volcano in the Philippines, with the Cagsawa Church tower bell ruins in the foreground.

CHAPTER 10

Back in Cebu

My sister and I were finally back in Cebu with Mama. We went directly to Mama's office as it was a Monday when we arrived. Aunt Lucy also arrived at Mama's office on the same day. She informed Mama that she was there to take us kids. I shouted at her angrily, asking her to let me and my sister have a break from all the fighting. I was very angry because I knew one of Mama's coworkers was too nosy and would report Mama's current activities, including the news of my sister and me arriving in Cebu.

We were exhausted from all the events that occurred in Mindanao and the ten-hour boat ride to Cebu. Both my sister and I just needed a little peace away from the drama of adult life.

Of course, my aunt went home empty-handed and shouted at me angrily. I could understand her frustration, but a soon-to-be twelve-year-old girl just wanted to reunite with her mother, as we had missed being with Mama for two years.

My sister and I just wanted to return to normal life, to how it used to be.

Mama rented a bed space together with a single lady named Ate Jing-jing. Ate Jing-jing is a pretty and smart Filipina who worked at a financial firm in Cebu. She was too kind to lend her space to us so we could sleep properly in a bed, although Juhan and I were fine sleeping anywhere as we were used to sleeping on the floor with a simple mat.

When we arrived in Cebu, Ate Jing-jing told her mother to let her younger brother visit her so we could have someone to play with, and his brother could be in the city, too. Kuya Jong-jong, Juhan, and I got along very well, but sometimes we also fought.

Juhan and Kuya Jong-jong always found ways to tease me about anything at all, and they even left me one time. I had to walk back alone, scared that

I could make it home. But I did, and I made sure to tell Ate Jing-jing about the incident. She has always been fair to all of us and was like an older sister to me and my sister, too.

The room that Ate Jing-jing and Mama rented was too small for all of us. Mama had to find a place to rent away from the city so my father's family couldn't easily find us.

One of her close officemates told her about a rental property owned by her in-laws in Naga. Mama decided to take it as it was near where her officemate lived, and the house was not far from our school.

After we were all settled in Naga, we asked Mama for a favor— we wanted to get our brother from Mindanao. We didn't want him to be all alone there. After all, we were all siblings and we cared about him and loved him. Mama left us for a couple of days and went to Mindanao to bring my brother back.

We were delighted to be together as a complete family, but the transition was not easy. My brother was still very young, and the toddler was so active that he needed a lot of attention. We found ourselves constantly running after him, which was quite a challenge for an eleven and twelve-year-old to handle on their own.

Mama spoke with our neighbors to seek help in taking care of my brother while my sister and I were at school. We would pick him up from our neighbor's house once we returned from school. However, one day, we noticed a slash on my brother's tongue. Juhan's classmate, who also happened to be our neighbor living beside the caretaker's house, mentioned that my brother had been crying a lot when she went home during lunchtime.

My brother was struggling to eat due to a horizontal cut on his tongue, and he had been in distress for many days. It was frustrating for him to put anything in his mouth. Surprisingly, my mother chose not to say anything about it. She was too afraid to speak up, fearing the caretaker's husband might react angrily.

In response to safety concerns, we moved to a house not too far from our previous location. Mama believed it was not a secure environment, and it was also challenging for her to balance her work and take care of us. She needed to find another family willing to watch over us while she was away.

Gratefully, the family living near the local road welcomed us and allowed us to stay with them for a while. The mother, Lola Tanya, and the third son, Kuya Ray, were exceptionally kind. Lola Tanya always treated my brother and us with kindness. Occasionally, I joined her in selling sticky rice around the area, a task I enjoyed doing since my younger days. I had also engaged in similar activities with my aunt in Mindanao.

During our time there, we found some relaxation and cherished moments with the youngest sister, Ate Stephanie, whenever she was in a good mood. At times, she hesitated to share their TV with us, but on other occasions, we got along well.

Lolo Aureo, my mother's father, had expressed a desire to see us all for Christmas, particularly the youngest grandchild. Having never met my brother Nimrod at that time, it was essential for us to fulfill Lolo Aureo's dream. Mama presented us with a choice: either buy an encyclopedia and a typewriter or use the money to visit our grandfather in Mindanao. Both of us decided to visit Lolo Aureo, as we knew he was already 94 during this time.

The trip was emotional but it was fun reuniting with everyone. Despite the large number of cousins on my mother's side (54 in total), I only had a few who were close to my heart, likely due to the age gap. Most of them were my mother's age, with only a handful close in age to us.

Lolo Aureo's face lit up when we arrived at his house for a two-day visit. It brought immense happiness to see and hug him and to converse with him again.

One morning, Lolo Aureo took the opportunity to share with me his life experiences, accomplishments, and the wisdom gained from surviving World War 1 and World War 2. He spoke about my mother being stubborn and my sister still being too young to understand certain things. He hinted that there was something different about me, assuring me that I would come to understand it someday. At that time, I was in the first year of high school, just thirteen years old. I simply nodded and said okay.

Upon our return to Cebu, Mama ended up purchasing the encyclopedia set and a typewriter, especially for my sister to complete her school assignments and projects. She faced difficulties in school as her classmates, initially friendly, turned resentful upon realizing her intelligence. Some top students made it challenging for her to access books at the library by passing these among themselves and refusing to cooperate.

Juhan began experiencing bullying from her classmates, resulting in daily tears and evident frustration. It was disheartening to witness her struggles in school.

Meanwhile, Mama started accumulating debts due to the purchase of the encyclopedia and typewriter. Despite the financial strain, these tools proved invaluable for our schoolwork.

After returning from our visit to Lolo Aureo, we had a dream about him, and upon stepping outside, we noticed a black butterfly circling the outdoor kitchen. The symbolism hinted at the possibility of Lolo Aureo's passing.

Returning to our routine, Mama received a long-distance call from one of her siblings confirming Lolo Aureo's death. She needed to return home to help prepare for the burial. To gather resources, Mama borrowed money for groceries and goods from Cebu to bring to Mindanao. Our financial situation was tight.

Due to financial constraints, Mama decided that we kids would stay in Cebu while she handled the preparations in Mindanao. She couldn't afford the fare for all of us, and Mama needed to focus on the arrangements without additional responsibilities.

Forty days after Lolo Aureo's burial, Mama attended the 40-day prayer in Cebu and she decided to bring the three of us this time. On our way there, Mama had to get my brother at Minglanilla, leaving Juhan to watch over the goods at the ship.

Unexpected traffic caused us to miss the ship we were supposed to take. It had left with only Juhan on board. Desperate to catch up, we found another ship leaving for Mindanao. Fortunately, there were available spots and we were allowed to board. The news spread at school that my sister couldn't take the test because she was on a boat. It was broadcast live on the radio. She was upset to have missed her final test.

Upon arrival the next day, Juhan pleaded with Mama to pay for her return journey, wanting to ride the ship alone and make it back to Cebu. Despite knowing how to take a jeepney back to Naga, we decided against it, as we would be taking a bus from Cagayan to Damulog immediately.

Initially upset about joining us, Juhan quickly shifted her mood and enjoyed the bus ride. She engaged with our cousins of the same age, showcasing her sociable and talkative nature. Fortunately, we all managed to attend Lolo Aureo's 40th-day prayer together.

After all the busyness surrounding Lolo Aureo's death, Mama struggled financially as a single mother burdened by significant debt. For about a month, we survived on porridge to manage our expenses and avoid accumulating more debt.

Mama had to extend her promise to stop eating porridge when a wealthy friend borrowed 500 pesos for gasoline. The friend was embarrassed to ride a jeepney, fearing judgment from others in her affluent circle. Mama, however, assured us that we were fortunate and blessed to know how to live with what we had.

My teacher, Mrs. Racaza, raised concerns about my well-being to Mama. She noticed my absence from playtime in the oval and during recess, expressing worry about my lack of interaction with my classmates.

It was just that I felt my friends were leading a typical kid's life while ours was different. Also, I tended to faint in the sun's heat, contributing to my reluctance to play outside. However, Mrs. Racaza was unaware that, in the absence of our teacher, I joined my friends at the beach.

During my elementary graduation, I spoke in front of the entire batch despite waking up late and attending unprepared. Rushing to dress and catch a tricycle to the church, Mama remained the only one looking presentable and pretty in her pink and white printed flowery business suit. I completed my elementary years with 5th honors, excelling in religion, service, obedience, and cooperation.

Juhan, facing bullying and lacking recognition of her potential due to being a new student, managed to secure a place in the top ten of her class during her elementary years. Financial constraints prevented her from participating in extracurricular activities.

Mama decided to enroll Juhan and me in a Youth for Christ group, a Catholic youth organization. Despite our initial resistance, Mama's determined attitude led us to attend and complete the three-day seminar, becoming part of the group. Despite my skepticism towards religious matters stemming from Mama's actions—having my brother and lying to us —we embraced the experience due to Mama's persistence.

Registration for the seminar was prohibitively expensive, but Mama ensured that both Juhan and I could participate, possibly influenced by my teacher noticing my behavior.

Following the three-day seminar, we attended several retreats that neither Juhan nor I wanted to be a part of. We resisted sharing our life stories with kids who experienced a normal childhood while we grappled with confusion about our own lives. However, our facilitator, Ate June, belonging to a well-off family, was patient and kind to us.

We would sometimes fabricate excuses to Ate June about lacking fare, even when Mama had provided it. In response, Ate June, still in high school at the time, would return with her family's vehicle, often giving us special attention. It wasn't a one-time occurrence; sometimes, she would generously offer extra money for our fare.

Occasionally, Juhan and I sought refuge at my aunt Riley's house, where we could take a break from porridge and enjoy ample food. During these visits, we packed burgers and delicious treats for Mama and Nimrod on our way home.

While at Aunt Riley's house, my father's sister, inquired if the rumors about Mama were true. She promised a better life and a safe environment for both of us if I spoke the truth. Knowing that my aunt was leaving the country and would therefore be unable to protect us from her other sister, I felt that being with our mother was the safest option. I also knew that our grandparents wouldn't live that long so if we were to stay with our father, it would be difficult because I knew our aunt Lucy was jealous of my sister and me. After all, our grandparents treated me and Juhan differently compared to how they treated Aunt Lucy's children.

So despite my aunt's persistence, I chose not to disclose anything. But deep inside, I wished I could talk to her, cry to her, hug her, and tell her everything. I feared a repeat of the beatings that happened before when the family accused me of lying when I was telling the truth.

Another turning point came when a letter from my sister's classmate revealed that the oldest son of Lola Tanya, the house's owner, said something to her mom. Attempting to clarify the gossip, my sister's classmate wanted to know if it was true. My mother discovered the letter while cleaning our space.

Mama confronted the mother and disclosed what was happening. The older brother reacted angrily upon learning about the gossip, and his younger brother, Ray, was furious with him. The two siblings ended up in a fight, with the younger brother attempting to protect us. Witnessing this family discord, we decided it was time to move again, not wanting their conflicts to escalate because of us.

REFLECTION

It was truly nice of my teacher to see beyond my silence and believe in me. I wasn't the brightest student in the class, and speaking in front of the entire elementary batch during our graduation was never part of my wildest dreams. However, being one of the students sharing my thoughts and experiences throughout my elementary years was a privilege.

Mama made the right decision by letting us join the YFC Camp! It shaped us into who we are today, helping us find like-minded individuals and turn towards God during the challenging and confusing moments of our lives.

Ate June, at a young age, was wise to follow God's mission for her. Through her hard work and sacrifices for us, we were able to continue treading the right path growing up.

"Sometimes parents have to do what they need to do for the good of their children."

- April Key

"When we invest well in our young ones, they will reap the benefits throughout their lifetimes."

- April Key

"Try to always be the positive person in somebody's life, as it multiplies a thousand times."

- April Key

PSYCHOLOGICAL ANALYSIS

"Juhan began experiencing bullying from her classmates, resulting in daily tears and evident frustration. It was disheartening to witness her struggles in school."

Bullying is the deliberate physical or psychological abuse inflicted by one person upon another. The perpetrator intentionally seeks to make the victim feel bad, aiming to intimidate and instill insecurity. Victims of bullying are often submissive, insecure, or struggle with self-esteem issues, lacking the ability to defend themselves. While bullying typically occurs in schools, it can also take place in public areas such as parks and sometimes even within one's own home.

The origins of bullying are diverse, as each harasser may have distinct reasons for their behavior. Some causes involve social or family problems, where the harasser comes from a violent home and learns these behaviors. Economic problems and general disorganization in the household are additional factors contributing to bullying.

To prevent bullying, it is crucial to recognize that a bullied child may struggle with handling frustrations, lack empathy, and face challenges in managing emotions. Children who engage in bullying behavior need clear rules to understand right from wrong. Parents play a fundamental role in bullying prevention, as values instilled at home often manifest in a child's behavior outside the home, particularly at school.

Parents can prevent their children from becoming bullies by teaching them appropriate behavior, emphasizing respect and kindness toward others, and instilling the importance of resolving conflicts healthily.

Guiding children in managing emotions and providing them with tools to navigate conflicts healthily is essential for parents.

Trauma and social anxiety resulting from bullying

Bullying is a complex issue that can cause severe emotional distress, leaving targeted adolescents feeling alone, alienated, vulnerable, and anxious. These effects persist even after the aggressor moves on to another victim.

Bullying significantly impacts a child's mental health, resulting in traumatic experiences and increased social anxiety.

Trauma. ———————— Bullying can lead to psychological trauma, causing symptoms such as flashbacks, anxiety, and depression. Research indicates a higher likelihood of post-traumatic stress disorder (PTSD) in adults who experienced bullying in childhood.

Social anxiety. ———————— Bullied children may develop social anxiety, making it challenging to form and maintain relationships. Studies show higher levels of social anxiety in bullied children compared to non-bullied counterparts.

Chronic victimization. ———————— Children experiencing chronic victimization may develop a sense of helplessness and hopelessness, leading to long-term mental health issues.

Gender differences. ———————— Boys and girls may experience different mental health outcomes due to bullying. Girls may be more prone to developing social anxiety and depression, while boys may exhibit aggressive behavior.

Dealing with the effects of bullying

Addressing the mental health impact of bullying can be challenging, but evidence-based approaches can help:

Seek professional help. ———————— Therapy or counseling can offer support and guidance in managing the mental health effects of bullying.

Build supportive relationships. ———————— Establishing supportive connections with friends and family can alleviate the adverse effects of bullying on mental health, fostering a sense of belonging.

Practice self-care. ——————— Engage in self-care activities, such as exercise, mindfulness, and relaxation techniques, to reduce stress and anxiety. Practicing self-compassion and self-acceptance aids in coping with the effects of bullying.

Address bullying directly. ——————— Reporting bullying to teachers or authority figures can help reduce its adverse effects on mental health. Standing up for oneself and setting boundaries contribute to building confidence and self-esteem.

JOURNAL

Have you or your children experienced bullying? How
did you handle the situation?

We detached ourselves from the world and attached ourselves to the Cross of our Lord Jesus Christ, we will be united to His will, and enduring our trials will have merit.

April Key

Pabasa is a tradition in the Philippines. It is a devotion and chanting of the passion of Jesus Christ during Holy Week.

CHAPTER 11

Fire

We moved to a place not too far from our previous residence but closer to our school. The new location made it easier for us to go to school, particularly for my sister, since we now lived just a few steps away.

Our new dwelling was a small bahay kubo, with space for sleeping upstairs and a designated area for a kitchen and dining table. Despite its modest size, it provided us with a sense of privacy, the smallest space we have ever lived in.

In this new place, there was no one to assist with the care of my brother. He, too, started going to school, with Mama occasionally bringing him along during her travels. Juhan and I took turns looking after him, bringing him with us to school.

Whenever I had to take tests or exams, some of my teachers helped by keeping an eye on him since he was so young and had a penchant for wandering. My classroom was located upstairs near a long staircase, and I was grateful for their help as it was challenging to focus on exams while constantly monitoring his whereabouts. I was sure my sister faced the same dilemma.

Despite my frail health, I completed the demanding training to become a Citizenship Advancement Training Officer in high school. Our weekend formations and training sessions became a routine, with my brother patiently waiting in the background or on the side, behaving well.

On one occasion, while returning from the bathroom with my brother, two unfamiliar schoolmates asked if he was my son. I smiled and clarified that he was my younger brother. When they directed the same question to him, he responded indignantly, "No, she's my older sister," and then they walked away.

For a time, my cousin Aurea, her husband, and four children lived with us. Aurea helped in caring for Nimrod and managing the house. Another niece, Ate Bebeth, also joined us in Cebu, offering valuable support to me and Juhan.

From Ate Bebeth, we gained insights into the challenges of being a teenager. Meanwhile, Mama's demeanor deteriorated, and her anger towards us escalated. Regardless of our achievements in school or the chores we completed, everything we did seemed wrong in her eyes.

Juhan and I found solace when Mama was away on trips, providing us with respite from her constant shouting and anger. The days wouldn't be complete if she wasn't able to find mistakes or reasons to shout at us.

We were fortunate, however, that Tatay Demy and Nanay Belen treated us kindly. At times, we would go to their house to watch our favorite TV shows. Sometimes, we would be too scared that Mama would come without us noticing because she would be angry that we were watching TV. But Tatay Demy would tell her to let us watch and have fun once in a while. She would then relent and go back to the house.

One day, my sister and I undertook a thorough cleaning of our house before heading to a worship event. To dispose of the trash, we opted for the unconventional method of burning it, eliminating the need to toss it behind our rented house. Believing the fire was extinguished, we prepared to leave, only to discover a blaze had ignited in the vacant lot where we had disposed of the ashes.

Despite our fear, we tried to remain calm. Fortunately, Nanay Belen and our neighbor from across the property assured us that we could proceed to the worship event without worry. Both of us were active members of Youth for Christ, serving as facilitators, and so we needed to attend. Thankfully, they allowed us to go.

Upon our arrival, the event had already started, but we made it in time for the baptism. The worship and baptism ceremonies took place outside, under a tree. However, the group next to us appeared as if they were not taking the event seriously as they were laughing constantly. To our disbelief, we saw two black devils with long tails appear, scaring them and us, too! Our eyes were open and from that moment, we believed in the existence of devils beyond mere stories or books.

After the event, my sister and I anxiously reflected on the fire incident. We were concerned about the possibility of our rented house burning down and facing reprimands from the adults in the compound. Fortunately, there were no complaints from anyone. Nanay Belen and Tatay Demy were understanding, and despite apologizing the next morning, their response was reassuring:

"It's okay, sometimes bad luck happens. What's important is that we prevented the fire and it's now extinguished."

Their understanding was truly comforting.

REFLECTION

Being a young teen responsible for a younger child is undoubtedly stressful. How wonderful it would be to enjoy childhood fully without the burden of caregiving. I express my gratitude and salute my teachers for their kindness and assistance when I had to bring my younger brother to school. I am likewise grateful to my brother for being well-behaved during long waits. Despite his young age, he could understand that I couldn't be disturbed during formation—such a good child.

Tatay Demy, Nanay Belen, and our neighbor were exceptionally kind. Witnessing our hard work and the unintended mistake that traumatized us, instead of compounding the trauma, they offered support and acted as compassionate adults.

We need more individuals like them, transforming adversity into a calming environment for children. Knowing when to intervene calmly and assuring children that everything is under control is crucial. Blame is not placed on the young ones.

"We need kind adults who will assure our children that everything is under control."

- April Key

"Every child deserves to be treated kindly and cared for."

- April Key

"Good people need to spread their wings so it can spread to many more after some time."

- April Key

PSYCHOLOGICAL ANALYSIS

"Juhan and I found solace when Mama was away on trips, providing us with respite from her constant shouting and anger."

Aggression is a commonly employed but ineffective parenting method used by many parents who lack effective coping skills. Parents resort to aggression, such as yelling, in an attempt to address issues.

While screaming may yield short-term results, it only creates an illusion of resolution, as the underlying problem is not addressed with a true understanding of what occurred. Short-term gains can transform into long-term issues that may surface later on.

Children raised in an environment where yelling is the usual form of communication may experience developmental problems. Some may adopt these communication patterns, potentially developing other aggressive behaviors.

Some parents mistakenly view yelling as a way to gain respect, but it breeds insecurity in children, diminishing their chances of leading successful lives.

The first step toward healthy parenting involves eliminating yelling as a tool to communicate with or teach children. Effective communication is crucial in the parenting process, requiring parents to learn how to express themselves to their children and healthily correct them.

Parents must exercise self-control. Aside from the lack of knowledge about healthy parenting strategies, yelling may also stem from parents' frustrations or concerns. Recognizing and addressing these underlying issues is essential.

Tips so you can avoid yelling at children when frustrated

1. Know your triggers
Identify indicators that signal a loss of emotional control, then establish a strategy to respond to them. Consider moments when you last yelled at your children and reflect on the why. Were you late getting somewhere? Multi-tasking or being asked numerous questions simultaneously? Or perhaps you were being interrupted during phone calls or while doing other tasks?

2. Be aware of physical cues
Pay attention to physical signs, including a tense jaw, congested upper chest, unsettled stomach, increased heart rate, altered breathing patterns, and the sensation of warmth spreading throughout your body. Recognizing these cues allows for the implementation of immediate strategies to reset when needed.

3. Ask yourself why these behaviors upset you so much
Reflect on your thoughts by delving into your past and fears for the future. Identify triggers from your past and the fears they evoke for the future. If your child's behavior makes you feel uncertain, helpless, out of control, scared, or overwhelmed, explore why. What can you do about these feelings? Determine whether these feelings are rational or irrational. When experiencing emotions associated with triggers, jot down possible actions to help calm yourself.

4. Try a physical reset

Recognize warning signs and employ quick-acting techniques to regain control.

Sigh with two breaths in and out. Offload carbon dioxide and increase oxygen to calm the nervous system. Take two nasal breaths, then let out an audible sigh as you exhale through the mouth. Do this twice or thrice.

Mindfulness exercise. Focus on your immediate surroundings using your eyes, ears, and nose to alleviate anxiety and promote calmness. This can help you focus on the present moment.

5. Give kids a warning
When bedtime delays or conflicts arise, warn children about your escalating frustration. Communicate the need for cooperation, warning them that you are about to get angry and shout at them. Warnings also allow children to mentally prepare for changes, fostering understanding.

6. Offer empathy when your child expresses any emotion
Empathy enhances cooperation, reducing the likelihood of resorting to yelling. It teaches children to recognize and accept their feelings, a crucial step in learning emotional control and behavior regulation.

7. Take a break from being a parent
Create distance to regain composure. Deep breaths, relaxation, or a change of environment can help manage emotions. Allow yourself to experience and release built-up emotions without reacting impulsively. Treat yourself with kindness. Allow yourself to experience what's driving the anger—without necessarily reacting to it in any way. This will help dissipate your anger.

8. Learn to rely on your judgment
Imagine a neutral guardian angel offering advice for the best outcome. Step back, view situations objectively, and seek guidance from this imaginary parenting coach. Adopt a mantra that shifts perspective positively. For example, "I don't need to be right," or "All I have to do is choose love."

9. Use "I" statements
Communicate feelings in a non-threatening manner by using "I" statements instead of "you" statements. For example, express frustration as, "I feel frustrated when the toys are left out," instead of, "You always leave the toys out." This helps promote understanding without making the child feel attacked.

10. Use positive reinforcement

Encourage positive behavior by praising children for their actions. Employ positive reinforcement through verbal praise or small rewards to motivate good behavior and reduce the need for yelling.

JOURNAL

Instead of resorting to yelling, what would be the other options you would consider to foster a healthy upbringing for your children?

It is not what we eat that harms us but it is what comes from our mouth. Our words are powerful it can destroy and it can heal.

April Key

Street food is popular on Philippines Island. There are a variety of rare foods that you will encounter in the Philippines such as Balut, Isaw (chicken intestine), Betamax (chicken blood), Tempura, and Fishball.

CHAPTER 12

Family Not By Blood

Mama found a place away from the main town through one of her sisters in Handmaids of the Lord and decided to move there as it was larger and was part of a compound.

The reason for leaving our old place was a disturbing incident. One night, an intoxicated man went to the small house we were renting and banged on the door, frightening us all. The man seemed to admire Ate Bebeth but perhaps felt too ashamed to express his feelings directly. He got drunk and then came to our small bahay kubo looking for Ate Bebeth, and since it was late at night, we were already in bed.

This incident frightened us, especially since it was just Mama who needed to stand up for all of us. Thankfully, Tatay Demy, the owner of the house, stepped in and addressed the situation. However, the experience left us feeling unsafe, given the need to walk a considerable distance to reach our rented house, passing by the guy's house at nighttime, through a tiny and potentially dark path.

We packed our belongings and moved to a new place with new people and neighbors. The house wasn't luxurious, but it provided enough space for us to breathe and have some privacy. We occupied the upstairs part of the house, with a total of three bedrooms. The residence was gated, and three other neighbors were also renting there. The property was extensive, allowing Mama to cultivate some vegetables with permission from Tita Thalia, who owned the land. Our neighbors were friendly, creating a good environment for everyone. We also had some fresh air as it was situated away from the highway.

Juhan continued her high school education, riding a tricycle to the main town for school, while I commenced my college education at the USJR. Despite facing challenges, Juhan excelled in high school, winning numerous science and math competitions. She became the valedictorian of her class and delivered an inspirational speech.

As Juhan's elder sister, I felt proud witnessing her hard work paying off, despite facing verbal attacks from an elementary teacher. The teacher, who happened to be the mother of our friend competing with Juhan, accused her of cheating, which was untrue. The competition involved high school students from all over Cebu, held in a different town. Our friend was the brightest student in a private school in the area. We had another intelligent friend from another private school in our area.

Juhan and these two students from different schools formed a close bond. They spent time together, studied, and supported each other. Despite wearing different uniforms, they became good friends and collaborated on studying the materials. The best student would win, and it was my sister who won!

Juhan's success was not new; she had a natural talent for academics and could excel even if she did not put a lot of time into studying unless it was subjects like Chemistry and Science that needed more attention. Despite being busy checking her classmates' papers, Juhan managed to maintain her strength in academics. Sometimes, I had to assist her, too.

While I, on the other hand, was occupied with caring for my siblings. I often found myself concerned about where to seek assistance or borrow rice to feed my two younger siblings when Mama was away, leaving us with no food on our table. She would simply instruct me, "Borrow where you can borrow. I would find ways to pay for it."

I assumed the role of the mother in our home at the tender age of thirteen. Occasionally, I struggled to formulate my words when requesting rice from neighbors or anyone willing to help. There were times when shame overcame me, and we would go to bed without any food.

However, Mama would express displeasure if I didn't make an effort to ask and allowed my siblings to go hungry. Therefore, I learned to overcome my embarrassment and ask for assistance to avoid her anger upon her return from work. Our happiness knew no bounds when she arrived home with fresh harvests from the farm. The farmers loved her so much as she not only cared for their needs whenever they would visit her office but also served as a great teacher to them.

My situation worsened. Limited public vehicles traveled to our town and the jeepneys quickly filled up. I had to fight my way into the jeepney or sometimes ride like a man just to get home. I sometimes had to walk three kilometers or more from school just so I could catch an empty jeepney before it reached the public terminal.

This challenging experience demotivated me from attending school. Waiting for jeepneys became exhausting, especially since they were mostly full by the time they reached our town. Returning home involved competing with other passengers for a safe journey, and I got too tired most of the time.

That was why I decided to take a break for a year to rest, not wanting Mama to waste her money on me. However, Mama insisted on investing in me, allocating funds for my attendance at various leadership events in different regions.

Juhan and I had the opportunity to travel to Negros for a leadership conference, Bohol, and many more locations around Cebu and the Visayas region. Mama was exceptionally supportive of our involvement, ensuring that we stayed active and connected with people while deepening our understanding of God. It was undeniably one of the best experiences for both of us.

Meanwhile, Mama's attitude continued to deteriorate. Our younger brother's midnight cries for peanuts would prompt Mama to shout at us and instruct the three of us to walk to the crossing to buy peanuts for him.

I observed that Mama was increasingly favoring him, complying with his every request without considering the safety of her daughters and grandniece going out to the crossing in the middle of the night. Fortunately, we remained safe.

Passing by Tita Thalia's house, I felt a sense of familiarity, unable to recall where I had seen it before. It wasn't until I started visiting their house, befriending her only daughter Nathalie and meeting some of Nathalie's friends, that I became their instant elder sister.

Then, I realized that it was in my dreams two years ago, and their faces appeared in my dreams as well. I even wondered how I met all those pretty girls and handsome boys and why they seemed so familiar to me.

Now, the Youth for Christ group was organizing another seminar for new members that summer, and we invited Nathalie and her friends to attend. Instead of aimlessly roaming around the mall and meeting other affluent kids, we now had a purpose—to attend an event, meet new friends, hear God's words, and follow His will.

I became their facilitator and household leader alongside my partner, Hansel. Tintin attended with her sister, whom we met during the seminar, and she became part of our group. Nathalie's best friend, Camille, also joined. We formed a close-knit circle, providing support to one another.

These friendships and groups stood the test of time. Many of us loved hanging out at Tita Thalia's house. She became like a mother figure to us all, often having to feed us when we gathered at their house, especially those close to Nathalie.

I became so close to Nathalie that I eventually stopped attending college. She constantly urged me to be at their house, so she had someone to talk to. During emergencies, she would let me borrow her clothes, saving me a trip home before accompanying her. However, a day came when my younger sister grew jealous and asked Nathalie to stop taking me away. Thankfully, we resolved the issue. Nathalie, being humble and kind, suggested, "Well, you can be my big sister, too." She needed a Math tutor, and my sister ended up spending more time with her, helping with her academic studies. From that moment on, she became our instant younger sister from another mother.

I celebrated my 18th birthday here, an event I thought I would never have. Tita Thalia and my friends secretly organized the celebration, inviting my crush and fellow Youth for Christ brothers and sisters from my household. It was a memorable and simple birthday celebration for all of us.

REFLECTION

This marked the first time that people from my dreams appeared in my life after some time. It was a surreal encounter, and I still couldn't believe it happened in real life.

I'm grateful for this kind of friendship and for an adult who opens her house to other children. Tita Thalia was like a friend when we needed one, a mother for motherly advice, and even an enemy when she needed to discipline us.

To be honest, this is where I learned how to handle my kids. Observing the positive impact Tita Thalia had on her child and on us who frequented her house influenced my parenting skills.

It was incredibly kind of Tita Thalia and my friends to prepare the food and secretly plan my 18th birthday, making it a special and surprising occasion. I felt blessed that God surrounded me with such sweet and kind people.

Tita Thalia's house was a blessing to many kids. We enjoyed our time there, feeling relaxed and heard whenever we visited. Her warm welcome to all of her daughter's friends was truly amazing.

She made every child feel safe and provided someone who would listen to them. This is where I learned the importance of listening and dedicating time to understanding your children!

"One of the greatest blessings a child can have is an adult who cares for another child aside from their own."

- April Key

"It's crucial for a child to observe how adults handle situations, so when it's their turn, they can distinguish between the good and the bad, perpetuating the good and changing the bad."

- April Key

"Living with friends who genuinely care is a blessing that money can't buy."

- April Key

PSYCHOLOGICAL ANALYSIS

"I assumed the role of the mother in our home at the tender age of thirteen."

When children are compelled or feel the need to take on the roles of mother or father in the house, we refer to it as parentification. The child assumes emotional responsibility, stepping into the parental role.

Parentification typically occurs in homes with unclear family roles, family conflicts, the absence of one or both parents and when a child feels obligated to act as a caregiver, especially for younger siblings.

While some aspects of parentification may not be entirely negative, assigning age-appropriate tasks to children by parents helps them become more responsible and develop into healthy individuals, progressing through their corresponding life stages.

Parentification can stem from various reasons, such as parents experiencing traumatic events that impact their parenting styles. Situations, where both parents work extensively or in a single-parent household, can lead a child to assume parental responsibilities.

When parentification occurs, children can be significantly affected, as they face adult situations that induce stress and anxiety. They may exhibit aggressive behaviors and encounter academic challenges, recognizing the difficulty for a child to navigate such circumstances.

Parentification can result in a series of symptoms that may impact a child's adult life. Stress, anxiety, depression, difficulties in interpersonal relationships, and codependency are signs that require attention. In managing these issues, therapy plays a crucial role, aiding both the child and the family in understanding and addressing the causes of parentification.

How to Cope with Stress and Depression

1. **Exercise.** Physical activity has demonstrated positive effects on both stress and depression. Exercise releases endorphins, enhancing mood and reducing stress levels.
2. **Social Support.** Building a support system, including friends and family, can help individuals cope with stress and depression. Emotional and practical assistance from a support network proves beneficial during challenging times.
3. **Relaxation Techniques.** Deep breathing, progressive muscle relaxation, and guided imagery are effective relaxation techniques that assist in lowering stress levels and promoting calm feelings.
4. **Sleep Hygiene.** Adequate sleep is crucial for maintaining physical and mental health. Poor sleep patterns can contribute to increased stress and signs of depression. Practicing good sleep hygiene, such as avoiding coffee and electronic devices before bedtime, can enhance sleep quality.
5. **Time Management.** Feeling overwhelmed by responsibilities can contribute to stress and depression. Effective time management helps individuals prioritize tasks, reducing feelings of stress.
6. **Nutrition.** A healthy, balanced diet positively impacts physical and mental well-being. Research suggests that a diet rich in fruits, vegetables, and whole grains is associated with fewer depressive symptoms.
7. **Gratitude.** A positive outlook and reduced depressive symptoms are linked to gratitude. Maintaining a gratitude journal or regularly expressing appreciation can be helpful.
8. **Creative Expression.** Engaging in painting, writing, or music has been shown to lower stress and increase feelings of fulfillment. These creative activities also serve as a form of self-expression, aiding in processing difficult emotions.
9. **Positive Self-Talk.** Negative self-talk contributes to stress and depression. Practicing positive self-talk, focusing on personal strengths and achievements, helps build resilience and improve self-esteem.
10. **Humor.** Laughter positively impacts mood and reduces stress. Engaging in activities like watching a funny movie, reading a humorous book, or spending time with friends who bring joy can be beneficial.

How to Cope with Codependency

Codependency can be described as a dysfunctional behavior pattern wherein individuals prioritize others' needs over their own, resulting in an unhealthy dependence on others' approval and validation.

Coping with codependency involves self-exploration and developing self-awareness to recognize and modify unhealthy behavior patterns.

One strategy to cope with codependency is practicing the establishment of healthy boundaries. This entails learning to say no to unreasonable or detrimental requests and taking responsibility for one's thoughts and feelings. Another crucial aspect is adopting self-care habits, including practicing self-compassion, engaging in enjoyable activities, and seeking support from trusted friends or professionals.

While codependency may initially manifest as "getting along" or "keeping the peace," the long-term effects often lead to resentment for sacrifices made for others. Despite the challenges in relationships, the desire is for individuals to be with someone who maintains their autonomy, acts according to personal beliefs, and establishes boundaries. Mutual strengths can compensate for each partner's limitations.

How to Overcome Codependency

1. Understand your actual needs
Identify and separate genuine needs from avoidance and anxiety. Assess whether it's more important to avoid offense or protect your emotional well-being. Establish a routine for taking breaks to relax, reflect, and evaluate your needs.

2. Study your past
Examine your family history to uncover experiences contributing to codependency. Explore potential events that may have led to disconnecting from your inner emotions. This process involves reliving childhood emotions and is best done in a safe therapy relationship.

3. Practice clear, direct communication

Develop a habit of being forthright and transparent to minimize misunderstandings. Cultivate open and honest dialogues with yourself. Share more of your true self with the world, moving beyond the "pleasing," peace-keeping, or diplomatic personas.

4. Maintain independence

Refrain from excessive concern about others' opinions or actions. Believe in people's ability to figure things out independently. Despite the disappointment, maintain confidence in your inherent decency.

5. Detach from unhealthy relationships

To facilitate personal growth, detach from obsessions. Acknowledge that you cannot change, control, or please others. Let go of the binding tether, experiencing a sense of freedom and lightness. Allow things to feel more effortless and lighter.

6. Learn self-care

Letting go of your need to please others is a good start to healing, but learning self-care is crucial. You must become aware of your thoughts, feelings, and needs and learn how to communicate them in a relationship. This may feel off at first like you're being incredibly selfish. But that's okay —it's to be expected. Allow space for this awkwardness to be present, but don't try to run from it. Simple mindfulness exercises and mindful breathing techniques are a great way to begin this process. To form healthy relationships with others, you must first form one with yourself.

Codependent Traits

1. Feeling responsible for solving others' problems

A codependent person feels the need to rescue the other person from any difficult situation they have created. They make excuses that don't hold water, try to get the other person out of jail, and operate under the mistaken assumption that if they can make the other person happy, they'll stop drinking or learn to control their temper. The codependent person believes they can fix the other person's issues and alter their negative behaviors, regardless of the nature of those issues.

2. Providing advice regardless of whether or not it is requested ——————

A codependent person frequently believes they know what is best in any given circumstance and will provide counsel even when it is not requested. In addition, they will often feel insulted if the person they are advising does not take their counsel or rejects their suggestion. After all, they are only trying to be of assistance.

3. Lack of ability to communicate feelings, wants or needs effectively ——

A person who is codependent often struggles to communicate their desires and requirements. This is because they were taught to value themselves and their wants less early on. The dependent individual believes that the only person who matters is the person who is reliant on them. Very frequently, the codependent person will reach a point where they cannot differentiate between their feelings and those of the other person. You are unable to communicate something that you do not first recognize.

4. Challenges in adjusting to new circumstances ————————

Change produces an environment in which things appear to be spinning out of control, and the codependent personality has an intense urge to maintain control of the situation. The fact that this is the case, any changes might throw the codependent person into a condition of despair or anxiety, which needs to be treated before the person can proceed. They manage to adjust, but not before experiencing tremendous mental and emotional anguish first.

5. Expecting other people to follow what you suggest they should do

Another matter that can be traced back to control problems is this one. As they mature, people who are codependent report feeling disoriented and unable to exert control over their lives. The individual should acknowledge that they are acting in a way that benefits the other person and complies with the recommendations being made to them. After all, it is evident that the other individual is not acting responsibly.

6. Difficulty making decisions ——————————————

A person can't make decisions when they are not in touch with their feelings and do not believe they deserve to have needs that are uniquely their own. This is especially the case if they have any clue that the decision might make the person they live for somehow angry or disapprove of them

Because one of the characteristics of codependence is a lack of trust in one's thoughts and feelings, someone who struggles with codependence often has difficulty determining whether or not they are hesitating in the right direction.

7. A constant state of rage ─────────────────────────

Many people who exhibit codependent tendencies also struggle with an underlying persistent rage. The anger may stem from a perception that the codependent person has been mistreated. However, more often than not, the anger is directed not only at the person for whom they feel responsible but also at themselves. Because the other person isn't responding to the codependent person's efforts to fix them, the codependent person may feel like they aren't strong enough or good enough on their own. They also experience resentment toward the person because, on some level, the codependent person believes they have been taken advantage of.

8. Having a sense of being mistreated and unappreciated ───────

Codependent people frequently find themselves in relationships where the other party does not seek excessive attention. They do not want any assistance. They are not necessarily interested in being the central focus of the life of another individual. They will accept what is offered to them but rarely give anything in return. The codependent individual recognizes that this is an imbalanced connection, and they report feeling used. They frequently think they are giving everything they possess, yet the other person is oblivious to how much they are attempting to assist. This helps contribute to the long-term anger that was discussed earlier. However, the codependent person's response is not to leave but to dig in their heels even further and make more effort to provide.

9. Trying to win the approval and affection of other people ──────

Codependent individuals often have the feeling that they are unlovable and unworthy. They will strive to achieve perfection, give until they are exhausted, and continue to look for ways to win the affection of the person who is the focus of their attention. They will do all they can to avoid making the other person unhappy or sparking a disagreement in any way they can. This holds especially true for a person with a history of being abused. From a young age, they instilled in their children the belief that the surest path to being "loved" was to be "good" and do nothing but what others desire. They focused their efforts on pleasing others. This involves believing solely what the other person wants them to think.

10. Lack of trust in self or others
In most cases, the codependent person has experienced numerous letdowns throughout their life. They learn that people often don't follow through and regularly lie to them. Unable to count on others to be there when needed, they refrain from asking for help. Furthermore, their own thoughts and feelings are distrusted due to past instances of heartache and disappointment. Their lack of self-esteem further undermines trust in their thoughts.

11. Fearing rejection or being unlovable
Fear of abandonment is a fundamental aspect of the codependent personality. This individual worries that asserting themselves and expressing desires will make others view them as unlovable. They fear that voicing disagreement will lead to others abandoning them, leaving them to fend for themselves. The anxiety of being intertwined with another person's essence makes them hesitant to establish personal boundaries, potentially leading to confrontations.

12. Having a sense of being a victim
When one doesn't feel loved and is used, it may foster a sense of victimization. The belief that giving without receiving is unfair and unequal persists, yet internalized thoughts of not deserving more keep them in the circumstance, even though they recognize its injustice.

13. Tending to take things personally
Unable to modify another person's behavior, a codependent person tends to blame themselves, feeling they fell short in some way or were too unlikeable to be lovable. Their actions and words are deemed inadequate to rectify the issue.

14. Lying to yourself and making excuses for others
A codependent person internalizes the shortcomings of those for whom they feel responsible and assumes accountability. Rarely is the person who caused the mistake held responsible for their actions.

15. Feelings of hopelessness, anxiety, or despair on a more general scale — Despite their lack of control, codependents wish to believe otherwise. Their focus is on taking care of others, convinced that their needs will be met and their messes cleaned up. As the dependent partner develops a sense of helplessness, anxiety, and a fear of abandonment or lack of love set in. Depression becomes prevalent, and codependent individuals often turn to addictive behaviors to cope.

What causes codependency?

It is believed that codependency originates in childhood and can be a disorder passed down through generations. Some circumstances that can lead to adults developing codependency include:

- having a history of physical, emotional, or sexual abuse
- having a parent or caregiver affected by addiction, mental health issues, or a debilitating illness that disrupts the normal parent-child roles
- having a parent who is overbearing, domineering, or overprotective, prioritizing their own needs over those of the children
- being deserted by one or both parents

JOURNAL

What differences do you think exist between parentification and children being assigned chores at home?

We are our children's heroes. Let us make sure that our actions and words are sincere, compassionate, and encompassing.

April Key

The Philippines is the land of strong, wise, and patriotic heroes. Jose P. Rizal is our national hero.

CHAPTER 13

Scholarship Result

We received the letter about Juhan's scholarship, stating that she passed the exam. She was thrilled, and her smile extended from ear to ear upon discovering that Civil Engineering was one of the preferred courses she could pursue. Becoming an engineer, like my father, had always been her dream.

During the scholarship orientation, Mama learned that the University of San Carlos offered a double major course. If a student enrolled in this program, the Department of Science and Technology in the Philippines, in collaboration with the government of the Netherlands, would provide a subsidized additional allowance. This would cover nearly the entire amount of tuition fees, books per semester, and an additional monthly stipend of P1,250.

As a single parent, Mama had to persuade my younger sister to undertake the education double course, choosing between Physics and Chemistry or Physics and Mathematics majors. This decision would increase our chances of completing college, given Mama's financial constraints. She couldn't afford the extra P7,000 per semester for Juhan's tuition if she pursued a Civil Engineering course.

My sister felt devastated and frustrated when she realized she couldn't pursue the course of her dreams. I saw the sadness on her face as she tore up the test results for the university where she wanted to enroll for Civil Engineering. If I remember correctly, her scores were almost perfect. I felt bad and guilty that she had to sacrifice her aspirations for both of us to obtain a degree.

There was nothing I could do, as I was frequently ill and not as academically proficient as her. She was intelligent, and her grades were consistently excellent. She didn't even need to study hard for other subjects!

With limited options, she reluctantly agreed and chose from the two available choices. Since she excelled in Mathematics, she decided to pursue a double major in BSED, focusing on Physics and Mathematics.

"Affirming words from mom and dad is like a light switch. Speak a word of affirmation at the right moment in a child's life and it's like lighting up the whole room full of possibilities."

- Gary Smalley

"It's not about how to achieve your dreams, it's about how to lead your life. If you lead your life the right way, karma will take care of itself, and the dreams will come to you."

- Randy Pausch

PSYCHOLOGICAL ANALYSIS

"As a single parent, Mama had to persuade my younger sister to undertake the education double course, choosing between Physics and Chemistry or Physics and Mathematics majors. This decision would increase our chances of completing college, given Mama's financial constraints. She couldn't afford the extra P7,000 per semester for Juhan's tuition if she pursued a Civil Engineering course."

Being a child of a single mother or father does not mean that the child will not receive a better upbringing, have access to better education, or have a better life in general. Still, it is a process that can generate a lot of stress for an adult.

When the separation between the parents occurs, and the child or children go to live with the mother or the father, the one who has custody and responsibility for the children may have a more significant burden. Because of the separation between parents, there may be a decrease in financial resources, leaving the adult in charge of the children with more significant difficulties in supporting the household.

A single parent juggling work and household responsibilities faces inevitable chaos. The desire to provide a better life for their children becomes a source of stress, especially when financial resources are insufficient. This compels the adult to dedicate more time to work, inadvertently reducing the time spent with their children.

The impact of single-parenting is felt both financially and emotionally. Children in such situations experience a lack of time with one of their parents, often missing the absent adult. Additionally, the challenges faced by parents during divorce proceedings and the introduction of new relationships further contribute to the emotional and psychological strain on children.

It's essential to note that not all children in single-parent households undergo these challenges. Some homes manage to maintain healthy relationships post-divorce, with parents actively involved in their children's lives and well-being. Nevertheless, it is crucial to recognize that single mothers or fathers encounter heightened stress in navigating the responsibilities of child-rearing and overall family welfare.

How to handle stress in single parenting

What are some ways that a single parent might alleviate the stress that comes with their role?

The job of parenting children can be made more difficult and stressful by the presence of a single parent in the household. Because they have no one else to help them with their day-to-day tasks or decisions, single parents have a greater responsibility to give increased support to their children, although they may feel isolated. The following are some ideas that might help minimize stress in your household.

1. Get a grip on your financial situation
Acquire the skill of managing your money effectively. Keep track of your home bills and be aware of when your paycheck or other sources of revenue will arrive. Make every effort to strengthen your financial situation. Contact employment and temporary agencies for assistance if you require a job. If you need more education, consider acquiring a college degree, a high school diploma, or specialized training.

2. Have conversations with one another frequently
Inform your children about the changes that have occurred in the family. Sit quietly with your kids and encourage them to talk about their feelings.

3. Discover help and put it to use
Refrain from fooling yourself into thinking you're capable of handling things on your own. It would help you to lean on your closest friends and family for support.

The best approach to connect and talk to other single parents is through support groups. You can also get great advice and information from your child's pediatrician.

4. Spend time with your loved ones

Being a parent all by oneself can be demanding. Every day, set aside some time to connect with your children. Spend time together in a relaxed setting, playing games, and reading, working on arts and crafts projects, or simply listening to music. The gift of your time is among the most meaningful items you can bestow upon your offspring.

5. Spend some time on your own

There is value in both you and your children benefiting from time spent apart from your children. Being a single parent does not exclude you from having a life of your own as an adult. Find a babysitter so that you can spend some time by yourself or with your pals. Engage in pursuits that bring you joy. Go to a movie. Find something you enjoy doing.

6. Maintain a daily routine

Your children will know what to anticipate daily if you establish routines for meals, chores, and bedtimes and stick to those schedules. They will have more confidence as they adhere to the practice.

7. Abolish "guilt" from your vocabulary

It's common for a single parent to feel overwhelmed by what they can't do or provide for their children and the limited time available. However, for your well-being, it's crucial to shift focus toward acknowledging your daily achievements and the care, attention, and comfort you consistently provide. Don't overlook the love and support you contribute to your children's lives. If doubts about your accomplishments arise, consider creating a list to remind yourself.

If you're grappling with guilt stemming from a divorce or other significant family changes, joining a support group for divorced parents can be beneficial. Redirect your focus toward obtaining the necessary assistance for both you and your child. Prioritize self-care and seek out the support you need.

8. Uphold a level of consistent discipline

It is essential for parents who are divorced or separated to cooperate in providing consistent discipline for their children. Check the parenting section of your local library for further information. Parenting classes are

are frequently sponsored by the community's medical facilities, YMCAs, and churches. Finding effective techniques to deal with your children's behavior will help lessen stress for the whole family.

9. Treat kids like kids
Even though being a single parent might be a lonely experience, you should try to avoid treating your children as if they were replacements for a relationship. It would be best not to count on them for consolation or sympathy.

10. Keep a good attitude
Remember that your disposition and attitude will invariably rub off on your children. They will require your love and praise during challenging circumstances more than before. It is acceptable to be open and honest about your experiences of grief and loss, but you should reassure them that happier times are ahead for all of you.

11. Be mindful of your well-being
You, too, are going through a challenging moment right now. If you want to deal better with stress, obtaining enough rest, maintaining a healthy diet, and getting regular exercise are essential. Make sure you get regular checkups, too.

12. Answer questions honestly
Inevitably, people will inquire about the alterations that have taken place in your family or about the absence of your partner. If your child has questions, you should respond to them straightforwardly, honestly, and age-appropriately. Make it a priority to provide your child with the assistance and support they need to manage challenging feelings.

13. Find a reliable childcare center
Finding reliable childcare is critical to ensuring your health and happiness as well as your mental well-being. Finding reliable childcare is the most challenging. Keep the following in mind:

- Never leave your kids at home alone. Find someone you can trust to look after them while you are at work.
- Don't rely on older kids to babysit the younger children.

- Be careful about asking new acquaintances or potential partners to look after your children, even briefly. It's possible that they don't have the patience for it, mainly if the child exhibits challenges in conduct.
- A responsible adult with previous work experience in childcare is necessary to be able to provide appropriate care for children. Visit the daycare facility or watch your babysitter whenever they have your children in their care.

How to support children in the process of divorce

Children might have a difficult and stressful experience due to their parents' divorce. Parents need to be there for their children throughout the divorce process to assist them in coping and adjusting.

Here are some strategies for supporting children during and after a divorce:

1. Communicate openly and honestly
Parents should communicate openly and honestly with their children about the divorce. This includes explaining the reasons for the divorce age-appropriately and answering their questions. A study published in the Journal of Divorce & Remarriage found that children who received honest and age-appropriate explanations about divorce reported fewer emotional and behavioral problems.

2. Reassure children of their safety and well-being
Children may feel insecure and anxious about their future after a divorce. Parents should reassure their children that they are loved and will be cared for. Researchers found that children who received emotional support from their parents after a divorce reported better mental health outcomes.

3. Keep routines consistent
Children benefit from consistency and routine, especially during stressful situations and life changes. Parents should keep routines consistent, including mealtimes, bedtimes, and school schedules. Researchers found that children with consistent routines and structure after a divorce reported better mental health outcomes.

4. Avoid putting children in the middle

It is best for parents not to place their children in the center of their disagreements and not to use them as messengers or spies in any situation.

This can create feelings of guilt and loyalty conflicts for children. Research has found that parental conflict significantly predicts children's adjustment problems after a divorce.

5. Seek professional support

Parents and children may benefit from seeking professional support from a therapist or counselor. A study published in the Journal of Divorce & Remarriage found that children who received therapy after a divorce reported better mental health outcomes.

6. Encourage children to express their feelings

Children may have a range of emotions about divorce, including sadness, anger, and confusion. Parents must acknowledge their children's sentiments and encourage their children to talk about how they are feeling. Children who claimed they were heard and understood by their parents reported better mental health outcomes.

7. Keep positive co-parenting ties

For the sake of their children, separated or divorced parents should make every effort to maintain positive co-parenting relationships with their former partners. This requires refraining from making critical remarks or acting antagonistically against the other parent when the child(ren) is/are present. Also included in this requirement is maintaining a neutral demeanor. Positive co-parenting relationships were shown to be connected to better adjustment outcomes for children following a divorce, according to a study published in the Journal of Family Psychology.

8. Create a safe and supportive home environment

Parents can create a safe and supportive home environment by providing their children with love, attention, and positive reinforcement. Their resilience and sense of self-worth will likely improve. According to the findings of a study published in the Journal of Child and Family Studies, children who had a supportive home environment after their parents divorced reported having better mental health outcomes.

9. Encourage healthy coping strategies

Children may benefit from learning healthy coping strategies to manage their stress and emotions. This can include exercise, relaxation techniques, or talking with a trusted adult. Research shows that children who used active coping strategies, such as problem-solving and seeking social support, reported better mental health outcomes.

10. Be patient and understanding

Children may need time to adjust to the changes in their families after a divorce. Parents should be patient and understanding and avoid putting pressure on their children to adjust quickly. A study published in the Journal of Divorce & Remarriage found that children who felt rushed to adjust after a divorce reported worse mental health outcomes.

How to support children in the process of new relationships

Parents are responsible for providing a child with attention and support before a divorce, as well as during and after a divorce. Divorce, by design, splits a family unit. The process is typically draining and has lasting effects on all family members. A parent's new romantic decisions significantly impact their child's mental and physical health during or after divorce.

1. Choose the right time to introduce your child to your new partner

Discussing a new relationship is not a casual dinner conversation. A thoughtful parent should plan when, where, and how to disclose their new relationship to the kids. Preparation helps parents avoid mistakes and minimize harmful outcomes for their children. A licensed family therapist could help a parent decide when to tell their children about a new romance and how to prepare for the occasion. A therapist could also gauge how well a parent and child have adjusted to the divorce and make recommendations accordingly. For example, a therapist could advise a divorced parent exhibiting psychological distress to slow down and prioritize their healing first.

2. Understand your child's feelings

When you start dating again after your divorce, your child may experience various feelings. They might also be jealous of you or furious with you. You must learn to comprehend what your child is going through and have a talk with them about it. It may be helpful for your child to consult with a therapist or counselor if they are having difficulty adjusting to their new environment. This is also true if your child has difficulty adapting to their new school.

3. Take things slowly
This will allow them to develop their bond with their new partner at their own pace and give them time to acclimate to the concept of their parent being in a new relationship. It will also give them time to adjust to the fact that their parent is in a new relationship.

In addition, it is essential to be sensitive to your child's feelings and to listen to any concerns they may have. Forcing them to spend time with their new partner can be damaging and only make them feel more resentful. Instead, try to introduce your child to your new partner gradually.

Start by having them over for dinner or a barbecue, for example. Consider letting your child get to know them as a friend before asking them to play the role of step-parent, and above all, be understanding if your child needs some time to adjust. They've been through a lot, and it's important not to rush them.

Taking things slowly can help make the transition to a new family unit easier for everyone involved.

4. Be sensitive to your child's feelings
Respecting your child's feelings about the divorce and your new relationship is essential. Only allow them to meet your new partner if they're ready. Let them take their time in getting to know the person, and this includes avoiding pressuring the child to form a relationship with the new partner and respecting the child's need for privacy. Doing things as a family is another excellent way to include your child in the bond.

Your youngster may feel more at ease because you are willing to do this for them. With some understanding and effort, you can help your child adjust to this new chapter in their life.

You can help them by saying something like:

- I know it's hard to see mommy/daddy with someone new, but we still love you just as much.
- We're still a family, even though things are different.
- It's okay to be scared/sad/mad about this. Let's talk about it now.

5. Don't expect them to trust your partner immediately
Trust takes time to build, personalities take time to blend, and chaos takes time to settle. Most children will not eagerly accept their parent's new partner. Research suggests that most children need about two years to deal with a divorce emotionally.

Divorce causes many children to manage new living arrangements and daily routines. These stressful changes often overwhelm a child's ability to cope. It is common for children of divorced parents to struggle with human connection and act out when their emotional cup overflows.

6. Protecting your child is your highest priority
Divorce often fractures a child's identity and shatters the world they know.

A child did not exchange "I do's," sign divorce papers, or start a new relationship. Nonetheless, they endure the stressful consequences of their parent's life decisions by proxy.

Every divorced parent has the right to pursue romance after a divorce. They don't need to turn their back on love because their wedding vows weren't actualized. Each child has the right to feel safe, loved, and prioritized. A compassionate and patient parent will protect their child's feelings regardless of their relationship status.

How can neighbors and surrounding adults play a crucial role in supporting children in these situations?

Neighbors and surrounding adults can play a crucial role in supporting children whose parents are divorced. The following are ways in which they can be of assistance:

1. Offer emotional support. Neighbors and surrounding adults can offer emotional support to children of divorced parents by listening to them and providing a safe space to express their feelings. Research has shown that emotional support from non-family members can positively impact children's well-being.

2. Provide positive role models. Surrounding adults can be positive role models for children of divorced parents by modeling healthy relationships and behaviors. A study published in the Journal of Divorce & Remarriage found that positive relationships with adults outside of the family can positively impact children's emotional well-being.

3. Encourage communication. Neighbors and surrounding adults can encourage communication between children and their parents by providing opportunities for them to spend time together or facilitating communication. Research has shown that positive communication between parents and children can positively impact children's emotional well-being.

4. Resources. Neighbors and surrounding adults can provide resources to families of divorced parents, such as information about support groups or counseling services. According to the research results of a study published in the American Journal of Marriage and Family, providing children with access to resources and social support can benefit their overall health and happiness.

5. Be a positive influence. Neighbors and surrounding adults can also positively influence children by engaging in activities with them and showing an interest in their lives. This can help children feel valued and supported and contribute to their well-being. According to the findings of a study that was presented in the Journal of Youth and Adolescence, positive adult involvement can protect against adverse outcomes associated with divorce.

6. Avoid taking sides. Neighbors and surrounding adults must avoid taking sides or bad-mouthing one parent to the child. This can create unnecessary conflict and stress for the child and can contribute to feelings of guilt and confusion. Instead, surrounding adults should remain neutral and support the child's emotional needs.

7. Be aware of signs of distress. Neighbors and surrounding adults should also be aware of signs of distress in children of divorced parents, such as changes in behavior, mood, or academic performance. If a child is struggling, offering additional support, or referring the child and their family to professional counseling services may be helpful.

JOURNAL

What has been the most challenging aspect you've faced as a single parent? If you haven't experienced single parenthood, what factors do you believe contribute to the increased burden faced by single parents compared to those in relationships?

Purity is one of the sweet virtues that is pleasing to God. Be chaste and live a happy life.

April Key

Sampaguita is the national flower of the Philippines. It symbolizes purity of heart. It's beauty and scent is enduring.

CHAPTER 14

Moving Back to the City

Now that Juhan has graduated from high school and is about to start college, it would be too expensive for Mama to pay for our transportation costs. It's time to move back to the city so that our daily commuting expenses won't cost Mama an arm and a leg.

Mama found a rental room in the city that was near her office. Sometimes, when she didn't have enough money, she could simply walk from the apartment to her office. It was also close to Juhan's school and to mine, too.

We shared the apartment with Ate Rita, who happened to be the security guard of a big cooperative in Cebu. Ate Rita was a tall lady with a fair complexion. She exhibited a strong personality while on duty, but you could never tell she was a security guard when she wasn't in uniform, as she was quite girly.

Here, I was able to relax, and commuting to school and the rental house was easy for me when I didn't have a class. I could go home and take naps if needed. For Juhan, she had to take two jeepney rides from her school to the house.

We had a normal life here, but our only issue was that we couldn't leave our clothes or belongings hanging outside, as they might be stolen. It was frustrating, and the cost of continuing to rent the place was adding up. So, we decided to move again.

In my second year of college, we moved to the other side of the city. Not too far from where we were before, still near Mama's office, and the commute for Juhan and me to our respective schools remained the same.

The house was owned by my mother's officemate, Tita Shayne, who was a kind person. She sometimes allowed Mama to miss the rent and pay it whenever she could. It was a good rental property, but our problem here was that when it rained, our things would often get wet due to the nearby water canal. It was frustrating to constantly clean the house from flooding.

The upstairs tenant was also a co-worker of Mama's, and we had a small issue as she would constantly steal water. The caretaker of the water assumed we were doing the same. We paid for our water by the tank, and the water supply ran on schedule.

One day, the caretaker and I met at the sari-sari store. She initiated a conversation, asking about our origin and family name. I told her about our father's family, and she excitedly replied, "Oh, my family is from the same area. What's your family name?" I responded, "Cortes!" She said, "Omg! There were no other Cortes family names left there! Who's your aunt and father? Let's see if I'm right." She smiled and said, "I know them; they are my second cousins!" She then continued to share how my grandparents were kind to her family and took care of them in the old days when they had nothing.

From that moment on, Ate Rowena listened to us, becoming one of the people we turned to when we lacked fare for school. Sometimes, when we were too busy with school and couldn't be present during the watering schedule, she assisted us by allowing us to place our pails and buckets at her house for retrieval later. She helped us in her way, despite the challenges of her modest living conditions.

We were deeply grateful to have had her nearby! She treated us as if we were her blood and was consistently there for us when needed.

Another fortunate acquaintance was Ate Cherry, our neighbor, and a skilled dressmaker. We felt blessed that she was just next door, so whenever we needed adjustments to our uniforms or had to have something sewn, we could easily approach her for help.

My younger brother, Nimrod, continued attending elementary school here, and fortunately, he found three brothers with whom he quickly formed friendships. They were well-behaved boys and the only kids who visited our house. I never had any issues when they hung out or played together.

These brothers were good kids, and my brother was fortunate to have found them in our new neighborhood.

During one summer, the eldest brother and my brother underwent circumcision together. Thankfully, they had each other for support and could talk through the experience. They were both nine years old at the time, wearing oversized shirts and being cautious not to let the fabric touch the wound.

Assisting my brother in cleaning and witnessing his pain wasn't an easy task. Fortunately, as the days passed, the wound healed, and they were able to resume normal play like typical kids.

Our rented house was within walking distance from the church. We enjoyed attending church services and volunteered to be catechists for the young children in our community. Teaching kids about God and the basic prayers of the Catholic Church was a fulfilling experience.

Every May, during Flores de Mayo, we attended daily masses and guided younger kids to the church. I used to buy a yellow rose and offer it to Mama Mary every day—a cherished activity during the summer season, especially in May.

Juhan and I remained active in the Youth for Christ. We continued to be leaders and facilitators in our youth groups, forming strong friendships with other youths in the area. We grew close and bonded like real sisters and brothers.

REFLECTION

Moving back to the city was one of the best decisions my mother made for me and my siblings. It provided us with the opportunity to easily rest after long days at school or work. It also allowed us to save money on transportation, as it's only a one-ride journey that took around 30 minutes, depending on traffic.

Honestly, it significantly contributed to my mental well-being, allowing me to rest between classes if needed. We enjoyed our time here and, once again, made new friends.

It's challenging to constantly move, meet new people, and adjust, but at this age, as adults, we've learned to adapt to this lifestyle and grow from it.

Having positive people around us was crucial in managing stress, especially during college when we had numerous responsibilities at home and in school.

Engaging in church activities, volunteering, and supporting summer programs for younger kids were among the best memories we shared with friends in this town.

"Surround yourself with positive people who are achievers because they will also help you achieve your goals"

- April Key

"When we're in the environment of like-minded people, there's a different energy, and you can feel the positive words that come out of their mouths to lift each other up."

- April Key

"One of the key factors influencing our mental and psychological health is our environment, including where we live and who we associate ourselves with."

- April Key

PSYCHOLOGICAL ANALYSIS

"We were deeply grateful to have had her nearby! She treated us as if we were her blood and was consistently there for us when needed."

The environment in which a child develops is crucial for their growth and formation as an individual. The relationships children establish with people in their daily lives can significantly impact their development.

A child's initial relationships are with their parents, from whom they gain knowledge about various aspects of life. As children grow, they encounter different environments, applying their prior learning and acquiring new knowledge.

Regrettably, not all children grow up in healthy environments with parental support that positively influences them. However, there are instances where children find support from individuals outside their homes, within their community.

Living in a community with neighbors can be beneficial for everyone. Human beings are social creatures and require interaction for their development. Establishing bonds of friendship and trust with neighbors provides a sense of security, knowing whom to turn to in times of trouble.

In some cases, neighbors become like family and not merely people who live next door. They become individuals who care for each other, offer support, and enjoy good times together.

Fostering relationships beyond the immediate family helps a child develop social skills, learn how to interact and behave with others, and gain a broader perspective that encourages discernment and critical thinking.

JOURNAL

Describe a situation in which someone from your community has assisted you. How did you feel?

Let our services be punctuated with love. When there is no love in our good works it become stale.

April Key

Malacañang Palace officially known as Malacanan Palace, is the official residence and principal workplace of the President of the Philippines.

CHAPTER 15

College Life

I continued to pursue my Hotel and Restaurant Management course for two years, and Juhan chose the course Mama wanted her to take. However, it reached a point where both Juhan and I decided to shift and pursue different majors.

I struggled physically in my course, particularly in the Housekeeping and Restaurant subjects. It escalated to the point where the dean of my department told me I would never finish the degree due to frequent sickness and absences. Besides the financial challenges in paying my tuition, my health posed a significant hurdle. I shifted to Bachelor of Science in Hospitality and Tourism Management, finding it the most feasible way to complete my studies with credit transfer for related subjects.

If money and health weren't an issue, my top preferred courses would be a Bachelor of Science Major in Psychology, a Bachelor of Science Major in Political Science, and a Bachelor of Science Major in Business Administration. Unfortunately, due to my commitment to my maternal grandfather to care for his property and fulfill our vision of helping Mama manage the rental property for future passive income, I chose a Bachelor of Science in Hotel and Management. On the other hand, Juhan cried and pleaded with Mama to switch to Physics and Chemistry as she found Mathematics too easy. She felt she never learned anything new in her course, consistently scoring perfect grades and straight A's, especially in Math.

Fortunately, Mama allowed her to switch. Despite not being content with her course, Juhan had no choice but to finish college and earn a degree. Despite her frustrations and anger with Mama for not allowing her the freedom to pursue her dreams, she excelled in school.

In Juhan's last year of college, she talked to me and decided to leave our house to live near her school, focusing on her studies and practice teaching to achieve her dream of becoming an honor student. The constant loudness from Mama was hindering her progress, and she feared not making it to the honor list if she continued living with us.

I was genuinely saddened when she opened up to me, but as her older sister, I agreed with and supported her decision. However, I knew it wouldn't be easy for me to be left alone with Mama and take care of my younger brother.

I've been constantly stressed since Juhan left us. I took on all the chores and cared for my stubborn brother, who wouldn't come home right after school. The stress took a toll on my health, leading to frequent illnesses. Fortunately, my sister and I would occasionally meet and cry together, finding solace in each other despite the hardships we faced.

Both of us were blessed to have close friends who provided financial and emotional support. Their presence was crucial as we were away from our own family.

Juhan's best friend, BJ, and his family were very supportive of her. Meanwhile, I was fortunate to have my best friend, Jez, when I shifted to Tourism Management. I was lucky to have a friend like her who was willing to sacrifice her wants, needs, and time for me, especially during sickness. She consistently walked me to the clinic, disregarding the time it took for her to return to her classes.

While we shared what we had, I was the one who often turned to her for financial support since she belonged to a wealthy family. I did this especially when I had no money for transportation or lunch.

Both of us had the opportunity to travel together around the country, not only in our major Tourism classes but also in our minor classes. Despite our differences, we managed to respect each other's personal lives and found common ground that strengthened our connection. This dynamic added an interesting, fun, and exciting dimension to our friendship. Of course, misunderstandings occurred at times, but we always found a way to talk it out when we were ready.

One of my close friends, Hazel, lived with us for a year after her father passed away. Since we shared the same room, it was easier for her to relate to my experiences with Mama. Despite these challenges, Hazel consistently showed respect towards Mama throughout her stay.

I got to know Genevie, another close friend, in one of our classes. We were the first two students to arrive outside one of our classes. While waiting, I realized we needed to pay P20 for a workbook. Since I only had enough money for my fare back home, I decided to approach Genevie, who was cool and easy to talk to. I asked her, "Classmate, what's your name? Is it okay to borrow money? I'll pay you back tomorrow for the workbook." Genevie turned around, surprised by my straightforward request, and responded with a big smile, saying, "What?" Fortunately, she was kind and agreed to lend me the money on the spot. This marked the beginning of the craziest friendship story in my life!

From that day forward, Genevie and I became close, hanging out more as we ended up living in the same town in Guadalupe. She invited me to her dorm, introducing me to her family and other friends. We formed a strong friendship, connecting with people in our department who lived nearby. Often, we agreed to go home together after school, especially if it was the last session at night, providing company and ensuring our safety. Genevie's dorm became a go-to place for everyone, particularly during major events at school.

I also had another group of friends, with all three of us belonging to different colleges. Others often asked us how we became friends and met each other. They thought it was rare to have such a diverse group of friends. Every semester, we made sure to sit down and plan our schedules to have time together. Two to three times a week, we enjoyed the same free time so we engaged in activities and conversations together. The two girls in this group loved to dance so they formed their group. I attended some of their performances to support them, and they attended mine as well.

Meanwhile, Juhan focused on her studies, working hard to achieve her goal of becoming an honor student. Her Physical Education was swimming, but she did not know how to swim so she and her classmates seized every opportunity to practice whenever the pool was open. The challenge was that it was in a different building and on a different side of the city, requiring travel to and from the Education campus. Fortunately, the Education campus was conveniently located near our residence.

She faced challenges in her new major, particularly in her laboratory classes. Being a clumsy person, she frequently ended up breaking laboratory beakers, test tubes, and other fragile instruments.

In her final years as a Physics and Chemistry major, the difficulty increased, pushing her to work harder to achieve her dream of becoming an honor student. Fortunately, everyone was supportive of one another, maintaining a balance of laughter and enjoyment throughout their college years. Despite the academic pressure, she and her best friend still found time to visit Ayala Mall or SM to visit the National Bookstore to read books, sometimes bringing their own, and relishing the free air conditioning while immersed in their studies. In jest, I used to inquire about how her "10 units" were at Ayala Mall. They also frequented the mall when their stipend was deposited into their account.

When she lived with us, it was frustrating for me that she often chose to go to the mall before coming home, instead of helping with chores and taking care of my younger brother. However, I came to understand that the mall served as her stress reliever. She found solace in reading books there.

During this phase of her life, Juhan became secretive about her crushes and love life, causing concern for me as her elder sister. She was someone we looked up to, and I didn't want her to make regrettable decisions. In a desperate move, I decided to grab her diary to learn more about her life.

One summer, she forgot her small pocket notebook in our room. Seizing the opportunity, I took it with me to school. Meeting Jez at one of the student hangouts near the canteen, I excitedly shared my plan to discover my sister's secrets. We enjoyed reading the well-written notes, which turned out to be a poem detailing stories about the person she admired. Despite being a poem, knowing the people she hung out with made it easy for me to identify the person she secretly loved. It was heartbreaking to realize her feelings were taken for granted, but thankfully, she moved on and embraced her college life.

On my end, I had a crush on a guy majoring in Mass Communication. However, it was merely admiration as I didn't have time for a relationship due to my full schedule of studies, dealing with illness, household chores, and caring for my younger brother.

I found joy in giving secret Valentine's chocolate roses to friends, especially to him, every Valentine's Day. Celebrating Valentine's Day had been a tradition for my sister and me since childhood but during college, we started including our younger brother in our celebrations as he had become more well-behaved and older. What was once a private celebration turned into a larger friends' Valentine's Day celebration as more friends joined us. Despite the challenges of finding a bigger table, the positive side was more laughter and meaningful conversations on this special day!

REFLECTION

"It's not impossible to reach our goals as long as we accept the challenges and work for them."

- April Key

"It's easier to navigate life and handle hardships when we have true friends who have our back."

- April Key

"True friends don't measure status in life; it's what is in their hearts that connects them."

- April Key

"Valentine's Day is for everyone to enjoy; it's not only for romantic couples."

- April Key

"When two or more people in the group gather at the table, there's so much more to talk and laugh about."

- April Key

"If you can find one true friend in your life, consider it a blessing. Others are surrounded by many, but none of them are true."

- April Key

PSYCHOLOGICAL ANALYSIS

"In a desperate move, I decided to grab her diary to learn more about her life."

Reviewing something as intimate as a person's diary is an invasion of privacy. As parents, there is often curiosity and the desire to know what is going on with their children, but going through their personal belongings without any justified reason can cause problems in the relationship between parents and children.

Parents have the right to monitor their children, to know how they feel, with whom they spend time, and how they are doing in their studies. When the father or mother perceives some strange behavior in the child, they may feel concerned and will want to get to the cause of it. When parents talk to their children about their concerns and see that they do not get an answer, wanting to go through their belongings such as a diary or cell phone can lead to the opposite effect.

If the child finds out that their father or mother has been looking at their things, they will be upset since they may feel that their privacy has been violated. Trust may deteriorate, negatively affecting the relationship between the parents and the child/ren.

It is natural for parents to be concerned about their children's well-being and to want insight into their lives. However, invading their privacy is not the solution. In situations causing distress, it is crucial to observe specific behaviors and pay attention to what they share. If the desire for more information arises, it is important to refrain from intruding on their privacy, as it could exacerbate the situation. Communication remains a primary and constructive means to understand the well-being of children.

JOURNAL

As a parent, what boundaries have you set to ensure the privacy of your children is respected?

To make your act of
kindness meritorious and
pleasing to God, make sure
you are helping those who
are serving God, and do it in
silence and your soul must
be in a state of grace.

April Key

Filipinos are known for having a
"Strong Work Ethic". Most of them are
hardworking individuals who cares
about the job and the profession that
was entrusted to them regardless of
their salary.

CHAPTER 16

Graduating with Honors

Before Juhan's graduation day, she needed to secure a total of P7,000 to cover all the expenses required for her college graduation. Mama couldn't afford it, as she also had to pay for my final tuition fee.

Juhan reached out to one of our aunts, asking for financial assistance. Our aunt instructed her to go back to the province, because she sent the money to my grandmother. Due to her busy schedule preparing for graduation, Juhan asked me to travel and collect the funds from my grandma.

However, upon my arrival, my grandma couldn't find the money in her pocket. Since she was too old to walk, she helped me to find the money for my fare back to the city. Fortunately, the wife of my cousin provided some money for my return trip.

It was a challenging day for all of us, especially for Mama and Juhan who didn't know where to borrow such an amount. Thankfully, Mama found someone willing to lend her the necessary funds, allowing Juhan to cover all the school expenses.

On her graduation day, Juhan, accompanied by Mama and my younger brother, attended the ceremony. She successfully graduated, fulfilling her dream of becoming an honor student and being one of the ten cum laude graduates in their department that year. I opted not to attend due to a disagreement with Mama and contemplated leaving the house. However, Juhan persuaded me to stay, so I cleaned the house instead and awaited their return.

Upon their arrival, we were surprised to see Papa's cousin and my father's aunt at our apartment. With all the money Mama collected spent on school expenses, we had nothing left for a celebration. We awaited the arrival of my aunt and grandmother to come and celebrate with us. While waiting, my father's aunt gave us money to buy sardines and noodles, and we enjoyed a simple celebration, sharing laughter while eating a can of sardines and two noodles.

As time passed, we realized it was late afternoon but my grandmother and aunt never showed up. She had hoped for her father's family to be proud of her, especially our grandma. However, they never came, leading her to tears. Despite this, we tried to remain positive, considering that maybe our grandma was just too tired to make the journey.

During the summer, Juhan and I visited our father and grandmother to check on them. Lola was busy gardening, and Papa was cooking in the back. We spent time with Lola, and Juhan asked her personal questions about motherhood and her feelings toward her children. It was an emotional moment that taught us the importance of giving back to our parents who sacrificed so much for us.

Returning to the city for my summer classes, I aimed to graduate on time, while Juhan embarked on her journey into the adult world.

After graduating from college, Juhan endeavored to find a job outside of teaching, which she didn't enjoy. I learned from the Department of Tourism that they were hiring an office assistant. I suggested Juhan apply, and she successfully passed the test, aided by my noisy study habits, which helped her memorize Tourism terms. She also assisted us in editing our thesis, making her more familiar with some tourism concepts.

We were able to work together because I was undergoing my "Airline Phase" on-the-job training at Mactan International Airport, while she was assigned to the DOT counter at the airport. Sometimes, my boss in the PA office would assign both Elien and me to the domestic and international arrival and departure counters, allowing us to work together and support each other. If Elien had to wait for more flights or assist someone, I would stay longer to help her wait for the last arrival or a delayed flight until we could both go home together.

VIPs often found it amusing to see us in our traditional Filipiniana costume while we adorned them with leis, the customary Filipino welcome for VIPs by the DOT in the Philippines. Many times, they mistook us for twins, a familiar occurrence that always made us smile. Juhan and I enjoyed wearing the dress, although it could be tiresome sometimes, especially if the flight was delayed and we had to change and walk back to the international arrival where the DOT airport office was located. Yet, it was part of the job, and we had no choice but to do it.

It was during this time that we met Tatay Felimon and Miss Christine, Juhan's co-workers. We grew close to them, often having lunch with Tatay and even walking together, each holding one of his arms. Tatay became an instant father figure to us, with some people at the airport thinking we were his twin daughters. Occasionally, we went home with Miss Christine, who treated us at her favorite pizza place.

Similarly, we would each hold Miss Christine's arms as we walked together. However, one thing that annoyed me was her insistence on making me eat bananas. I wasn't fond of them, so Juhan would sometimes grab them as she's the certified "banana girl." Over time, I learned to eat this fruit through her encouragement. We were grateful for people who offered help even when we didn't ask; it felt like God was guiding us through them.

The PA office at the airport was responsible for airport tours for the kids. One day, they had a scheduled tour, leaving Elien and me alone at the office. The person in charge of the tour didn't return as promised. Faced with a decision, Elien and I closed the office temporarily and took the children to the deck where they could see airplanes. Fortunately, the kids enjoyed the impromptu tour and we were praised by our big boss for handling the situation well.

Working at the airport provided exciting experiences, including encounters with numerous celebrities. One unforgettable memory was seeing my favorite childhood actors, John Lloyd, and Kaye Abad, in person. Although nervous, I found them to be approachable, allowing us to take pictures with them as they waited for their luggage.

Being at the frontline counter at the airport brought both positive and negative experiences, especially in handling various types of travelers, both international and domestic. Sometimes, it was rewarding, particularly when other people appreciated our beauty and service.

One irksome experience was dealing with foreigners who had too many questions, which took me so much time to address. My boss would tell me they were just finding ways to talk to me. It could be frustrating, especially because my English vocabulary was limited.

The most frightening incident occurred when I, along with Miss Daphne, waited for the last flight and there were two handsome young pilots in their uniforms who passed by the counter and tried to ask someone to obtain my cellphone number. Naturally, I declined, as they were strangers. Miss Daphne and I didn't pay much attention, assuming they had already left and the van taking them to their hotel had departed. We took our time cleaning up the counter, and I helped her with the items that needed to be placed in the DOT airport office. As we walked from the international arrival to the domestic arrival, the two pilots emerged from their hiding spots, surprising us. They have been waiting for us.

We both hurriedly returned to the international arrival area, exiting the building. Running was a challenge, given that we both wore short pencil skirts and high heels. We had to take off our shoes and run frantically, making sure to cross the street away from the airport building, which was now quiet and dark. Despite their tall, handsome, and young appearance, we were genuinely scared.

Miss Daphne estimated they were around 6 feet or taller as she tried to catch her breath. "Oh my goodness, April, it's so hard to be with you as all these giants always want you!" she exclaimed. It was one of the crazy experiences of being a Filipina beauty and working at the frontline.

While I enjoyed assisting tourists to know more about our province, there were instances when I felt intimidated by foreigners who seemed more interested in personal interactions than seeking assistance. I found relief when I wasn't stationed all day at the information booth, avoiding the need to entertain foreigners seeking my attention.

REFLECTION

In life, it's essential to work on self-improvement not to alter others' perceptions of us, but to foster personal growth. Regardless of how much we prove ourselves to others, their opinions may remain unchanged. In their eyes, we consistently appear as the person they have envisioned.

Many siblings do not have the privilege to work together or be near each other. We were fortunate to have had the opportunity to work together. The silver lining is that our colleagues became like a family to us.

In the tourism industry, one of the privileges we enjoyed was the opportunity to showcase our country and culture to arriving tourists at the airport. As a traditional Filipino imbued with the values and qualities of a Filipina, it was a blessing to authentically represent these traits when travelers landed in our city and our country.

"In life, it's important to work on ourselves for personal growth, not to change others' perceptions."

- April Key

"There are positive and negative experiences related to being a Filipina beauty; just go with your values."

- April Key

"Nurture your children's confidence in their youth; it's crucial for decision-making in adulthood."

- April Key

"Many siblings do not have the privilege to work together; if you have it, treasure each moment and the memories you make outside your home."

- April Key

PSYCHOLOGICAL ANALYSIS

"After graduating from college, Juhan endeavored to find a job outside of teaching, which she didn't enjoy."

After completing university, many aspire to secure a job, a process that can be frustrating when the perceived opportunities do not align with the reality of the job market.

University graduates often hope to find employment related to their field of study. However, faced with limited opportunities in their desired area, desperation and concern arise during the job search, compounded by the need to meet basic expenses. Consequently, many individuals opt for jobs unrelated to their academic background, solely to generate income and cover their financial needs.

There are individuals who, post-college, encounter difficulty securing any job. Days, weeks, months, and even years may pass without finding job opportunities, leading to heightened anxiety and potential depression.

Obtaining employment after completing university is challenging for many, but not impossible. To transform this process into a less frustrating and more learning-oriented experience, it is essential to recognize that perceptions may not align with reality. While some individuals do find work post-graduation, others may not. It's crucial for those who don't secure a job to understand that it's not a reflection of their capabilities. Rejection from interviews can impact self-esteem, but it's vital to realize that not receiving a callback doesn't inherently signify personal or professional inadequacy.

The job market is dynamic, and a lack of job offers doesn't imply a deficiency in an individual's qualities. Each company has specific criteria and rejection shouldn't be taken personally. Some people erroneously believe they chose the wrong career when struggling to find a job, but this is not accurate. While certain careers may face higher demand, the difficulty in finding a job does not invalidate the chosen career path.

Job searching may take time, but persistence and recognizing the uniqueness of each experience are crucial.

Graduates feeling frustrated about not finding a job must understand that success is a process, and a longer timeframe does not negate the possibility of achieving dreams. Maintaining healthy self-esteem is essential, acknowledging that job searches are not personal and that the process itself cultivates valuable skills and awareness.

Completing a degree in a field one dislikes may be a necessary step for economic support, serving as a platform to pursue one's true passions and dreams in life. Gratitude for the opportunity to attend college and earn a degree is crucial, recognizing it as a privilege that is not universally accessible.

JOURNAL

Reflecting on your personal experience, how did you find the process of finding your first job? Share the emotions you went through and the lessons you learned.

Mother must always be the support to the family. Her nurturing love dissipates the fears and worries of the children.

April Key

Birhen sang Barangay (Virgin of Barangay) is a Marian image in the Philippines, it is transferred from home to home, and a family must pray the Rosary while this sacred image is at their home.

CHAPTER 17

Confrontation

One day, while on duty at the airport, I received a text message from my mother informing me that my paternal grandmother was hospitalized. Given my close relationship with her, immediately after my airport duty, I rushed to Cebu Doctor's Hospital to visit her. She was confined in a private room, where I found her, my aunt Lucy, and my father. Surprisingly, my aunt had not informed my mother that my father was with them.

Fortunately, I was the first to visit, not my mother, and I appreciated that they told us they were in the hospital. The location was convenient as it was en route to my school, within walking distance from my mother's office, and easily accessible for a jeepney ride home.

I spent time with my grandmother, even assisting in cleaning her body which needed some TLC due to the effects of medication. My aunt Lucy was occupied with answering long-distance calls from her sisters abroad, allowing me to overhear conversations about Lola's condition. Strangely, she did not say anything about my presence and assistance, before anyone else arrived, but instead told them that her daughters were there taking care of Lola. She lied to my aunts as I didn't see them around at that time.

After some time, her eldest daughter arrived, and then my other aunt along with some of our relatives and cousins. They brought some rice and vegetable soup, turning the gathering into a mini-reunion.

The discussions led to the attitude of Lola's grandchildren. Lola declared that I was the most maldita (mischievous) among the grandchildren. "But you are different," she said, "In time you will know what I mean, and I salute you for that." I let it go, but from that moment, I never really forgot what she said. That statement echoed a similar sentiment from my maternal grandfather before he passed away when I was thirteen.

As the night progressed, I had to leave as I had my duty the next morning. But saying goodbye to Papa was always problematic, as he disliked our departure. We could not let him come with us either as it would be a big problem for Mama. Fortunately, my aunt discreetly helped me exit the hospital without Papa's knowledge. I had to take off my heels and run barefoot in my Airline Phase uniform as I navigated the dark street at the back of the hospital. I kept praying for safety as I walked and ran for about ten to twenty minutes until I reached the main street without any problem.

Toward my graduation, Lola passed away but the news reached us late, a recurring pattern that frustrated and saddened my sister and me. Despite our family issues, we attended the burial in Tabogon since we knew Papa would be happy to see us. Mama also urged us to go to avoid blame from our aunts.

Upon arrival, some aunts and cousins were present, except for one aunt in the USA who was facing travel difficulties at the time. We went directly to see Lola, crying our hearts out as we said goodbye to her. Then my sister and I talked to Papa to ask him if he was going to be okay staying in the house now that Lola was gone. He mentioned that he was going to be fine as his older sister Lucy was going to be with him. We knew that he lived with his parents most of his life and that it would be hard for him now that both parents were gone.

The next day, my aunt and I were busy cleaning the kitchen cabinets beneath the sink. Juhan and I had learned household chores from her during our younger years as she dedicated time to teaching us and assigning daily tasks whenever we visited her place. As we prepared for Lola's burial, she convened a meeting upstairs with Aunt Eden and some cousins, excluding Papa. She initiated, "Now that the last grandparent is deceased, it's time for all of us to decide how to move forward."

Addressing Juhan and me in front of everyone, she declared that we were obligated to take care of our father as we would be the heirs to his inheritance. I felt my blood boiling, witnessing her demeanor and the way she delivered her message in front of the family. Swiftly, I retorted with anger, asserting that we were working hard to earn degrees to buy our properties and didn't need material possessions.

Aunt Eden interjected, saying, "Don't say that because if your father were well now, he would give everything to both of you." Aunt Riley said that she would get a lawyer to make sure it's one paper, telling us never to return home, see our father, or interact with any of our relatives since we were a disgrace to the Cortes family and unworthy of the family name.

Juhan remained silent. She would later say that she was ready to respond, but since I had already spoken, she stayed quiet.

To diffuse the tension, the meeting concluded, but I could sense the satisfaction on one cousin's face. Maybe they felt victorious. It was heartbreaking to see Aunt Riley, my closest aunt on my father's side and my only godmother, easily manipulated by my other aunt.

After the confrontation, we all acted as if nothing had happened and proceeded to prepare for Lola's funeral mass. We went to the church service and walked to the cemetery together. While at the gravesite, we postponed lowering Lola's coffin into the grave as we had to wait for Aunt Mama Marydel's arrival from the USA. The journey from the airport to Tabogon would take four to five hours, depending on traffic.

Juhan and I contacted Miss Christine to confirm Aunt Marydel's arrival on the day and time she specified. Fortunately, Miss Christine verified her arrival and informed us she was on her way home in a rented car. Juhan conveyed this information to our aunts, but Aunt Riley insisted on proceeding with the burial.

As workers began applying cement, Aunt Del arrived and ordered them to stop and remove the cement so she could see Lola for the last time. I empathized with her effort to travel many hours and spend a significant amount on fare, only for Aunt Riley to proceed despite knowing her sister was on her way. The behavior displayed in front of us and our deceased grandmother left me confused.

We left Aunt Mama Del at the cemetery as darkness fell. Juhan and I promptly returned to the house, packing our belongings for the last bus trip home.

One older cousin approached us, attempting to explain to us the situation inside the house and Papa's behavior. According to him, Papa's deteriorating mental state was exacerbated by the treatment from his parents and sisters. Their words and handling of his situation contributed to his declining health. He shared positive memories of Papa when he was younger and mentally well.

He pleaded with my sister and me to lend an ear and care for our father, emphasizing his belief that Papa's current condition was a result of mistreatment and mishandling. Juhan and I attentively listened, feeling unsure of what actions to take, given Papa's heavy reliance on his older sisters. Moreover, our limited means made it challenging to provide for ourselves, and we were still striving to survive.

After our conversation with Papa, during which we bid our goodbyes, we sat on the bench outside until the late-night arrival of the bus. Thankfully, Papa understood and did not hinder us from returning to the city so I could attend my classes, and Juhan could resume work.

REFLECTION

Living abroad and knowing the truth about one's family back home is a challenging task. It is often easier to believe than to investigate what's happening. One could only hope that all of the information being fed to you was true.

Individuals, especially those raised away from their families, face difficulties surviving without familial support. For these children, the responsibility of caring for an ailing father due to inheritance issues adds another layer of emotional burden. They are concerned about the presence, love, and care of the adults in their lives more than material possessions.

Jealousy within a family can be a destructive force, damaging relationships throughout. It spreads like a disease, fueled by gossip, which, when directed at absent family members, can be akin to condemning them without allowing them to explain their side of the story.

One of the saddest scenarios in a family is when a family member fabricates stories and lies about other family members to tarnish their reputation and lead to them being disowned. It is a regrettable reality that, unfortunately, occurs.

Children who endure neglect and grow up amidst such pain must embark on a journey of healing, self-forgiveness, and moving forward.

"Children don't have the power to control the adults' behavior in their life, but all they can do is learn from them."

- *April Key*

"Jealousy can do a lot of damage to anything; strive to be happy for others instead."

- April Key

"Presence is more valuable than presents."

- April Key

"We don't need to give our kids material things on every occasion because all they need is someone to run to when they don't feel safe."

- April Key

PSYCHOLOGICAL ANALYSIS

"One older cousin approached us, attempting to explain to us the situation inside the house and Papa's behavior. According to him, Papa's deteriorating mental state was exacerbated by the treatment from his parents and sisters. Their words and handling of his situation contributed to his declining health."

Individuals who fall victim to physical or verbal abuse are more prone to developing mental illnesses like depression, a genuine condition that impacts over 300 million people globally.

Mental illnesses significantly impact a person's well-being, hindering them from conducting their daily activities as they used to. Providing additional care becomes essential to aid the individual in returning to their previous lifestyle.

Caring for family members with mental illnesses poses a challenge to the rest of the family. Whether psychological or physical, diseases introduce unexpected daily situations that generate uncertainty among family members.

Often, those with mental illnesses do not receive the necessary care, partly because their families may not know how to act. Sometimes, they interpret the affected member(s)' behavior in a non-disease-related manner, leading them to overlook or mistreat the affected individual(s).

Another obstacle to receiving care arises when individuals with mental illnesses are aware of the problem but hesitate to seek help due to the difficulty they face in doing so. Feelings of shame, isolation, or a sense of being misunderstood can hinder seeking help. They may believe that others won't comprehend their family's situation and, as a result, choose to remain silent.

Having a relative with mental illness is not a cause for shame. Contemporary awareness about mental health has grown, and there are more support groups available for individuals to obtain help and better navigate the challenges faced by the affected family member/s. To assist family members with mental illnesses, it is crucial to initiate a quest for information. If there is no diagnosis yet, consulting professionals in the field is imperative.

JOURNAL

Do you think some people have problems accepting a family member who is mentally ill? Why do you think this is so?

Completing a project is no simple task, but with exceptional teamwork within the group, success is achievable without a shadow of doubt.

April Key

"Bayanihan" is a Filipino word come from the word 'bayan' meaning town, nation, or community. "Bayanihan" literally means, "being a bayan," and is used to refer to a spirit of communal unity and cooperation.

CHAPTER 18

Divergent Thinking

During my senior year, finishing my thesis writing became more challenging due to a change in our class adviser. The new adviser disapproved of continuing our initial topic, rendering a whole semester of work wasted. Faced with this setback, I proposed a new and ambitious idea of shifting our research focus to "Tabogon as an Ecotourism Destination."

Having experienced disappointment in changing my first course, I saw an opportunity to align our research with our teacher's expertise in tourism. I believed that exploring my father's birthplace, which boasted abundant natural resources, could contribute to the local community's income through future tourism revenue.

Our university was the first to offer this major in the whole of Cebu. I wanted to grab the opportunity to work with a teacher who was knowledgeable in this matter. I wanted our team to make a difference, knowing that many people could benefit from it.

However, the proposal created disagreement within the group. The size of the area and the associated travel time and expenses further divided opinions, especially since some group members needed to graduate within six months. We had limited time to finish the work and make sure we could present it before graduation.

To resolve the conflict, we held a vote, ultimately separating from our previous leader, Josh. Most of our group members chose to pursue my proposed topic, but I could understand Josh's hesitation as time was, indeed, limited. Aside from that, he was sending himself through college and it would certainly be difficult for him to afford numerous trips.

As we delved into our new topic, we prioritized visiting the Municipal Hall and meeting Tabogon's government leaders to communicate our mission and gather essential information for our thesis. While the initial interactions went smoothly, challenges arose due to some members not cooperating and fulfilling their responsibilities, despite my mother offering financial support for our travels to the Municipality.

Feeling pressured and questioning my decision to pursue this research, Xhrystnn's positive attitude kept us going, while Rey's frequent requests for favors, coupled with his other commitments, added to the strain. I became particularly frustrated when Rey prioritized watching a TV show over project-related responsibilities, leaving Xhrystnn and me to work on the project alone in the middle of the night.

An incident in Colon, Cebu City, where Rey failed to meet us as promised, triggered my anger. Concerned for our safety as two women in a dangerous area at night, I confronted Rey the next day, publicly expressing my frustration. Fortunately, he remained calm, apologized, and understood the need for his support, especially as he was the only man in the group.

Following the incident, Rey became more helpful, prioritizing our safety during late-night work sessions despite his busy schedule with work and varsity practice.

The challenges in pursuing this topic extended beyond monetary expenses, technological limitations, and time constraints associated with traveling to the area. Our safety was also a concern, given the prevalence of rebels in the mountainous regions during that period. There were instances when Rey would rush towards us with a pale and frightened expression as if he encountered a rebel who resisted progress in the town.

The most challenging aspect of our research was the lack of a dedicated vehicle for travel between locations. We mostly traversed on foot, moving from one barangay to another for house-to-house visits to conduct surveys, enduring the scorching sun. To ensure accurate data, we carefully documented the percentage of people supporting our idea in each place.

During a few of our visits to mountainous areas, the municipality driver sensed danger, prompting a sudden halt in our activities as we realized the potential risk. The driver's urgency became clear when he signaled us to go right away. I had to run and grab my two groupmates, telling them to run to the van immediately.

As we sped away, the driver shared that the area had a history of conflict between the military and rebels. Fortunately, we reached the national highway safely, unharmed by any untoward incident. He looked so relieved and happy the moment we reached the national highway. By God's grace, we arrived in town, safe and sound.

The following morning, tensions rose, leading to a significant disagreement between Xhrystnn and me. Seeking solace and clarity, Neslie and I decided to visit in the spring. As the group leader, I grappled with conflicting perspectives, especially after Neslie chose to quit and drop the subject, leaving Xhrystnn and me as the main contributors.

During our final visit to Tabogon, while summarizing potential ecotourism sites, emotions ran high. The three of us shared a heartfelt moment, embracing each other and acknowledging the challenges and struggles overcome during the six months. We stood united, having weathered the tests of our senior year.

Our perseverance allowed Xhrystnn to graduate on time. Our research fostered a strong bond between us. Despite knowing we would part ways after the project, we vowed to revisit the place once our vision materialized.

The positive outcomes of our research extended beyond academic achievements. It provided me the opportunity to reconnect with my father, sleep at my grandparents' house with the research team, and strengthen familial ties. The project served as a pretext for subsequent visits to Tabogon in 2005, enabling me to meet more relatives on my father's side.

I was grateful for the chance to learn about my paternal great-grandparents leadership during the old times in Tabogon. I felt blessed to be able to uncover my roots. The older generations spoke highly of the Cortes family's contributions to the community in Sugod before Tabogon gained town status in Cebu province. They couldn't stop praising the continuing leadership of the Oberes clan, as well. This significant experience, shared with my research team, became a cherished memory, emphasizing the value of teamwork in achieving what I could never have accomplished alone.

REFLECTION

In life, events unfold with purpose, and when circumstances compel us to shift our decisions and goals, it may be a divine attempt to align us with our true purpose.

Frankly, undertaking research in Tabogon is a source of pride for me as a young adult. The challenges faced during the process became the catalyst for choosing such a topic.

Our journey tested our courage, perseverance, determination, and friendship over those six months. It was far from an easy path, and we willingly took risks to complete the research.

"We can't accomplish great things alone; we need teammates. However, we don't have to conform to trends; instead, we must be courageous to envision and create a remarkable future."

- April Key

"Don't hesitate to act on what you believe can be achieved and yield positive results; the true outcome remains unknown unless you take that leap of faith."

- April Key

"When people mock your ideas, it signifies your ideas' extraordinariness, requiring extraordinary individuals to comprehend and believe in them."

- April Key

"In the pursuit of great accomplishments, a multitude of people isn't always necessary; sometimes, one or two exceptional individuals are sufficient to surround yourself with to achieve it."

- April Key

PSYCHOLOGICAL ANALYSIS

"Our perseverance allowed Xhrystnn to graduate on time. Our research fostered a strong bond between us."

Teamwork is the collaborative effort of individuals coming together to achieve a shared objective. When people choose to work as a team, they leverage the unique skills of each member, fostering mutual learning. Establishing rules within a teamwork framework enhances the dynamics, promoting greater organization and preventing potential obstacles that may hinder the desired goal.

For successful teamwork to happen, clarity in objectives is paramount. Team members need a clear understanding of their goals, focusing their strengths and knowledge toward a common aim. Once objectives are well-defined, the next step involves devising strategies to attain them.

Maintaining order in a team is crucial, necessitating a strategic plan outlining the process of achieving objectives. Creating a plan with assigned dates and actions for each member helps individuals concentrate on specific aspects, leading to the desired results.

Cooperation plays a pivotal role in achieving goals. A unified force significantly increases the likelihood of reaching the shared objective. Instances of non-cooperation among group members can lead to conflicts, which, when handled appropriately, can result in positive outcomes. It is essential to understand the reasons behind any reluctance to cooperate.

JOURNAL

Describe a situation in which you had to work as part of a team, and the outcome was successful.

Faith is a gift from God that propels a person to follow God's will and guides a person toward the path of righteousness.

April Key

Simbang Gabi is a 9 Dawn Masses as anticipation for the birth of our Lord Jesus Christ on Christmas Day.

CHAPTER 19

Government Position

After graduating from college, I found myself at a crossroads, uncertain about my career path and where to seek employment. My dream of turning Lolo Aureo's property into a business with Mama had seemingly crumbled. It was then that I recalled my passion for helping others in need. Armed with a degree in Tourism, I decided to explore opportunities at the Department of Foreign Affairs (DFA). Without hesitation, I visited the department on a rainy day, despite being ill-prepared for an interview due to the unexpected downpour.

Clad in a white Island Souvenir t-shirt with a colorful fish print, paired with blue jeans and flip-flops, I sought information from the security guard about personnel names and details of the lower positions so I could write my cover letter. Surprisingly, the security guard informed me that the Director wanted to see me immediately. Despite feeling ashamed and drenched in the rain, I embraced the impromptu opportunity for an on-the-spot interview. The Director recognized my potential and willingness to work, advising me to dress appropriately in the future.

Embarking on this journey was no easy feat, demanding long hours at the office, sacrificing meals, and coping with overwhelming responsibilities. Despite the challenges, the experience was enriched by the proximity of my sister Juhan, who had transferred to the Marketing Department of the Department of Tourism, conveniently located nearby. Our lunchtime rendezvous became a respite from the daily grind.

Working alongside Juhan allowed me to liaise with Miss Cindy from their Accounting Department, addressing payables owed by DFA Cebu to various suppliers. Coordinating efforts, we successfully resolved issues and strengthened our working relationships. The Finance Department, with only my boss and me handling most tasks, presented its own set of challenges, including overseeing the release of passports.

Despite my initial aversion to being near money due to its smell, my close bond with my boss made the financial responsibilities more manageable. We worked as a cohesive team, accomplishing tasks efficiently.

One day my boss took a leave of absence so I was left alone in our office. It meant overseeing everything that would happen in our room that day. So I made sure to lock the door every time I got out. But one time, after lunchtime, as I tried to get back to work, I forgot the key inside our office and since we couldn't open the door, I could not go inside to do my job. Handling keys has always been my weakness. I always tend to forget my keys since I was a child. So there were no surprises here.

It scared me that our director would find out about what happened and would be so upset and angry with me. But I didn't have any choice but to tell him the truth so I could go on and do the things that needed to be done. Fortunately, he did not shout at me or get angry with me. He simply told me to do what I needed to do so I could continue my work. Ah, it was a relief!

Working at the DFA taught me patience, instilled a strong work ethic, and emphasized the importance of loving one's job. I obtained insights into the diverse personalities within the department, revealing the true character of individuals. Director Esperanza's leadership left a lasting impression, fostering a non-toxic, team-oriented environment. I was fortunate to have a supportive boss who believed in my potential and provided growth opportunities.

An example of such an opportunity was representing our director at a reception in preparation for the ASEAN Summit. He appointed me and Miss Arlene to attend the reception on his behalf. This experience exposed me to high-ranking officials and ambassadors, challenging me to build confidence and face individuals without intimidation. The journey at the DFA became a lesson in resilience, hard work, and gratitude for the people who shaped my professional growth.

Aside from being a good boss, he was also a devoted husband and father to his sons. They maintained close family ties, and his family always visited and extended a helping hand whenever needed.

It has been six months since I joined the Department. Unfortunately, my paperwork was still pending. I knew that it was not the fault of the local office, as the main office in Manila processed these documents. All they could do was inquire about the status at the main office.

Despite their efforts, it came to a point where I had to seek another job. I had contributed significantly to the office and I needed to support my family with food and bills. I submitted my resignation letter, and although the Director and some others were not pleased, citing the progress of the pending documents, I had to prioritize my family's well-being. I no longer knew if I could trust their assurances, given the prolonged delay in receiving the necessary documents.

Dealing with government offices in the Philippines often involves such challenges. Seasoned employees shared with me their own stories of lengthy waits for paperwork, and advised me to endure and be patient.

Rumors circulated that the Director intended to appoint me as his secretary once the paperwork was finalized. However, considering the three responsibilities I was already juggling in the Department, I doubted my ability to take on additional tasks. Exhausted after work, I couldn't even change my clothes or eat a proper dinner. The thought of assuming more responsibilities as a secretary seemed overwhelming.

The Director suggested I take a break from work while waiting for the paperwork to be completed, assuring me they would call me back when it was ready. He believed I was merely burnt out from my tasks and daily responsibilities. Although they kept their promise, my decision to leave the job remained unchanged.

The Director, in a fatherly manner, spoke to me about patience and my untapped potential. Despite his kind words and genuine concern, my stubborn response remained a firm "No." I was truly grateful for his kindness and couldn't fault his leadership; he was true to his words and actions. Leaders with such compassion for their employees are a rare find.

REFLECTION

In life, it is crucial to discern when to persist and when to take a detour or alter our course. Confidence in ourselves is important as it helps us to move forward and navigate challenging decisions.

My boss may be correct—I lacked the patience required to wait for the legal papers for my official acceptance into the Department. Nevertheless, I was grateful for the time spent working with him and others, as it has contributed to my personal growth and allowed me to test my work ethic.

Having a boss like him was truly a blessing; the day-to-day work environment was peaceful and well-organized. However, as the eldest in my family, hailing from a financially challenged background, I must carry the responsibility of putting food on the table and assisting with bills. Taking action and making decisions became imperative for the sake of both myself and my family.

"Don't hesitate to take risks and explore alternative paths; you'll never know what happens until you try."

- April Key

"Having a great boss is akin to winning a jackpot; it creates a peaceful workplace."

- April Key

"Regrets can foster self-pity; instead of regretting, learn the lessons and know that everything happens for a reason."

- April Key

PSYCHOLOGICAL ANALYSIS

"After graduating from college, I found myself at a crossroads, uncertain about my career path and where to seek employment."

After completing university, many individuals face uncertainties regarding their next steps. Post-graduation, people often grapple with doubts stemming from factors such as choosing a degree that doesn't align with their aspirations, lacking defined goals for the future, or simply fearing the unknown in taking the next step.

Feeling adrift after university is a common experience, and parents play a crucial role in helping their children navigate this transitional period. Identifying the individual's interests is a key consideration when selecting a career path.

For parents, understanding their child's passions enables them to provide more targeted guidance, aligning potential careers with their preferences. Some parents may impose specific career choices on their children, believing it guarantees success, overlooking the fact that success transcends the selection of a particular career.

Once interests and applicable fields have been identified, it becomes essential to establish goals for the chosen career. University serves as a knowledge hub, with the acquired knowledge being applied in the real world after graduation. Students should envision their future roles and aspirations, recognizing that these goals may evolve due to exposure to new experiences. Thinking about what to do after graduation helps in charting a meaningful path forward.

When finishing a university career, the most important thing is to understand that a job may not appear overnight, that the beginnings will be difficult, and that there will be moments of doubt about whether the career was a good choice or not.

JOURNAL

What advice would you offer to someone grappling with impatience and confusion regarding their post-graduation plans?

Let us teach children about God and virtues. This will flourish and help them when they grow.

April Key

Flores De Mayo is a customary event in every Catholic community in the Philippines. Every May 1st to 31st, kids will attend a whole month of Catechism as preparation for first communion.

CHAPTER 20

Separated but Reunited

The Department of Education was seeking scholars and graduates, offering them priority and permanent positions to fulfill their required service years. My sister, despite her reluctance, had no choice but to submit her resignation letter to the Department of Tourism (DOT) and begin teaching at her high school alma mater, where science and math teachers were needed. She cried and didn't like the idea of teaching. She cherished her work at DOT despite the modest salary.

Committed to honoring the contract she signed for her scholarship, my sister gradually developed a passion for teaching. She found joy in sharing her talents and skills, not only academically but also in areas like dancing and coaching students for science and math quiz competitions. Her teaching salary improved our living conditions and supported our younger brother's education in a private Catholic high school.

Meanwhile, I applied for a position at DOT with two friends, but the interview coincided with the arrival of my first foreign boyfriend. Opting to wait for him before pursuing another job, I missed the interview. Following our trip, I secured a role as one of the Sales Agents at Plantation Bay Resort. The workplace, equipped with modern computers, tables, and chairs, fostered positive relationships with my Filipina coworkers, who became like big sisters to me.

My coworkers, especially Miss Lenny and Miss Del, contributed to a harmonious work environment. Miss Lenny and I, with similar physical attributes, occasionally confused people. A shared camaraderie with Miss Del, our energetic supervisor, brought optimism to the team. I sometimes visited and slept over at her house to talk, laugh, and do card readings. We used to go out and spend time with each other outside work to have fun. The workplace culture was refreshing, devoid of gossip, and characterized by direct communication to resolve concerns.

Despite the positive work environment, my challenges, including a recent breakup and conflicts with my mother affected my performance at work. Mama's lack of emotional support during difficult times, coupled with family disapproval of my relationship, led me to decide to move out of the house. I rented a bed space with my friend Genevie, providing me with a calm and relaxed space after work. Her cousin, the owner of the house she was staying in, allowed me to rent with them.

The daily two-hour commute to Plantation Bay Resort from Cebu City, and another two hours to go back home, was alleviated by the free rides offered by the resort, saving me both time and money. The job also came with free lunch vouchers. Our monthly salary was intact as we didn't have to spend money on fares and lunch. Sometimes, the perks of the job included the option to stay overnight at the resort. However, I often declined due to the inconvenience of commuting late at night just to get clothes for the next day. It was difficult to get a ride late at night and I couldn't afford to hire a taxi. Besides, I would be too tired to have fun anyway so I always said no.

The emotional turmoil from working at a resort where I had fond memories with my first boyfriend, combined with the lack of emotional support from my mother, made this period challenging. However, I found solace in the unwavering support of my younger sister during the toughest moments of my personal life.

After the breakup, I entertained the idea of working abroad. I applied for a front desk clerk position in Dubai and got accepted. However, my mother, my ex-boyfriend, and my new boyfriend Nathan, who is now my husband, dissuaded me from going. I listened to them and decided not to pursue the opportunity. I began searching for a local job.

I secured a position in one of the prominent travel agencies in Cebu City. However, I left after a few months due to a toxic environment, particularly because of the way they conducted sales among the agents. The competition to secure clients for extra commission created a hostile atmosphere, and I felt guilty about quitting after the company had invested in training me.

Frustrated by the attitude of my colleagues and their interference with my daily tasks, I sought guidance from my mentor. She concurred with my assessment and supported my decision to leave. I only lasted three months there before my boyfriend Nathan visited the country.

Within four months of knowing each other, we traveled together across the Philippines, exploring places like Kawasan Falls in Cebu, island hopping in Puerto Princesa, Palawan, enjoying the picturesque sunset and white powdery sand in Boracay, embarking on an all-day countryside trip in Bohol, and engaging in dolphin watching, swimming, and snorkeling with my family.

Several months later, Nathan returned to the Philippines. Due to the expedited processing of his visa petition, his flight details were changed. Instead of heading to Hong Kong as originally intended, we explored more of the Philippines. We rented a motorbike on Camotes Island to visit the Volcano Center and hiked Mount Vulcan on a rainy day. We got stuck on the island for a day or two due to the weather, which allowed us to discover additional tourist attractions in the region.

We explored the white powdery islands in El Nido, Palawan, and enjoyed a discounted stay at Shangri La Mactan, inviting my mother and sister to join us here for one night before we left for the USA. Nate and I got married, and shortly after arriving in the USA, I became pregnant. Keira, our eldest child, was born nine months after I arrived in the USA.

However, my sister Juhan was upset about me leaving her with Mama in the Philippines. She got so upset when I got pregnant and couldn't work. She felt alone back home so I encouraged her to prioritize her own life, suggesting she use social media or Facebook to connect with friends and find potential relationships. She had messaged me to say that she couldn't live her life as she was left with the responsibility of being the eldest in the family.

A few months later, she shared that she found her crush in 6th grade, and added each other as friends on Facebook. They started talking, and he recognized her face but couldn't recall where they had met. She pretended not to remember him and engaged in conversations about their school days.

Then, they decided to enter into a relationship. Later on, she confessed to the man, who is now her husband, that she recognized him from their elementary years when she used to have a crush on him. He returned to Cebu to meet and spend time together.

Fortunately, she had already fulfilled the required four years of service as a teacher. The government imposed restrictions on government scholar graduates, preventing them from leaving the country if they hadn't completed their contractual service, enforced through a hold departure order in the Immigration Department.

It seemed as if God was orchestrating all the pieces for her because while waiting for the processing of her husband's US citizenship papers, she was preparing for her final year of teaching and handling the paperwork at the embassy. She arrived in the USA on a fiancée visa, and they had their civil wedding in NJ. We were able to attend it together with her husband's family.

She then stayed with me for a month and helped to prepare the house and care for me at the hospital during the birth of my second child, Kyle.

Living in adjacent states allowed us to visit each other frequently. We explored various family-friendly tourist attractions with our kids as they have two boys now.

Although we didn't realize our dream of having adjacent houses in a compound, God placed us near each other and offered the opportunity to live in the same country known as the "Land of the Free," a dream for many.

Residing in the US enabled us to communicate with one of our aunts and share our side of the story. It was a blessing to be able to express what we carried in our hearts for so long. Despite struggles and challenges, our childhood journey prepared us to face new obstacles in our lives away from our family and friends.

Juhan experienced various jobs in New York City and currently works from home as a Logistics Manager for a wholesale company while being a full-time mom to her two intelligent kids. On the other hand, I spent several years as a full-time mom and worked as a content editor for a grocery store for two years. To support my talented daughter and be with my younger son, I postponed applying for another job. Currently, I am working on my blog page "Rodes On The Road" and a member of the John Maxwell Team, certified as a speaker, coach, and teacher, and allowed to teach the twelve topics from John Maxwell's book. As my kids are growing older, I am gearing towards personal growth and aspiring to launch a class to guide kids, tweens, teens, and young adults in navigating life.

Juhan and her husband are happily married and have overcome financial struggles early in their marriage. Through Juhan's perseverance and determination to navigate the unfamiliar financial system, she helped her husband develop financial literacy. They now own a house in Pennsylvania, USA, and are financially stable compared to the early years of their marriage. Nathan and I, on the other hand, own two houses, one in New York and one in the Philippines.

Managing two mortgages required considerable adjustment and sacrifice. In 2021, with hard work, perseverance, courage, determination, and the risks we took a few years back, particularly Nathan joining a startup company with his boss, we were able to pay off our mortgages and other debts. We are now embarking on a new chapter of our lives. Nathan and I are now separated and is living in two different States. Still we both manage to work together to support the emotional well beings of our children. In God's grace and lots of prayers, we managed to co parent our children with no drama that makes our children still supported, love and cared from both of us.

REFLECTION

Sometimes in life, we must separate from our loved ones to build our own families. This process can be challenging for those who leave and those left behind, especially when the distance is significant. No matter how meticulously we plan our lives, if it's not aligned with God's purpose, it may never come to fruition.

Moving to another country, getting married, and adjusting to new people, weather, environment, culture, language, and food is particularly challenging, especially when faced with an immediate pregnancy and the steep learning curve of becoming a mother. Managing everything at once is an overwhelming task, but through perseverance, I've been able to navigate it all.

For Juhan, taking time for herself allowed her to find the love of her life and build a happy family.

God always has His plans. While we may not comprehend the process and may feel impatient, blaming others for our unhappiness and difficulties, facing these hardships has made us stronger in faith and everyday decisions.

Our visit to the USA and our aunt's home allowed us to release the anger, pain, and childhood baggage that we've carried since a young age. We now understand their side of the situation. Living away from family back home and establishing a family in a foreign country is no easy feat. It was difficult to know whom to trust, and of course, it made sense to trust their kin more than other people.

It's essential to prioritize personal goals over someone we don't know well. Prioritizing oneself is necessary because people might take us for granted, disregarding our efforts. If someone truly loves you, they will wait and avoid doing anything that might cause doubts.

"Trust God's process because His way is better than our own ways."

- April Key

"Sometimes, we have to leave someone behind to start living the dreams we have for ourselves."

- April Key

"Don't base your decisions on someone you don't know well, as you can't be sure if they value what you sacrifice for them."

- April Key

"Life is unpredictable; all we have to do is be flexible."

- April Key

PSYCHOLOGICAL ANALYSIS

"Despite struggles and challenges, our childhood journey prepared us to face new obstacles in our life away from our family and friends."

Resilience is the capacity of an individual to confront adversity, encompassing events such as the loss of a family member, job termination, divorce, illness, or any catastrophic occurrence.

A resilient person can surmount any catastrophic event they encounter. It's crucial to understand that being resilient doesn't imply the absence of emotions like sadness, fear, or anger. Instead, it signifies that despite experiencing these emotions, the individual can move forward.

Even amid the discomfort generated by the challenges they face, strong individuals can cultivate resilience. The development of resilience is a learned process, wherein the person adopts a set of thoughts, actions, and behaviors enabling them to cope with traumatic events.

Support from friends and family stands out as a significant factor contributing to resilience. Having a support network empowers individuals navigating difficult times to rise above their problems and confront them.

Another vital factor in fostering resilience is self-confidence. Individuals who believe in themselves, and their capabilities, and possess the ability to handle challenging circumstances are resilient.

JOURNAL

Reflect on the most challenging situation you have faced and outline the lessons you learned from it.

POEMS

MY LOVE OF BASKETBALL
by April Key

My love of basketball started with you!

Seeing you play full of energy and enthusiasm,
running from one side to the other,
No matter what angle and distance,
you can shoot that ball in an instant.

As the crowd went crazy, clapping their hands,
cheering you on as they jumped for joy
Every time you grabbed that ball from somebody's hands.
I was confused and never understood
How that game worked,
but the sport left imprints in our hearts!

Living far away from you was very hard.
All a little girl could ask was wish you were with us.
I always held on to that Atlas ID stating,
"The daughter of Engineer Cortes" –
the only thing that connects me to you.
You brought me to your workplace as a very young child.
It honestly meant a lot to me.
The basketball league has been a part of our life!
Even if you weren't there with us,
we would continue to be there.

Despite your absence in our lives,
we reminded ourselves to be strong and to hold on!

Your weakness made us strong!
We took a less-traveled road,
and that's what makes it a great story to tell!

It indeed was hard — pain that nobody could understand.
But despite everything, we are grateful —
thankful that God gave us the strength
that everyone struggled to have.

I know you are longing for our love and presence.
And we dream of having a father by our side.

We wish and pray that God will grant our favor
and give us a chance at the end of this heavy road.

I hope there is still time to make up for everything we missed.
Your grandson, Kyle, hopes that you'll live up to 150 years. Lol.

Indeed, I laughed so hard and at the same time was surprised.

God is full of surprises. Let's hope for a better tomorrow!
May you live longer and stay strong as we fix the wrong!

BORN TO SUFFER
by April Key

I wanted to escape these feelings that took hold of me for so long.
It's too much for me to handle and I can take it no more.
It isn't great. It isn't great, all I know is I was born to suffer.

But now, I am strong and I can break every storm
that is trying to shake and trying to break me.

I am born to live. I am born to lead.
I am born to guide, and I am not born to suffer.

I am born to write... I am born to inspire...
I am born to preach, and I am not born to suffer.

Born... Born... Born... Yeah...Yeah... Yeah...

NO MATTER
by April Key

No matter how grey
No matter how dark, always find a way to follow the path!
No matter how grey,
No matter how dark, always look for a sign to light!

No matter how grey,
No matter how dark, always know that you made it this far!
No matter how grey,
No matter how dark, always know that you lead this road so far!

No matter how grey,
No matter how dark, always put a smile to life!
No matter how grey
No matter how dark, there is light somehow down the path!

No matter how grey,
No matter how dark, the more you come strong,
the more you stand tall!

YOU RAISED US

by April Key

You raised us well despite all the struggles you had to endure.

You raised us based on each of our individual
strengths and weaknesses.

You raised us to be strong and equipped us
with strengths that others wouldn't have.

You raised us to be good citizens to our community
and to our country.

You raised us to be content with what we have,
to live off what we're given.
To learn to enjoy the things that we do have
and not compare with the things others have.

You raised us to cling to God in moments of distress.
To continue to have hope and faith in Him
by simply picking up your guitar and singing praise songs
when you have no one to turn to.

You raised us and showed us how powerful God's miracle is in our lives.
And how important it is to offer all our sorrows to Him.

You raised us and showed us how to surrender everything to Him
by praying, singing, praising and serving Him.

You raised us well with the help of the many good people
who came to help, to rescue you without asking anything in return.
Through you and all the kind people we met on our broken path
you were all able to mold us into who we became.

You and many others on your journey raised us well!

LORD, HOW I LOVE YOU
(Psalms Collection)
by Monica

Can he who made the ear not hear?
Can he who formed the eye, not see?
On the day I called, you answered
You increased the strength of my soul.

This poor man called
The Lord heard him and rescued him from all his distress.
If the Lord were not to help me, I would soon go down to silence.

Your mercy, Lord, holds me up.
The Lord will bless His people with peace.
From where shall come my help?
My help shall come from the Lord who made heaven and earth.
For you have been my help
In the shadow of your wings, I rejoice.

I FEEL FINE BECAUSE I HAD WORSE

by Juhan

In times when I feel down, I remember that I had worse...

When I am too lazy to cook dinner, I remember the time when I
and my sis had to gather kangkong (river spinach) from a swamp
and sell it to the neighbors to buy corn grits for food.

When I begin to complain about the laundry and folding of clothes,
I remember the time when I had to glue my shoe
and patch my school uniform because my family
cannot afford to buy a new one.

When I am too tired from going here and there for errands,
I remember the time when I and my sis had to walk 3km (1.9 mi)
to and from school because we didn't have the fare
to ride the habal-habal (motorcycle).

When I get frustrated with all the mess in the house,
I remember the time when my family had to salvage our belongings
because our house was flooded.

When I am stressed from my delayed work pay,
I remember the time when my scholarship allowance
was months delayed and I had to skip lunch at school
and borrow money for the fare.

When I feel sad about not being able to go out for date nights,
I remember my college graduation when I received a medal
but had canned tuna for dinner at home.

In times when I feel down, I remember that I had worse...

Then I feel fine and grateful that what I have at present
is a lot better than what I had in the past.

QUESTIONS AND ANSWERS

For Their Friends

Question 1: *As a friend, classmate, or schoolmate of a survivor of domestic abuse who experienced trauma at a young age, how are April and Juhan as a friend to you? What positive and negative traits have you noticed about her/them and how did she/they handle meeting your family and other groups of friends?*

"How is April as a friend?"

Maricor: April has been my BFF since the second year of high school. Both she and Juhan have big visions and dreams for their family. They both work hard for their future and the future of their family. They're not selfish and always look forward to helping others.

Faith: April is one of my friends in grade 6. She's a maldita and the strict type. She's been good at setting boundaries since she was very young. She knows what she wants.

Camille: Ate April is true, thoughtful, and one of my kindest friends by far.

Karen: I can't remember how we became friends because we were never classmates. We used to walk together on the way home. All I can remember is April is still the same person I used to know in high school, a very humble person.

Ma. Charito: I was April's classmate but even if we're not in the same group of friends I noticed that in every assignment we had she was always so organized and was always performing well. She worked hard on tasks that she liked and wanted to do. She's ambitious, hardworking, caring, loving, and understanding. I also noticed she doesn't like to socialize with others. She will simply sit at her desk or in any corner, busy with her book.

Lorena: I have known April since high school because we were classmates. She's smart, friendly, and religious, and most of all, she has a good heart for her friends, family, and the people who need her help. She has a big heart for everyone.

Dearmie: I met April when she became my classmate in sixth grade. Being friends with her was unexpected as she was a transferee and a very silent type of person. I honestly just learned about her and her sister's situation, that they have been going through domestic abuse at a very young age. The positive side to that is they were able to go through the trials with the help of their mother who is a very strong person. She's ready to fight for the welfare of her children and, looking back, her sacrifices have paid off. As we can see they both live now compared to how life was when they were in the elementary grades.

I remember how their mother supported them, no matter how hard it was for her to carry her youngest son to school just to make sure the two girls were both safe. Even though we separated in college, we were reunited during our high school reunion and I was surprised to see how much they accomplished in life and how far they have come. I can't imagine how they were able to overcome the abuse and trauma, but I know they are both strong and so focused on their goals.

Elien: I have known April since college and she's always a jolly and optimistic person. She is the kind of friend who sees the brighter side of things. She also has that relentless determination, which I admire most about her. Her distinct trait is her being vocal and straightforward; speaks genuinely from the heart.

For others who do not know her well, she can be easily misunderstood as being insensitive or direct. I believe it is all part of the package that came with being herself. This is what makes her April Key, and this is also the very reason why her friends, including me, love her dearly.

Rhea: I remember that time when we were in 6th grade, Key was a quiet young lass. She was such an achiever and a loving sister. She was also active in religious and spiritual activities. She was a truly protective older sister, classmate, and friend. I was trying to recall the times when we played this game and she approached her sister to tell her that we cheated on her. She is still an approachable, helpful, well-mannered young person in class, which was why our adviser used to admire her because of these characteristics.

Theresa: April is more courageous and difficult to understand, but the longer we were together we understood why. We came to know each other more as she opened up to us about their experiences in life.

"How is Juhan as a friend?"

Mylin: Juhan is my best friend! You can tell her anything. She is very positive despite the hardships she went through and she is a very happy character, always finding ways to innovate and solve problems. She cries when you cry and laughs with you during good times!

Gemma: Juhan and I were friends for so long. She has a strong fighting spirit despite all the experiences she had in life. What I love most about her is her positive attitude and motivation in life. Despite the distance, we are still connected and our love for each other as friends remains.

Miss Zafra: At the onset, I can honestly say Juhan is not defined by her past or her origin. She sets herself a goal to be achieved despite seemingly insurmountable odds. Having known her since 1997, this is how I assessed her as a student/friend, teacher/friend, and now as a friend.

Humble. Brainy and smart, she is not an attention-grabber. She topped her class, yet she's content to stay on the sidelines. She's neither assertive nor aggressive unless she thinks she needs to be.

Achiever, Go-getter. She was consistently on the honor roll from elementary to college despite the circumstances surrounding her. She could also easily land a job and make the best of it; she's never mediocre in whatever job she handles. Her student output was out of the ordinary.

Self-reliant. She practically sent herself to school, up to college. She was able to land scholarships in high school and college seemingly on her own.

Accepting, Open-minded. She got lemons, she made lemonade. Life threw her curve balls all the time, but she dealt with the shots face-on and survived. She has no bitterness about what life served her; she rose above them and became a better person.

Resilient. She swims in the water, flies in the air, and climbs mountains. She's a chameleon who adjusts to her surroundings, never sacrificing her principles but always finding ways to blend in and not disrupt the balance.

Responsible. A middle child, she doesn't act like one. Instead, she tried to fill the shoes of a missing parent and was instrumental in helping with the family's sustenance even when she was still a student. She sacrificed her personal comfort and financial sustainability for her family. Balancing both academic and family survival is not a small challenge, but she did it, and she emerged successful.

Cheerful, Optimistic, Tactful. She always shows a radiant face despite going through a mood inside. She also speaks so softly that one can barely hear what she's saying. If she reproaches you about something, she does it with her version of tactfulness. When a problem is put forward, instead of dealing with the whys, she steers the discussion to how it could be solved or made better. She always sees the good in others, no matter what.

Ailene: Ate Juhan's life is such a blessing to us. She is the kind of friend who will be with you through the ups and downs. Despite her experiences, she always exudes positivity. She is a real friend who will tell you the truth, her listening heart gave me so much comfort and love. Her persistence and determination are very evident in her life right now. She handles her challenges with grit. She is also a good encourager, telling her stories to inspire others.

Jade: Ga Juhan is more than a friend to me, she's my sister from another mother. She treated me, my family, and the rest of her close friends as her family, too. She is very down to earth, enjoys simple things, and most of all, has a very big heart for others. We've been friends for many years, and you will not feel that she has had this not-so-good experience in the past because her goodness radiates. Being frugal, generous, and valuing everything, even the smallest things, are just a few of the many things I admire her. I love her dearly and I miss her so much. I hope she's staying safe with her family.

Harley: Ate Juhan is a rare gem. She is one of the first few people who accepted me for who I was, without judgment. God led me to her. She is my sister, someone I shared great memories with - happiness, struggles, laughter, and tears. She made me realize that there are still sincere people in this world.

Before I met her, I never had friends because I didn't trust anyone. She made it so easy that I did not notice that we were already friends. She welcomed me with open arms both in school and in their home.

My high school days were tough, especially since I was not part of the smart group and had no moral support from my parents. I was all alone when I started and all I had was guts, a thick face, and pretensions, that I could do it! But my days became less stressful and became memorable because I had her support. I was assured through her kind heart and genuine friendship that she would be there all the way, and indeed she was!

No words can express how grateful I am to have met such a wonderful human being— the smartest, kindest, most down-to-earth person, who is also always willing to give even if nothing is left for herself. She is indisputably the best Ate! We may now be miles away from each other, but I will always be here for her beyond infinity. Whether she likes it or not! I love her a zillion times and I wish her happiness, good health, and peace of mind because she deserves so much. Again, I love you, Ate.

Jaja: I think I shouldn't be asked since I am not her friend. I am her sister! I don't know how our friendship started. We're not even classmates in high school. But one thing is for sure, I am so lucky to have her beside me while growing up. I don't know if she has any idea, but she's one of the people whom I consider to have molded me into what I am today. She always taught and showed me good values and she has always guided me toward God. She brings me to church and keeps reminding me to always pray because He listens, even if we think He doesn't. And I want to thank her for that because I've been doing it to this day. She's not just a friend but a wonderful great big sister. And that now she has come before God to have her marriage blessed, I can't be happier. I wish her all the happiness in the world with her great family. May she be happy always and love her husband more even if he says he loves her even more. Cheers to two more baby girls!!!

"How are the sisters as friends?"

Ate June: I have known Juhan and April since they were in elementary. I admire the resilience of these two. They don't easily give up on any challenge that comes their way and they always put God at the center of everything.

Joseph: My only answer is... both April and Juhan are the loveliest people I've met, and I hope to visit them in New York one day. Thank you for your friendship all these years.

Chrizyl: These two young girls are very kind and good to me and to my family. Way back when we were young, I still remember how they struggled with a lot of challenges, but despite this, they still managed to show goodness to us. They never treated us badly, the way other people treated them, and because of that, I am thankful to them. Even now that we are all grown up, they are still very good to us.

Demosthenes: Both of them are good individuals, as friends, neighbors, and as part of the community. I have known Juhan more since she was my classmate in grade six until we graduated high school. Juhan is intelligent and very competitive. She is also caring and loving towards her friends. As for April, I have observed that she was the silent type and I think she preferred to be alone. She's a good sister to her siblings. I have never seen them fight.

Question 2: How would you describe Monica?

Abeth: Mana Monica, as we fondly called her, was nice to us. Despite having a traumatic experience with her husband, she still knew how to handle things, especially regarding her kids. There were times, however, when she seemed to be preoccupied and muttered things that I didn't understand during that time. As a single parent, she knew how to raise the kids by herself, of course with the help of relatives because she was working at the same time.

Jing-Jing: Nang Monica, as I fondly call her, is a sweet and loving person. She treated me and my brother as her children. She helped me cope with my issues with my mom. She is funny and loving, yet a lonely person. Although she has plenty of issues in life, she seems like a normal person without any issues because she handles her problems well! She is a superwoman to her children. She always talked about them when they were away. She loves her children so much that she will do everything for them.

For the Adults They Encountered and the People They Lived With

Question 1: *Since you have known the two kids since they were young and have seen them when they were still trying to get to safety, how would you describe their attitude towards you and the rest of your family?*

Abeth: Both are sweet kids but, somehow, the older one seems aloof sometimes and defensive.

Jing-Jing: When I first met April and Juhan, I didn't know that they were in that situation because they seemed like any other normal kids. They treated me as their big sister. They treated us (me and my brother) like relatives.

Marsden: They are both good girls. They are so good to me and to the rest of the family. They respected me for being an older brother and called me Kuya. They followed the house rules and my do's and don'ts. Inday April is serious and Inday Juhan is a comedian. They are not like other children who use swear words. They did not go outside the house or wander around without us by their side.

Mary Anne: I lived with the two in Mindanao and the two sisters were inseparable. They both looked after one another and were buddies to each other.

April is striving to become somebody and she does her best. She has a strong attitude and is the type of person who doesn't like it when others treat her, or someone close to her, unjustly. She won't keep quiet and will indeed speak up if she has to. April will show her emotion and anger, while Juhan will hide it and keep quiet. But when the two fight, April won't let her guard down and will be insistent.

The older sister is way more particular when it comes to clothing and physical attributes; she's talented but physically weak. Juhan is smart, talented, and a sweet girl. She was always mindful of April's health and was always looking out for her. Juhan is always ready to help her big sister.

April is a great leader, but Juhan is a good planner. April has a good heart but is quite strict!

Juliet: Being the eldest of the 5 siblings of Mama Tata and Papa Toto, having April and Juhan around made the family happier. I do not remember any unpleasant thing that happened because of their presence. Although my parents were not financially stable, they still raised us well. Papa and Mama loved April and Juhan so much. They were like their own children. There were times when I got jealous as they prioritized them over us. Looking back, I think they were doing the right thing as Mama Monica trusted them to take good care of the two. When Mama Monica decided to bring them back to Cebu, we were sad as we were used to having them live with us. But Nimrod wins because he is Papa Toto's favorite. I am thankful that God blessed us with great parents!

Question 2: How did you meet the two sisters, and how do you think they were affected by their circumstances?

Abeth: I knew them when their mom brought them to the house of a relative where I was staying as a working student. Then I knew that they were relatives, too. My heart melted when I learned why they were there and how they escaped from their father. The kids were traumatized, including their mom, because they were afraid of even the sound of footsteps of people passing by. (The house we lived in was located beside the road.)

Jing-Jing: For April, I noticed that she was somewhat rebellious to her mom, but she's so sweet to me. As for Juhan, she was this hardworking and studious little kid who helped her mom. I noticed that they were affected by the situation because they were not like the usual kids who were happy; they had these sad faces. They just wanted to help their mom.

Question 3: *Was there anything you noticed about their attitude?*

Abeth: I saw in their eyes the fear, and how they felt like running for their lives. I was thankful that they eventually trusted us.

Ate Jing-Jing: April was rebellious but sweet, hardworking, and studious, while Juhan was sweet, intelligent, and hardworking. Juhan is more understanding of her older sister when she has tantrums. But both used to have tantrums which I couldn't understand because their mom didn't disclose anything that happened to her and the two children.

AFTERWORD

"Parenthood... it's about guiding the next generation, and forgiving the last."

- Peter Krause

ACKNOWLEDGEMENT

To my parents, thank you for bringing us into this world. This book wouldn't be here today if it weren't for the two of you.

I'm thankful for my siblings for helping me be strong and by not going through the battle alone. Especially for my brother Nimrod, who made us grew faster and stronger as we took care of him. Thanks for each of their strengths that makes their character unique and interesting. It made this book more inspiring to read.

For my family that I build thanks for the encouragement and all the support you shared for enticing me to write this book believing that it can help many children and or families learn to navigate life in a way that is less traumatic to their young ones.

Our sincere thanks to Ate Jing-Jing and Kuya Nick for being kind to us and sharing their space with me and Juhan. Ate Jing-Jing treated us as her own younger sisters listened to us, and rightfully reprimanded those who needed to be scolded. To Kuya Jong-Jong, thanks for being a good older brother to me and Juhan. Thank you for the laughter we shared and for patiently listening to us talk about our crushes.

To our family friends, close friends, and friends, especially Ate June, who made extra effort to make us feel that we mattered and that we were loved. Auntie Dionne and family, Tita Tessie and Tash, Tita Shayne, Tita Nanette, Tita Cris, Miss Jing, Miss Christine, Tatay Felimon, Lola Tanya and family, Tatay Demy and family—thank you for being there for us in those trying times without asking for anything in return. We're so blessed to have met you all.

And to all the friends I and my sister have made along our journey, thanks from the bottom of our hearts for being kind to us. The emotional support and kindness you gave helped us focus on our goal and keep going despite the hardships we encountered along the way.

To my therapists, my fellow writer, editor, and proofreader, thank you for giving your time and saying yes to me, and helping me make this book happen. Above all, my gratitude to God Almighty for surrounding me with talented individuals and for giving me the wisdom to put this publication together.

REFERENCES

- How Children Process Grief and How to Help Them/ Medically reviewed by Nathan Greene, PsyD — By Nancy Lovering on February 21, 2022 https://psychcentral.com/lib/children-and-grief
- All about prolonged grief disorder/Medically reviewed by Matthew Boland, PhD — By Hilary I. Lebow on August 11, 2021 https://psychcentral.com/depression/all- about-complicated-grief
- Helping Kids Cope With Grief: 6+ Tips to Support Children by Gabriella Lancia, Ph.D. Scientifically reviewed by William Smith, Ph.D. May 17, 2021 https://positivepsy- chology.com/grief-for-children/#books
- What is Prolonged Grief Disorder? Complicated, Chronic, Traumatic, and Pathological Grief By Geralyn Dexter, LMHC Medically reviewed by Steven Gans, MD Published on April 06, 2022 https://www.verywellhealth.com/prolonged-grief-disorder- 5218745
- How Children Process Grief and How to Help Them/ Medically reviewed by Nathan Greene, PsyD — By Nancy Lovering on February 21, 2022 https://psychcentral.com/lib/children-and-grief
- Domestic violence against women: Recognize Patterns, Seek Help By Mayo Clinic Staff April 14, 2022 https://www.mayoclinic.org/healthy-lifestyle/adult
- How to Recognize Emotional Abuse By Amanda Kippert Nov 30, 2015 https://www.domesticshelters.org/arti- cles/...
- Domestic Violence by US Department of Justice https://www.justice.gov/ovw/domestic-violence
- 10 Patterns of Verbal Abuse By Amanda Kipper on Sep 23, 2016 https://www.domesticshelters.org/articles/
- What Is Domestic Violence? By AmandaKippert Jan 13, 2021 What Is Domestic Violence? (domesticshelters.org
- How to Recover of Emotional Trauma of Domestic Abuse by KELLIE JO HOLLY /May 31, 2015 https://www.healthyplace.com/blogs/verbalabusei...
- Healing and Empowerment after Domestic Violence and Abuse by Christina Cannes Healing & Empowerment After Domestic Violence & Abuse - Big Beautiful Sky

- 7 Steps of Healing from Domestic Violence Medically reviewed by Scientific Advisory Board — By Christine Hammond, MS, LMHC on November 17, 2017 https://psychcentral. com/pro/exhausted-woman/2017/...
- Reclaiming Your Life After Domestic Violence By Lisa Esposito March 30, 2018, at 12:22 p.m. Reclaiming Your Life After Domestic Violence (usnews.com)
- How to Heal After an Abusive Relationship Medically reviewed by Janet Brito, Ph.D., LCSW, CST — By Morgan Mandriota — Updated on Sep 8, 2021 https://psychcentral.com/health/how-toheal-after-an-abusive-relationship
- Stages of Recovery After Trauma By Amanda Kippert Jan 30, 2019 https://www.domesticshelters.org/arti-cles/after-abuse/stages-of-recovery-after-trauma
- Three Systems Model of Emotion in Compassion Focused Therapy-Talking Heads by Dr M. Tolfrey Post published: January 7, 2019 https://www.talkingheads.org.uk/three-systems-model-of-emotion-in-compassion-focussed-therapy/
- What is Compassion Focused Therapy (CFT)? Last updated on 12 March 2020 Compassion-Focused Therapy: What is it and who is it for? (welldoing.org)
- Applying the 3 Circles Model of Emotion to Help Clients Heal Shame https://www.nicabm.com/3circles/
- 3 Systems CFT Formulation- Master Your Emotions With This Neuroscience Superpower By: Dr. Justin in CBT July 29, 2021 3 Systems CFT Formulation - Master Your Emotions With This Neuroscience Based Superpower! - CBT Gym
- Three Systems Model of Emotions in Compassion Focused Therapy By Dr. M. Tolfrey January 7, 2019 https://www.talkingheads.org.uk/compassion-focussed-therapy/
- American Psychiatric Association. (2014). Practice guideline for the treatment of patients with major depressive disorder (3rd ed.). https://psychiatryonline.org/pb/as-sets/raw/sitewide/practice_guidelines/guidelines/mdd.pdf
- American Psychological Association. "What Is Exposure Therapy?" Https://Www.apa.org, 2017, www.apa.org/ptsd-guideline/patients-and-families/expo- sure-therapy.

- American Psychological Association. (2017). Understanding psychotherapy and how it works. Retrieved from https://www.apa.org/topics/psychotherapy
- Barker, S. B., & Dawson, K. S. (1998). The effects of animal-assisted therapy on anxiety ratings of hospitalized psychiatric patients. Psychiatric Services, 49(6), 797-801. doi: 10.1176/ps.49.6.797
- Bäuml, J., Froböse, T., Kraemer, S., Rentrop, M., & Pitschel-Walz, G. (2014). Psychoeducation: A basic psychotherapeutic intervention for patients with schizophrenia and their families. Journal of Affective Disorders, 156, 23-29. doi: 10.1016/j.jad.2013.12.023
- Bayanihan - Massachusetts Institute Technology- https://groups.csail.mit.edu/cag/bayanihan/bayanword.html
- Bögels SM, Wijts P, Oort FJ, Sallaerts SJ. Psychodynamic psychotherapy versus cognitive behavior therapy for a social anxiety disorder: an efficacy and partial effectiveness trial. Depress Anxiety. 2014;31(5):363-73. doi:10.1002/da.22246
- Braun J, Strunk D, Sasso K et al. Therapist Use of Socratic Questioning Predicts Session-to-Session Symptom Change in Cognitive Therapy for Depression. 2015 May 05
- Brubacher, L. L., & Lafrance, A. (2015). Emotionally focused family therapy: An overview. Journal of Family Psychotherapy, 26(4), 310-326. doi: 10.1080/08975353.2015.1064934
- Chand SP, Kuckel DP, Huecker MR. Cognitive Behavior Therapy. [Updated 2020 Oct 15]. In: StatPearls [Internet]. Treasure Island (FL): StatPearls Publishing; 2021 Jan. Available from: https://www.ncbi.nlm.nih.gov/books/NBK470241/
- Cognitive Behavior Therapy Techniques. https://cog-btherapy.com/cognitivebehavior-therapy-techniques
- Cramer, H., Lauche, R., Langhorst, J., & Dobos, G. (2013). Yoga for depression: A systematic review and meta-analysis. Journal of Psychiatric Research, 47(5), 742-748. doi: 10.1016/j.jpsychires.2013.01.013
- Craske, M. G., & Stein, M. B. (2016). Anxiety. The Lancet, 388(10063), 3048-3059. Davis, M., & Lang, P. J. (2015). The extended amygdala and fear conditioning. In The Neurobiology of Learning and Memory (pp. 31-51). Elsevier.

- Dein, S., Cook, C. C. H., Powell, A., & Eagger, S. (2010). Religion, spirituality, and mental health. The Psychiatrist. Retrieved from https://www.cambridge.org/core/journals/the/psychiatrist/article/reli gionspirituality-and-mental health/593DAFFEFE80F7819A8451BF7FD878BC
- De Jongh A, Ten Broeke E, Renssen MR. Treatment of specific phobias with eye movement desensitization and reprocessing (EMDR): Protocol, empirical status, and conceptual issues. J Anxiety Disord. 1999;13:69–85.
- Driessen E, Van HL, Peen J, Don FJ, Twisk JWR, Cuijpers P, Dekker JJM. Cognitive-behavioral versus psychodynamic therapy for major depression: Secondary outcomes of a randomized clinical trial. J Consult Clin Psychol. 2017;85(7):653-663. doi: 10.1037/ccp0000207
- Ehlers, A., & Clark, D. M. (2000). A cognitive model of posttraumatic stress disorder. Behavior Research and Therapy, 38(4), 319-345.
- Exposure therapies for specific phobias. (2016). div12.org/treatment/exposure-therapies-for-specific-phobias/
- F. Shapiro (2001) Eye movement desensitization and reprocessing: Basic principles, protocols and procedures (2nd edition) New York: Guilford Press.
- Fenn K, Byrne M. The key principles of cognitive behavioural therapy. 2013 September 06
- Foa, E. B., Hembree, E. A., & Rothbaum, B. O. (2007). Prolonged exposure therapy for PTSD: Emotional processing of traumatic experiences. Oxford University Press
- Gabatz RIB, Schwartz E, Milbrath VM, Carvalho HCW, Lange C, Soares MC. Formation and disruption of bonds between caregivers and institutionalized children. Rev Bras Enferm. 2018;71(sup pl6):2650-2658. doi:10.1590/0034-7167-2017-0844
- Gosselin P, Matthews WJ. Eye movement desensitization and reprocessing in the treatment of test anxiety: A study of the effects of expectancy and eye movement. J Behav Ther Exp Psychiatry. 1995;26:331–7.
- Greenberg, L. S., & Johnson, S. M. (1988). Emotionally focused therapy for couples. New York, NY: Guilford Press.
- Gupta MA, Gupta AK. Use of eye movement desensitization and reprocessing (EMDR) in the treatment of derma- tological disorders. J Cutan Med Surg. 2002;6:415–21.

- Haggerty, J. (2016). Psychodynamic therapy. Psych Central. Retrieved from https://psychcentral.com/lib/psycho- dynamic-therapy/
- Hall CB, et al. (2018). Brief therapist-guided exposure treatment of panic attacks: A pilot study. journals.sagepub.com/doi/10.1177/0145445518776472
- Hofmann, S. G., Sawyer, A. T., Witt, A. A., & Oh, D. (2010). The effect of mindfulness-based therapy on anxiety and depression: A meta-analytic review. Journal of Consulting and Clinical Psychology, 78(2), 169-183. doi:10.1037/a0018555
- "Interpersonal Psychotherapy IPT." CAMH, www.camh.ca/en/health-info/mental-illness-and-addiction-index/interpersonal-psychotherapy.
- Jayasinghe N, et al. (2017). Systematic review of the clinical application of exposure techniques to community dwelling older adults with anxiety. ncbi.nlm.nih.gov/pmc/articles/PMC6072459/
- Johnson DC, Krystal JH, Southwick SM. Chapter 19: Posttraumatic Stress Disorder and Acute Stress Disorder. (https://accessmedicine-mhmedical-com.ccmain.ohionet.org/content.aspx?secsectionid=
- 200980381&bookid=2509#200980513) In: Ebert MH, Leckman JF, Petrakis IL. eds. Current Diagnosis & Treatment: Psychiatry, 3e. McGraw Hill; 2019. SAGE Publications, Inc. Accessed 3/29/2022.
- Johnson, S. M., Hunsley, J., Greenberg, L., & Schindler, D. (1999). Emotionally focused couples therapy: Status and challenges. Clinical Psychology: Science and Practice, 6(1), 67-79. doi: 10.1093/clipsy.6.1.67
- Johnson, S. M., Makinen, J. A., & Millikin, J. W. (2001). Attachment injuries in couples' relationships: A new perspective on impasses in couples therapy. Journal of Marital and Family Therapy, 27(2), 145-155. doi: 10.1111/j.1752- 0606. 2001.tb01149.x
- Johnson, S. M., Whiffen, V. E., & Makinen, J. A. (2012). The attachment injuries workbook: Powerful tools to heal the injuries that sabotage your relationship. New Harbinger Publications.
- Johnson, S. M., Moser, M. B., Beckes, L., Smith, A., Dalgleish, T. L., Halchuk, R. E., & Hasselmo, K. (2013). Soothing the threatened brain: Leveraging contact comfort with emotionally focused therapy. PLoS ONE, 8(11), e79314. doi: 10.1371/journal.pone.0079314

- Johnson, S. M., Makinen, J. A., & Millikin, J. W. (2019). Attachment injuries in couples relationships: A new perspective on impasses in couples therapy. Journal of Couple & Relationship Therapy, 18(3), 185-204. doi: 10.1080/15332691.2019.1561778
- Johnson, S. M. (2019). Attachment theory in practice: Emotionally focused therapy (EFT) with individuals, couples, and families. New York, NY: The Guilford Press.
- Jones, L. K. Emotionally focused therapy with couples — the social work connection. Social Work Today. 2019;9(3):18.
- Kaimal, G., Ray, K., & Muniz, J. (2016). Reduction of cortisol levels and participants' responses following art making. Journal of the American Art Therapy Association, 33(3), 74-80. doi: 10.1080/07421656.2016.1182289
- Kliem, S., Kröger, C., & Kosfelder, J. (2010). Dialectical behavior therapy for borderline personality disorder: A meta-analysis using mixed-effects modeling. Journal of Consulting and Clinical Psychology, 78(6), 936-951.
- Lancaster CL, et al. (2016). Posttraumatic stress disorder: Overview of evidence-based assessment and treatment. mdpi.com/2077-0383/5/11/105/html
- Leichsenring, F., & Rabung, S. (2011). Long-term psychodynamic psychotherapy in complex mental disorders: update of a meta-analysis. The British Journal of Psychiatry, 199(1), 15-22.
- Linehan, M. M. (1993). Cognitive-behavioral treatment of borderline personality disorder. New York, NY: Guilford Press.
- Linehan, M. M., Comtois, K. A., Murray, A. M., Brown, M. Z., Gallop, R. J.,Heard, H. L., ... Lindenboim, N. (2006). Two-year randomized controlled trial and follow-up of dialectical behavior therapy vs therapy by experts for suicidal behaviors and borderline personality disorder. Ar- chives of General Psychiatry, 63(7), 757-766
- Linehan, M. M. (2014). DBT® skills training manual (2nd ed.). New York, NY: Guilford Press.
- Little, H., Tickle, A. C. & das Nair, R. (2017) 'Process and impact of dialectical behavior therapy: A systematic review of perceptions of clients with a diagnosis of borderline personality disorder,' In Psychology and Psy- chotherapy, 91 (3), pp. 278-301.

- Liu, J. J., Galfalvy, H., Cooper, T. B., Oquendo, M. A.,Grunebaum, M. F., Mann, J. J., & Sublette, M. E. (2015). Omega-3 polyunsaturated fatty acid (PUFA) status in major depressive disorder with comorbid anxiety disorders. Journal of Clinical Psychiatry, 76(6), 848-854. doi: 10.4088/JCP.14m09186
- MacIntosh, H. B., Johnson, S. M., & Wiebe, S. A. (2019). A randomized clinical trial of emotionally focused therapy for couples with chronic illness. Journal of Marital and Family Therapy, 45(4), 606-620. doi: 10.1111/jmft.12352
- Makinen, J. A., & Johnson, S. M. (2006). Resolving attachment injuries in couples using emotionally focused therapy: Steps toward forgiveness and reconciliation. Journal of Consulting and Clinical Psychology, 74(6), 1055-1064. doi: 10.1037/0022-006X.74.6.1055
- Milad, M. R., & Quirk, G. J. (2012). Fear extinction as a model for translational neuroscience: Ten years of progress. Annual Review of Psychology, 63, 129-151.
- Rogers, Kristen. "The Psychological Benefits of Prayer: What Science Says about the Mind-Soul Connection." CNN, 17 June 2020, edition.cnn.com/2020/06/17/health/benefits-of-prayer-wellness/index.html#:~:text=Prayer%20can%20fos- ter%20a%20sense.
- Sarris, J., O'Neil, A., Coulson, C. E., Schweitzer, I., & Berk, M. (2014). Lifestyle medicine for depression. BMC Psychiatry, 14, 107. doi: 10.1186/1471-244X-14-107
- Schuch, F. B., Vancampfort, D., Richards, J., Rosenbaum, S., Ward, P. B., & Stubbs, B. (2016). Exercise as a treatment for depression: A meta-analysis adjusting for publication bias. Journal of Psychiatric Research, 77, 42-51. doi: 10.1016/j.jpsychires.2016.02.023
- Shapiro, F. (2014). Eye Movement Desensitization and Reprocessing (EMDR) therapy: Basic principles, protocols, and procedures (2nd ed.). New York, NY: Guilford Press.
- Shedler, J. (2010). The efficacy of psychodynamic psychotherapy. American Psychologist, 65(2), 98-109.
- Smith, C. A., Armour, M., Lee, M. S., Wang, L. Q., & Hay, P. J. (2010). Acupuncture for depression. Cochrane Database of Systematic Reviews, 1, CD004046. doi: 10.1002/14651858.CD004046.pub3

- Stiglmayr C, Stecher-Mohr J, Wagner T et al. Effectiveness of dialectic behavioral therapy in routine outpatient care: the Berlin Borderline Study. Borderline Personal Disord Emot Dysregul. 2014;1(1):20. doi:10.1186/2051-6673-1-20. https://www.ncbi.nlm.nih.gov/pmc/articles/ PMC4579507/. Accessed March 28, 2022.
- Summers, R. F., & Barber, J. P. (2010). Psychodynamic therapy: A guide to evidence-based practice. Guilford Press.
- Taylor, E. J. (2017). The spiritual dimensions of mental health. Journal of Psychiatric and Mental Health Nursing, 24(2-3), 65-69. doi: 10.1111/jpm.12361.
- Telephone coaching: Behavioral Tech. (2019) Phone Coaching in DBT - part 1 [online] Available at: https://behavioraltech.org/phone-coaching-in-dbtpart-1/ [Accessed 9 November 2020]
- Telephone coaching: Behavioral Tech. (2019) Phone Coaching in DBT - part 2 [online] Available at: https://behavioraltech.org/phone-coaching-in-dbtpart-2/ [Accessed 9 November 2020]
- Thoits, P. A. (2011). Mechanisms linking social ties and support to physical and mental health. Journal of Health and Social Behavior, 52(2), 145-161. doi: 10.1177/0022146510395592
- Wilensky M. Eye movement desensitization and reprocessing (EMDR) as a treatment for phantom limb pain. J Brief Ther. 2006;5:31–43.
- What happens during a DBT session: Essex behavioral therapy. Dialectical Behavior Therapy (DBT) Skills for Borderline Personality Disorder (BPD) individual therapy. [online] Available at: http://essex-behavioural-ther-apy.-co.uk/article.asp?topic=dialectical-behaviour-therapy-dbt-skills&id=39 [Accessed 9 November].
- What happens during a DBT session: Chapman, A. L. (2006) 'Dialectical behavior therapy: current indications and unique elements,' In Psychiatry (Edgmont), 3(9), pp. 62 - 68.
- "What Is Exposure Therapy?" The Light Program, thelightprogram.pyramidhealthcarepa.com/what-is-exposure-therapy/#:~:text=During%20exposure%20therapy%2C%20a%20therapist. Accessed 7 Apr. 2023.

- "What Is Cognitive Behavioral Therapy (CBT)?" Www.mind.org.uk,Sept. 2021,www.mind.org.uk/infor-mation-support/drugs-and treatments/talking-therapy-and-counselling/cognitive-behavioural-therapy-cbt/#:~:text=Cognitive%20behavioural%20ther-apy%20(CBT)%20is.
- Winston, A., & Rosenthal, R. N. (Eds.). (2018). Psychotherapy essentials to go: Psychodynamic psychotherapy for depression. WW Norton & Company.https://journals.sagepub.com/doi/full/10.1177/1755738012471029 https://www.ncbi.nlm.nih.gov/pmc/articles/PMC4449800/
- Amato, P. R., & Keith, B. (1991). Parental divorce and adult well-being: A meta-analysis. Journal of Marriage and Family, 53(1), 43-58.
- American Academy of Pediatrics; CompleteMom.com; Parents Without Partners; Single Mothers by Choice; the Women's Institute for Financial Education
- Arseneault, L., Bowes, L., & Shakoor, S. (2010). Bullying victimization in youths and mental health problems: 'Much ado about nothing'? Psychological Medicine, 40(5), 717- 729.
- Bates, E. A., & Carthy, T. (2017). Children's experiences of relocating to a new home: A systematic review of qualitative research. Child and Adolescent Social Work Journal, 34(2), 115-129.
- Beattie, M. (1987). Codependent No More. Hazelden Publishing.
- Beattie, M. (1992). Beyond Codependency. Hazelden Publishing.
- Mellody, P. (1989). Facing Codependence. HarperCollins.
- Bennett, M. P., & Lengacher, C. A. (2008). Humor and laughter may influence health: III. Laughter and health outcomes. Evidence-Based Complementary and Alterna- tive Medicine, 5(1), 37-40
- Benson, H., Rosner, B. A., Marzetta, B. R., & Klemchuk, H. M. (1974). Decreased blood pressure in borderline hypertensive subjects who practiced meditation. Journal of Chronic Diseases, 27(3), 163-169.
- Christensen, A. M., & Brooks, D. (2011). Parental expectations, relationship satisfaction, and coping as predictors of psychological adjustment among children of divorce. Journal of Divorce & Remarriage, 52(1), 41-58.
- Cohen, S., & Wills, T. A. (1985). Stress, social support, and the buffering hypothesis. Psychological Bulletin, 98(2), 310-357.

- Copeland, W. E., Keeler, G., Angold, A., & Costello, E. J. (2013). Traumatic events and posttraumatic stress in childhood. Archives of General Psychiatry, 70(8), 913- 920.
- Darling, N., & Steinberg, L. (1993). Parenting style as context: An integrative model. Psychological Bulletin, 113(3), 487-496.
- Dvorakova, A., Kocourkova, J., & Javurkova, A. (2020). Bullying as a traumatic event: Review of the literature and current research. International Journal of Environmental Research and Public Health, 17(17), 6257.
- Espelage, D. L., & Hong, J. S. (2017). Bullying and peer victimization: An overview of the constructs, prevalence, and associated correlates. In D. L. Espelage & S. M. Swearer (Eds.), Bullying in North American schools (3rd ed., pp. 1-20). Routledge.
- Fiese, B. H., Tomcho, T. J., Douglas, M., Josephs, K., Poltrock, S., & Baker, T. (2016). A review of 50 years of research on naturally occurring family routines and rituals: Cause for celebration? Journal of Family Psychology, 30(5), 571-590.
- Fite, P. J., Williford, A., Cooley, J. L., DePaolis, K. J., & Rubens, S. L. (2008). Trajectories of aggression and victimization across middle school among urban, minority adolescents. Aggressive Behavior, 34(2), 161-176.
- Gordon. "Bullying Can Lead to Anxiety Disorders." Verywell Family, 2019,www.verywellfamily.com/bullying-and-anxiety-connection-460631.
- Grych, J. H., & Fincham, F. D. (1990). Marital conflict and children's adjustment: A cognitive-contextual framework. Psychological Bulletin, 108(2), 267-290.
- Hassmen, P., Koivula, N., & Uutela, A. (2000). Physical exercise and psychological well-being: A population study in Finland. Preventive Medicine, 30(1), 17-25.
- Hetherington, E. M., & Stanley-Hagan, M. (1999). The adjustment of children with divorced parents: A risk and resiliency perspective. Journal of Child Psychology and Psychiatry, 40(1), 129-140.
- Holt, M. K., Jaggi, L., & Kubicek, L. F. (2021). Addressing the mental health impact of bullying: What supports do youth perceive as helpful? Journal of Interpersonal Vio- lence, 08862605211000752.

- Hunt, C., Hames, J. L., & Molnar, D. S. (2018). An examination of the relationship between bullying and social anxiety in adolescents. Journal of School Violence, 17(4), 401-414.
- "I Used to Be Codependent. Here's How I Stay True to Myself in Relationships." Mindbodygreen, 5 May 2021, www.mindbodygreen.com/articles/how-to-stop-being- codependent.
- Jacobs, Shannon. "12 Ways to Make Moving with Kids a Good Experience for All." PODS Moving and Storage Blog, 20 Oct. 2022, www.pods. - c o m / b l o g / 2 0 2 2 / 1 0 / m o v-ing-with-kids/. Accessed 14 Apr. 2023.
- Kadane, Lisa. "10 Proven Ways to Finally Stop Yelling at Your Kids." Today's Parent, 28 Aug. 2019, www.to-daysparent.com/family/discipline/provenways-to-finally-stop-yelling-at-your-kids/.Sherri Kashdan, T. B., Uswatte, G., & Julian, T. (2006). Gratitude and hedonic and eudaimonic well-being in Vietnam War veterans. Behaviour Research and Therapy, 44(2), 177- 199.
- Kazdin, A. E. (2019). Positive reinforcement, praise, and other rewards. In Parent management training: Treatment for oppositional, aggressive, and antisocial behavior in children and adolescents (pp. 73-102). Oxford University Press.
- Kelly, J. B., & Emery, R. E. (2003). Children's adjustment following divorce: Risk and resilience perspectives. Family Relations, 52(4), 352-362.
- Killian, James. 5 Ways to Overcome Codependency Anxiety Therapist in New Haven. 23 May 2020, arcadiancounseling.com/5-waysto-overcome-codependence/.
- Knappe, S., Beesdo, K., Fehm, L., Stein, M. B., & Lieb, R. (2010). Low and high trait anxiety in individuals with social anxiety disorder: Differences in reappraisal, emotional suppression, and affective flexibility. Journal of Abnormal Psychology, 119(3), 886-897.
- Knox, M., & Schacht, R. (2013). Children's coping with parental divorce: Perspectives of young adults. Journal of Divorce & Remarriage, 54(1), 1-18.
- Kostrzewa, R. M., Nęcka, E., & Lizińczyk, S. (2021). Time management and stress among teachers: An overview of research. International Journal of Occupational Medicine and Environmental Health, 34(2), 143-159.

- Kristenson, Sarah. "15 Codependent Personality Traits and Characteristics." Happier Human, 18 July 2022, www.happierhuman.com/codependent-traits/.
- Ladd, G. W., & Ettekal, I. (2013). Peer-related loneliness across early to late adolescence: Normative trends, intraindividual trajectories, and links with depressive symp- toms. Journal of Adolescence, 36(6), 1269-1282.
- Lansford, J. E., Criss, M. M., Pettit, G. S., Dodge, K. A., & Bates, J. E. (2014). Friendship quality, peer group affiliation, and peer antisocial behavior as moderators of the link between negative parenting and adolescent externalizing behavior. Journal of Research on Adolescence, 24(2), 305-320.
- Lassale, C., Batty, G. D., Baghdadli, A., Jacka, F., Sánchez-Villegas, A., Kivimäki, M., & Akbaraly, T. (2018). Healthy dietary indices and risk of depressive outcomes: A systematic review and meta-analysis of observational studies. Molecular Psychiatry, 23(5), 1189-1199.
- Leopold, Bryan. "How to Help Your Child Accept a New Relationship." Overcomers Counseling, over-comewithus.com/parenting/how-tohelp-your-child-accept-a-new-relationship. Accessed 17 Apr. 2023.
- Luecken, L. J., & Appelhans, B. M. (2006). Early parental loss and salivary cortisol in young adulthood: The moderating role of family environment. Development and Psychopathology, 18(1), 295-308.
- Mackenzie, M. J., Carlson, L. E., & Ekkekakis, P. (2018). Effects of an exercise program on self-esteem in children: A randomized controlled trial. Journal of Pediatric Psychology, 43(6), 643-652.
- McCready, Amy. "We're Moving?!" 7 Tips to Help Kids Thrive during a Move." Positive Parenting Solutions, 27 Apr. 2020, www.pos i t i veparent ing -s o l u t i o n s . c o m / p a r e n ting/tips-to-help-kids-thrive-during-a-move. Accessed 14 Apr. 2023.
- Opie, R. S., Itsiopoulos, C., Parletta, N., Sanchez-Ville- gas, A., Akbaraly, T. N., Ruusunen, A., & Jacka, F. N.(2015). Dietary recommendations for the prevention of depression. Nutritional Neuroscience, 18(3), 120-131.
- Riggs, S. A., & Kaminski, P. L. (2010). Childhood family instability and adult well-being: The mediating roles of childhood cumulative risk and adulthood stress. Journal of Family Psychology, 24(6), 667-677.

- Sandler, I., Tein, J. Y., Mehta, P., Wolchik, S., & Ayers, T. (2000). Coping efficacy and psychological problems of children of divorce. Child Development, 71(4), 1099- 1118.
- Sandler, I. N., Tein, J. Y., Mehta, P., Wolchik, S. A., & Ayers, T. S. (2011). Coping efficacy and psychological problems of children of divorce. Child Development, 82(3), 677-693.
- Seligman, M. E. P. (2012). Flourish: A visionary new understanding of happiness and well-being. Simon and Schuster.
- Sherri Gordon. "Bullying Can Lead to Anxiety Disorders." Verywell Family, 2019, www.verywellfamily.com/bullying-and-anxiety-connection-460631.
- "Stresses of Single Parenting." HealthyChildren.org, 2019, Single Parenting (Copyright © 2007 American Academy of Pediatrics, Updated 5/2007) www.healthy-children.org/English/family-life/family-dynamics/types-of- families/Pages/Stresses-of-Single-Parenting.aspx.
- Stuckey, H. L., & Nobel, J. (2010). The connection between art, healing, and public health: A review of current literature. American Journal of Public Health, 100(2), 254- 263.
- Teubert, D., & Pinquart, M. (2010). The association between coparenting and child adjustment: A meta-analysis. Parenting: Science and Practice, 10(4), 286-307.
- Towe-Goodman, N. R., Stacks, A. M., Porter, B., & Chen, C. (2014). The role of therapists in mitigating the negative effects of divorce on children. Journal of Divorce & Re- marriage, 55(1), 1-15.
- Ttofi, M. M., Farrington, D. P., Lösel, F., & Loeber, R. (2016). Do the victims of school bullies tend to become depressed later in life? A systematic review and meta-analysis of longitudinal studies. Journal of Aggression, Conflict and Peace Research, 8(4), 209-222.
- Wallerstein, J. S., & Kelly, J. B. (1979). The effects of parental divorce: Experiences of the child in later latency. American Journal of Orthopsychiatry, 49(1), 1-19.
- Wallerstein, J. S., & Kelly, J. B. (1980). Effects of divorce on the parent-child relationship. Developmental Psychology, 16(4), 382-390.
- Wallerstein, J. S., & Kelly, J. B. (1980). Surviving the breakup: How children and parents cope with divorce. Basic Books.

- Ways on How to Help Your Child Accept a New Rela-tionship." Farzad & Ochoa Family Law Attorneys, LLP, farzadlaw.com/how-help-your-child-accept-new-relationship#. Accessed 17 Apr. 2023.
- Wood, A. M., Froh, J. J., & Geraghty, A. W. A. (2010). Gratitude and wellbeing: A review and theoretical integration. Clinical Psychology Review, 30(7), 890-905.
- https://www.nspcc.org.uk/what-is-child-abuse/types-of-abuse/emotionalabusehttps://www.thehotline.org/re-sources/types-of-abuse/
- https://ocfs.ny.gov/programs/domestic-violence/
- Childming.org
- Unep.org
- Mayoclinic.org
- aifs.gov.au
- ncadv.org
- parents.com
- empoweringparents.com
- kidshealth.org
- counselingcenter.illinois.edu
- atlassian.com
- apa.org

APPENDIX

Philippine Hotlines to call for Domestic Violence

Luna Legal Resource Center for Women and Children
https://www.facebook.com/lunalegalcenter/ (082) 306-5761

Gender Watch Against Violence and Exploitation (GWAVE)
https://www.facebook.com/GWAVEPhilippines/
(035) 422 84 05 | +63 915 259 3029 | +63 999 576 6679

ING MAKABABAYING AKSYON (IMA) Foundation
https://www.facebook.com/Ing-Makababaying-Aksyon-IMA-
Foundation-131515322286/ (045) 323 4750

National Domestic Violence Hotline
Hotline: 1 (800) 799 SAFE – 7233
(206) 518-9361 = (Video Phone Only for Deaf Callers)
Available 24 hours a day, 7 days a week via phone and online chat.

The National Domestic Violence Hotline (The Hotline) is available for anyone experiencing domestic violence, seeking resources or information, or questioning unhealthy aspects of their relationship.

Love is Respect – National Teen Dating Abuse Hotline
Available 24 hours a day, 7 days a week via phone, text, and online chat.
Hotline: 1 (866) 331 – 9474
Text: 22522

StrongHearts Native Helpline
Available Monday through Friday, 9:00am to 5:30pm CST via phone.
Hotline: 1 (844) 762 – 8483

Pathways to Safety International
Available 24 hours a day, 7 days a week via phone, email, and online chat.
Hotline: 1 (833) 723 – 3833
Email: crisis@pathwaystosafety.org

Gay, Lesbian, Bisexual and Transgender National Hotline
Hours vary, available via phone and online chat
Hotline: 1 (888) 843 – 4564
Youth Talkline: 1 (800) 246 – 7743
Senior Helpline: 1 (888) 234 – 7243 Email: help@LGBThotline.org

Sexual Assault
Rape, Abuse, and Incest National Network (RAINN) –
National Sexual Assault Hotline
Available 24 hours a day, 7 days a week via phone and online chat.
Hotline: 1 (800) 656-4673

Department of Defense (DOD) Safe Helpline for Sexual Assault
Available 24 hours a day, 7 days a week via phone and online chat.
Hotline: 1 (877) 995 – 5247

Human Trafficking
National Human Trafficking Hotline Hotline: 1-888-373-7888
Text: 233733

The National Human Trafficking Hotline is a national anti-trafficking hotline serving victims and survivors of human trafficking and the anti-trafficking community in the United States. The toll-free hotline is available to answer calls from anywhere in the country, 24 hours a day, 7 days a week, every day of the year in more than 200 languages.

Children, Youth, and Teenagers
National Runaway Safeline
Available 24 hours a day, 7 days a week via phone, email,
forum, and online chat.
Hotline: 1 (800) 786 – 2929
Email: info@1800runaway.org

The National Runaway Safeline provides crisis and support
services for homeless and runaway youth in the United States.

National Center for Missing and Exploited Children (NCMEC)
Hotline: 1 (800) 843 – 5678
Cyber Tipline: http://www.missingkids.com/gethelpnow/cybertipline

Child Help National Child Abuse Hotline
Available 24 hours a day, 7 days a week via phone and text.
Hotline: 1 (800) 422 – 4453

The Child help National Child Abuse Hotline is dedicated to the
prevention of child abuse. Serving the U.S. and Canada, the
hotline is staffed 24 hours a day, 7 days a week with professional
crisis counselors who—through interpreters—provide assistance
in over 170 languages. The hotline offers crisis intervention,
information, and referrals to thousands of emergencies, social
service, and support resources. All calls are confidential.

Boystown USA – Your Life Your Voice Helpline
Available 24 hours a day, 7 days a week via phone, email,
text, and online chat.
Hotline: 1 (800) 448 – 3000
Text: Text VOICE to 20121 (hours vary)

Your Life Your Voice is a program of Boystown USA and is available to children, parents, and families who are struggling with self-harm, mental health disorders, and abuse.

National Suicide Prevention Lifeline
Available 24 hours a day, 7 days a week via phone and online chat.
Hotline: 1-800-273-8255

Philippine Red Cross
Emergency Hotline: 143
IN Touch Crisis line:02- 790-2300 local 604

National Alliance on Mental Illness (NAMI) Helpline
Available Monday through Friday, 10:00am to 6:00pm
Eastern Standard Time.
Hotline: 1 (800) 950 – 6264
Text "Help Line" to 62640
Email: helpline@nami.org

Substance Abuse and Mental Health Services Administration (SAMHSA) Helpline
Available 24 hours a day, 7 days a week via phone in
English and Spanish
Hotline: 1 (800) 662 – 4357

Contact the Victim Connect Hotline by phone at 1-855-4-VICTIM or by chat for more information or assistance in locating services that can help you or a loved one.

HOTLINES FOR OFWS

Action Line Against Human Trafficking
-1343 or +632(1343) if outside Metro Manila or Philippines Contact No:
(02)525-2131/(02)527-2363
Email add: iacat@g.mail.com

Department of Social Welfare and Development

DSWD Central Office (CO)
Office of the Secretary
Contact Person: Erwin Tulfo, Secretary
Trunkline : 8-931-81-01-07 local 10046;10256;10047;10048
Email: osec@dswd.gov.ph
Tel no: 8-931-80-68,8-931-79-16
Tel/Fax: 931-81-91

Office of the Undersecretary for Operations Group
Contact Person: Jericho Francis L. Javier, Undersecretary
Trunkline : 8-931-81-01-07 local 10004;10002:10003
Email: ousoperations@dswd.gov.ph
Tel no: 8-952-71-21
Tel/Fax: 931-81-38

Office of the Assistant Secretary for Social Welfare and Development
Contact Person: Rodulfo Santos, CESO II Assistant Secretary
Trunkline: 8-931-81-01-07 local 10313; 10311:10312
Tel no: 8-931-63-66

DSWD Field Offices and SWAD Satellites

DSWD Region 1 Field Office
Contact Person: Marie Angela S. Gopalan CESO III Regional Director
Tel/Fax: (072) 687-8000
Website: https://fo1.dswd.gov.ph

DSWD Region 1 SWAD Satellites

Province of Ilocos Norte
Contact Person: Lorna P. Rafanan, SWO II SWAD Leader
Office Address: Jomel Bldg., 3rd floor, Brgy., 14, Laoag City, Ilocos Norte
Tel: (077) 670-0342, (077) 774-2100

Province of Ilocos Sur
Contact Person: Ryleen Gadong, SWO II SWAD Leader
Office Address: Luisa Bldg., Quezon Avenue, Salcedo St., Brgy. 111, Vigan City, Ilocos Sur
Tel: (077)674-0137

Province of La Union
Contact Person: Ma. Bernadette B. Arcangel, SWO II SWAD Leader
Office Address: 4rth floor, Dona Pepita Bldg., Quezon Avenue, City of San Fernando, La Union
Tel: (072) 607-0326

EASTERN PANGASINAN
Contact Person: Danicar C. Maleon, SWO II SWAD Leader
Office Address: Governor Robert B. Estrella Memorial Stadium, Zone 4, Rosales, Pangasinan and Sta Maria, Binalonan, Pangasinan
Tel no: +63 9976120632

Central Pangasinan

Contact Person: Ma. Concepcion F. Narag, SWO II SWAD Leader
Office Address: AVRC 1, Russia St., Bonuan Binloc, Dagupan City, Pangasinan
Tel: (075) 653-4910

Western Pangasinan

Contact Person: Emil B. Cabudoy, SWO II SWAD Leader
Office Address: Jomel Bldg., 3rd floor, Brgy., 14, Laoag City, Ilocos Norte
Tel: (077) 670-0342, (077) 774-2100

DSWD Region 2 Field office

Contact Person: Celso L. Arao, Jr., OIC Regional Director
Tel no: (078) 304-0586
Website: https://fo2.dswd.gov.ph

DSWD Region 2 SWAD Satellites

Province of Batanes

Contact Person: Miryan Tumanguil, SWAD Team Leader
Office Address: 3rd Floor PSWDO Cum Bahay Pag-asa building, Barsana St. San Antonio, Basco, Batanes
Email: tumanguilmiryan@gmail.com
Tel: 09976649268

Province of Cagayan

Contact Person: Ursula Orpilla, SWO II SWAD Team Leader
Office Address: DSWD Fiel Office 2, Regional Government Center, Tuguegarao City, Cagayan
Email: swadcagayan.dswd02@gmail.com
Tel: (0917) 389 9622

Province of Isabela
Contact Person: Rosario N. Corpuz, SWO II SWAD Leader
Office Address: Sports Complex, Brgy. Alibagu, Iligan City, Isabela
Email: swadisabela@dswd.gov.ph
Tel: (0995) 205 2912

Province of Nueva Viscaya
Contact Person: Rochel I. Puddunan, SWO II SWAD Leader
Office Address: Capitol Compound, Bayombong, Nueva Vizcaya
Email: swadnuevaviscays.fo2@dswd.gov.ph
Tel: (0915)6526428

Province of Quirino
Contact Person: Rosita Malabad, SWO II SWAD Leader
Office Address: 2nd floor, PSWDO Building, Capitol Hills, San Marcos,
Cabarroguis, Quirino
Email: quirino.fo2@dswd.gov.ph
Tel: (0906) 9315010

DSWD Region 3 Field Office
Contact Person: Venus F. Rebuldela, Concurrent OIC Regional Director
Tel: (045) 8-961-21-43 loc 108
Website: https://fo3.dswd.gov.ph

DSWD Region 3 SWAD Satellites

DSWD Provincial Extension Office-Aurora
Contact Person: Margie Y. Nortez, OIC-Provincial Team Leader;
Joanne P. Mateo, Provincial Link
Office Address: Quezon Highway, Former Asia Pacific Building,
Amihan Suklayin, Baler, Aurora
Email: dpeoaurora.fo3@dswd.gov.ph

DSWD Provincial Extension Office-Bataan

Contact Person: Chasmalyn G. Francisco, Provincial Team Leader;
Elena G Dones, Provincial Link
Office Address: Palihan Publik Markt, Hermosa, Bataan
Email: dpebataan.fo3@dswd.gov.ph

DSWD Provincial Extension Office-Bulacan

Contact Person: Cynthia G. Alfonso, Provincial Team Leader;
Josefina David, Provincial Link
Office Address: DSWD-SWAD Bulacan, Capitol Compound ,Malolos City
Email:dpeobulacan.fo3@dswd.gov.ph

DSWD Provincial Extension Office-Nueva Ecija

Contact Person: Aurelia C. Senayo, Provincial Team Leader;
Marites Javate, Provincial Link-operations;
Office Address: Mabini St. Extension, Cabanatuan City (Near Wesleyan
University), Nueva Ecija
Email: dpeonuevaecija.fo3@dswd.gov.ph

DSWD Provincial Extension Office-Pampanga

Contact Person: Maria Fe C. Evarista, Provincial Team Leader ;
Fritzie Joy Cunanan, Provincial Link
Office Address: Rosal St. , San Isidro Village, San Isidro, City of San
Fernando, Pampanga
Email: dpeopampanga.fo3@dswd.gov.ph

DSWD Provincial Extension Office-Tarlac

Contact Person: Raul Regalado, OIC-Provincial Team Leader; Daisy Madrid,
Provincial Link
Office Address: A & R Building, Zamora St. San Roque, Tarlac City
Email: dpeotarlac.fo3@dswd.gov.ph

DSWD Provincial Extension Office-Zambales

Contact Person: Rosemarie M. Hebron Provincial Team Leader;
Jasper Nicolas, Provincial Link
Office Address: SWAD Office-Zambales Gordon Avenue, corner
10th St., Brgy. Asinan
Email: dpeozambales.fo3@dswd.gov.ph

DSWD Region 4A Field Office
Contact Person: Myla S. Gatchalian, Concurrent OIC Regional Director
Tel: (02) 807-71-02
Website: https://fo4a.dswd.gov.ph

DSWD Region 4A SWAD Satellites
Crisis Intervention Section Field Office
Contact Person: Rodolfo V. Narciso Jr. -OIC CIS
Office Address: DSWD FO IV-A Regional Office, Zapote-Alabang Road,
Alabang Muntinlupa City
Contact: 0968-768-8392

SWAD Batangas
Contact Person: Billy O. Angayen
Office Address: Province Capitol Compound, Capitol Site New Building,
Brgy. Kumintang Ibaba, Batangas City
Contact: 0968-768-8389

SWAD Cavite
Contact Person: Alnida D. Fernandez
Office Address: Bacoor Gov. Center, Molino Blvd., Bacoor City Cavite
Contact: 0968-768-8385

SWAD Laguna
Contact Person: Erica Joana L. Agcanas
Office Address: G. De Leon St., Brgy., Pagsawitan, Sta. Cruz, Laguna
Contact: 0968-768-8404

SWAD Quezon
Contact Person: Marynel B. Calabit
Office Address: QPGOE MPC Quezon Capitol Bldg., 2nd floor Brgy. 10,
Lucana City, Quezon
Contact: 0968-768-8384

SWAD Rizal
Contact Person: Shaira Q. Minas
Office Address: Annex Bldg. Rizal Provincial Capitol, Sumuling Circumferential Rd. Brgy. San Roque, Upper Antipolo
Contact: 0968-768-8388

DSWD Region 4B Field Office
Contact Person: Leonardo C. Reynoso, CESO III Regional Director
Tel: (02) 852-24-45 loc. 110
Website: https://fo4b.dswd.gov.ph

DSWD Region 4B SWAD Satellites

Department of Social Welfare and Development Field Office IV-(MIMAROPA) Regional Office
Office Address: 1680 F. Benitez Cor. Malvar St. Malate, Manila
Email Address: fo4b@dswd.gov.ph
Contact: (632)336-8106/07

Department of Social Welfare and Development Field Office IV-(MIMAROPA) Youth Center
Office Address: Poblacion Bansud, Oriental Mindoro
Email Address: myc. fo4b@dswd.gov.ph

Department of Social Welfare and Development Field Office IV-(MIMAROPA) Marindoque SWAD-T
Office Address: Capitol Compound. Brgy., Bangbangalon, Boac, Marindoque
Email Address: marindoqueswadt.fomimaropa@dswd.gov.ph
Contact: (642)754-0015

Department of Social Welfare and Development Field Office IV-(MIMAROPA) Occidental Mindoro SWAD-T

Office Address: M.H. Del Pilar St. Brgy., 7, San Jose, Occidental Mindoro
Email Address: ocmindoroswadt.fomimaropa@dswd.gov.ph
Contact: (643)732-0451

Department of Social Welfare and Development Field Office IV-(MIMAROPA) Oriental Mindoro SWAD-T

Office Address: 2nd floor RKT Building, JP Rizal St. cor. Bayabas St. Lalud Calapan City, Oriental Mindoro
Email Address: ormindoroswadt.fomimaropa@dswd.gov.ph
Contact: (643)441-8370 or (643) 441-9147

Department of Social Welfare and Development Field Office IV-(MIMAROPA)Palawan SWAD-T

Office Address: 3rd Floor Building Carandang St. corner Mendoza St. Brgy Manggahan, Puerto Princesa City, Palawan
Email Address: palawanswadt.fomimaropa@dswd.gov.ph
Contact: (648)4339216

Department of Social Welfare and Development Field Office IV-(MIMAROPA)Romblon SWAD-T

Office Address: 2nd fr. Servanez Bldg., General Luna St., Liwayway, Odiongan, Romblon
Email Address: rombloneswadt.fomimaropa@dswd.gov.ph
Contact: (642)752-5583

DSWD Region 5 Field Office

Contact Person: Arwin O. Razo, Concurrent OIC Regional Director
Tel: (052) 8-480-04-25
Website: https://fo5.dswd.gov.ph

DSWD Region 5 SWAD Satellites

Contact Person: Shereen Mae R. Morasa, SWAD Team Leader

Province of Camarines Norte
Contact Person: Claudio A Villarea Jr., SWAD Leader

Province of Camarines Sur
Contact Person: Harry Jay B. Daet, SWAD Leader

Province of Camarines Catanduanes
Contact Person: Edlyn L. Noble, SWAD Leader

Province of Masbate
Contact Person: Laramie M. Ocharan, SWAD Leader

Province of Sorsogon
Contact Person: Cecil G. Mapa, SWAD Leader

DSWD Region 6 Field Office
Contact Person: Dalia V. Bagolcol, Concurrent OIC Regional Director
Tel: (033) 8503-37-03/ (033) 8-337-62-21
Website: https://fo6.dswd.gov.ph

Office of the Regional Director
Email Address: fo6@dswd.gov.ph
Contact: (033) 330-7860 loc 16001
Contact PersonMa. Evelyn B. Macapobre, CESO III Regional Director
Email Address: mebmacapobre.fo6@dswd.gov.ph
Contact: (033) 330-7860 loc 16001

Contact Person: Delia V. Bagolcol, Assistant Regional Director for
Operations
Email Address: dvbagolcol.fo6@dswd.gov.ph
Tel. No: (033) 330-7860 loc. 16003

Contact Perso: Ryan A. De La Gente, OIC-Assistant Regional Director for
Administration
Email Address: radelagente@dswd.gov.ph
Tel. No: (033) 330-7860 loc. 16024

DSWD Region 6 SWAD Satellites

AKLAN
Contact Person: Lluva R. Gallofin, SWAD Team Leader
Email address: swadaklan.fo6@dswd.gov.ph
Contact: (036) 268-2620

Antique
Contact Person: Melrose Amaran, SWAD Team Leader
Email address: swadantique.fo6@dswd.gov.ph
Contact: (036) 540-9701

Capiz
Contact Person: Josephine P. Degala, SWAD Team Leader
Email address: swadcapiz.fo6@dswd.gov.ph
Contact: (036) 621-5566/552-9372

Iloilo
Contact Person: Mary Joy M. Acana, SWAD Team Leader
Email address: swadiloilo.fo6@dswd.gov.ph
Contact: (033) 508-4103

Negros Occidental
Contact Person: Mrlyn L. Porras, SWAD Team Leader
Email address: swadbacolod.fo6@dswd.gov.ph

Guimaras
Contact Person: Elena G. Salazar, SWAD Team Leader
Email address: egsalazar@dswd.gov.ph

Disaster Response and Management Division
Email Address: drmd.fo6dswd.gov.ph
Tel No: (033) 330-7860 loc. 16006
Contact Person: Judith T. Barredo, OIC-Division Chief

Disaster Response and Rehabilitation Section
Contact person: Lisa B. Camacho
Tel No: (033) 330-7860 loc. 16006

Protective Services Division
Email Address: protective.fo6@dswd.gov.ph
Tel No: (033) 330-7860 loc. 16007
Contact Person: Lucita J. Villanuava, Division Chief

Crisis Intervention Section
Contact Person: Josilito G. Estember
Email:assistance.fo6@dswd.gov.ph
Contact: (033) 330-7860 loc 16014

Center Based Services
Contact Person: Delia V. Bagolcol, Center Coordinator (Concurrent)
Email Address: dvbagolcol.fo6@dswd.gov.ph

Regional Center for Women
Contact Person: Remelyn S. Niadas
Email Address: rcw.fo6@dswd.gov.ph

Home for Girls
Contact Person: Rhea B. Valdellon
Email Address: hfg.fo6@dswd.gov.ph
Tel. No: (033)522-8941

DSWD Region 7 Field Office
Contact Person: Shalaine Marie S. Lucero, CESO IV OIC Regional Director
Tel: (032) 8-231-2172
Website: https://fo7.dswd.gov.ph

Regional Rehabilitation Center for Youth
Contact Person: Haydee C. Canilla, SWO IV
Email Address: rrcy.fo6@dswd.gov.ph

DSWD Region 7 SWAD Satellites

Office of the Assistant Regional Director for Administration
Contact Person: Antonio R. Dolaota
Email Address: oarda.fo7@dswd.gov.ph loc. 107

Office of the Protective Service Division
Contact Person: Rosemarie Salazar
Email Address: Proserv.fo7@dswd.gov.ph
Contact: loc 116

Office of the Disaster Response Management Division
Contact Person: Lilibeth A. Cabiara
Email Address: drmd.fo7@dswd.gov.ph

SWAD Bohol
Contact Person: Jimmy Crusio
Office Address: Barangay Poblacion III, Tagbilaran City
Email Address: swad-bohol.fo7@dswd.gov.ph
Contact: (038) 501-9365, 427-1405

SWAD Cebu
Contact Person: Evain Gladys L. Manzano
Office Address: M.J Cuenco Avenue corner General Maxilom Avenue, Brgy., Carreta Cebu City
Email Address: swadcebu.fo7@dswd.gov.ph
Contact: (032)233-0261, 231-2172 loc 17147

SWAD Negros Oriental
Contact Person: Rosalina Coritico
Office Address: Solon Apartment, Brgy. Bantayan, Dumaguete City
Email Address: swad-negros.fo7@dswd.gov.ph
Contact: (034) 420-9555

SWAD Siquijor
Contact Person: John Michael Rollorata
Office Address: Brgy. Pangi Siquijor
Email Address: swad-siq.fo7@dswd.gov.ph
Contact: (035) 480-9261

DSWD Region 8 Field Office
Contact Person: Grace Q. Subong, Director IV Regional Director
Tel: (053) 321-30-90
Website: https://fo8.dswd.gov.ph

DSWD Region 8 SWAD Satellites

Department of Social Welfare and Development Field Office VIII
Office Address: DSWD Field Office VIII, Candahug, Palo, Leyte
Contact Person: Grace Q. Subong, Director IV Regional Director
Email Address: gqsubong@dswd.gov.ph
Contact: (053) 888-0330

DSWD Field Office VIII Social Welfare Office
Office Address: DSWD Field Office VIII, Candahug, Palo, Layte
Contact Person: Natividad G. Sequito, OIC-Assistant Regional
Director for Operation
Email Address: ngsequito@dswd.gov.ph
Tel.No. (053) 888-0330

OIC-Division Chief, Disaster Response Management Division
Office Address: DSWD Field Office VIII, Candahug, Palo, Leyte
Contact Person:Lucia G. Balantad, Social Welfare Officer IV
Email Address: lgbalantad@dswd.gov.ph

OIC-Division Chief, Protective Services Division
Office Address: DSWD Field Office VIII, Candahug, Palo, Leyte
Contact Person: Gina D.Ogay, Social Welfare Officer IV
Email Address: gdogsy@dswd.gov.ph
Contact: (053) 888-0330

OIC-Head, Crisis Intervention Section
Office Address: DSWD Field Office VIII, Candahug, Palo, Leyte
Contact Person:Irene A. Permejo, Social Welfare Officer II
Email Address: iapermejo@dswd.gov.ph
Tel. No: (053)321-3322

Children and Youth Sector
Office Address: DSWD Field Office VIII, Candahug, Palo, Leyte
Contact Person: Leo Nito L. Caliba, Social Welfare officer II/Focal Person
Tel No: (053)880-0330

Regional Rehabilitation Center for Youth
Office Address: DSWD Field Office VIII, Candahug, Palo, Leyte
Contact Person: Georgina M. Bulasa, Social Welfare Officer III
Email Address: rrcy.fo8@dswd.gov.ph
Tel. no.: (053)880-9005

Home for Girls
Office Address: DSWD Center and Institution, Pawing, Palo Leyte
Contact Person: Delia P. Aguirre, Social Welfare Officer III
Email Address: hfg.fo8@dswd.gov.ph
Tel No.:(053) 323-3145

SWADT Leader 1st and 2nd District Leyte

Office Address: DSWD Complex, New Building, Brgy. Cogon, Ormoc City
Contact Person: Hermanito S. Mangalao, Project Dev. Officer
Email Address: hsmangalao@dswd.gov.ph

SWADT Leader 3rd, 4rth and 5th District Leyte

Office Address: Government Center, Candahug, Palo, Leyte
Contact Person: Raquel J. Bateo, Social Welfare Officer III
Email Address: jrbateo@dswd.gov.ph

SWADT Southern Leyte

Office Address: Barangay Asuncion, Maasin City
Contact Person: Benjie P. Belen, Project Development Officer II
Email Address: bbpelen@dswd.gov.ph

SWADT Western Samar

Office Address 1st District: Brgy. San Policarpio, Calbayog City, Samar
Office Address 2nd District:Brgy. 13, San Francisco St.,
Catbalogan City Samar
Contact Person: Ma. Joyce A. Flora, Social Welfare Officer III
Email Address: mjaflora@dswd.gov.ph

SWADT Northern Samar

Office Address: 2nd. Flr. Philhealth Building, Brgy. San Jose Abad
Santos, Catarman, Northern Samar
Contact Person: Nena L. Getalado, Social Welfare Officer III
Email Address: nlgetalado@dswd.gov.ph

SWADT Eastern Samar

Office Address: 2nd Floor, Chinabank Building, Brgy. Balud, Borongan
City, Eastern Samar
Contact Person: Edizon R. Cinco, Social Welfare Officer II
Email Address: ercinco@dswd.gov.ph

SWADT Biliran
Office Address: Castin St. Barangay Santissimo Rosario, Naval, Biliran
Contact Person: Raquel J. Bateo, Social Welfare Officer III
Email Address: rjbateo@dswd.gov.ph

DSWD Region 9 Field Office
Contact Person: Riduan P. Hadjimuddin, CESO IV Concurrent
OIC Regional Director
Tel: (062) 991-10-10
Website: https://fo9.dswd.gov.ph

DSWD Region 9 SWAD Satellites

Office of the Field Director
Office Address: DSWD Field Office VIII, Candahug, Palo, Leyte
Contact Person: Atty. Sittie M. Pamaloy- Hassan,Regional Director
Email Address: srphassan@dswd.gov.ph

Regional Juvenile Justice Welfare Committee
Contact Person: Jacqueline R. Julpi, RSW, Social Welfare Officer III
Email Address: jackyrjulpi@gmail.com

Regional Council for the Welfare of Children
Contact Person: Raquel Jumig, RSW, Social Welfare Officer III
Email Address: rjumig@gmail.com

Protective Service Division
OIC-Division Chief
Contact Person: Ma. Socorro S. Macaso, MSW, Social Welfare V
Email Address: nenettemacaso@gmail.com

Crisis Intervention Section
Contact Person: Aisa T. Askalani, RSW, Social Welfare Officer IV
Email Address: sataskalani@dswd.gov.ph

Home for the Elderly
Contact Person: Fatnohalda J. Padih, RSW, Social Welfare Officer III
Email Address: fjpadih@dwsw.gov.ph

Area Vocational and Rehabilitation Center III
Contact Person: Evangeline Poquita, MSW, Social Welfare Officer V
Email Address: eapoquita@dswd.gov.ph

Home for Women
Contact Person: Evelyn Lingatong, RSW, Social Welfare Officer III
Email Address: dswdhfw123@gamil.com

Regional Rehabilitation Center for Youth
Contact Person: Eva E. Avila, RSW, Social Officer IV
Email Address: meeavila@dswd.gov.ph

Balay Dangpanan sa Kabataan
Contact Person: Rebecca P. Guillermo, RSW, Social Welfare Officer III

SWADT Isabela
Contact Person: Aisyl A. Sagoso, Social Welfare Officer II
Email Address: krjespos@dswd.gov.ph

SWADT Ipil
Contact Person: Junila O. Reganon, Social Welfare Officer II
Email Address: junilareganon@dswd.gov.ph

SWADT Pagadian
Contact Person: Edward Espenosa, RSW, Social Welfare Officer II
Email Address: eoespinosa@dswd.gov.ph

SWADT Liloy
Contact Person: Mary Ann B. Mag-abo, RSW, Social Welfare Officer II
Email Address: marbongcarasmagabo@yahoo.com

SWADT Dipolog
Contact Person: Alex Z. Sabal, Project Development Officer II
Email Address: dswdswadtdipolog@dswd.gov.ph

DSWD Region 10 Field Office
Contact Person: Ramel F. Jamen, OIC Regional Director
Tel: (088)8-858-81-34: 8-858-89-59
Website: https://fo10.dswd.gov.ph

DSWD Region 10 SWAD Satellites

DSWD Field Office 10
Office Address: Masterson Ave., Upper Carmen, Cagayan de
Oro City, Misamis Oriental
Contact Person: Ramel F. Jamen, OIC Regional Director
Email Address: fo10@dswd.gov.ph
Tel. No: (088) 565-5795
Mobile: 0926 793-9942

Protective Service Division
Contact Person: Rosemarie P. Conde, Concurrent Division Chief
Email Address: opd.dswdregion10@gmail.com

Regional Rehabilitation Center for Youth
Contact Person: Sonia E. Ipang, Center Head
Email Address: dswdrrcyfo10Gmail.com

Home for Girls
Contact Person: Armelita M. Paye, Center Head
Email Address: dswdhome4girls@gmail.com

Regional Haven for Women
Contact Person: Janet B. Ganzan, Center Head

Bahay Silungan
Contact Person: Richelle Gay A. Magatao, Center Head
Email Address: bsdswd10@gmail.com

Misamis Oriental
Office Address: Arturo Lungod Gym, Barangay 22-A, Gingoog City

Bukidnon
Office Address: National and Provincial Offices , Old Hospital, Capitol Compound, Barangay 9, Malaybalay City, Bukidnon.
Office Address: 2nd Floor Dacayana Building, Hagkol, Valencia City
Office Address: Municipal Hall, Anahawon, Maramag, Bukidnon

Lanao Del Norte
Office Address: Kwon Residence, Purok 5, Poblacion, Tubod, Lanao Del Norte
Office Address: Macapagal Avenue, Brgy. Tubod, Iligan City

Misamis Occidental
Office Address: Provincial Operations office, #295, Gov. Anselmo Bernad St., Poblacion 1, Oroquieta City, Misamis Occidental
Office Address: DSWD Building, City Engineers Compound, Barangay Aguada, Ozamis City, Misamis Occidental

Camiguin
Office Address: Plaza Corales building, B. Aranas Street, población, Mambajao, Camiguin

DSWD Region 11 Field Office
Contact Person: Vanessa B. Goc-ong, Regional Director
Tel: (082) 226-28-57
Website: https://fo11.dswd.gov.ph

DSWD Region 11 SWAD Satellites
Office Address: D. Suazo St. cor. R. Magsaysay Ave., Davao City
Email Address: fo11@dswd.gov.ph
Tel. No: (082) 227-1964/ 255-0911/224-2643/227-8764/227-1435

SWAD Davao City, Mintal
Contact Person: Analyn Romero
Office Address: 3rd District Office, Old Barangay Hall, Mintal
Davao City
Contact Number: 0917 3893975

SWAD Davao Del Sur, Digos City
Contact Person: Nida Bolilan
Office Address: Ground Floor Wilvil building corner G. Lim, 6th St.
Contact Number: 0915887008

SWAD Davao Oriental, Mati City
Contact Person: Renante Cruz
Office Address: Capitol Hills, Barangay Central, Mati City,
Davao Oriental
Contact Number: 09151333400

SWAD Davao de Oro , Nabunturan
Contact Person: Karen Kate Nunez
Office Address: Purok 14, Poblacion, Nabunturan, Davao del Oro
Contact Number: 0945 975 3102

SWAD Davao del Norte, Tagum City
Contact Person: Candelaria Tingson
Office Address: Macario P. Bermudez St. Tagum City
Contact Number: 09976300694

SWAD Davao Occidental, Malita
Contact Person: Arris Madrano
Office Address: Davao Occidental Provincial Capitol Compound, Malita
Contact Number: 0956 0322987

DSWD Region 12 Field Office
Contact Person: Restituto B. Macuto, Regional Director
Tel: (083) 8-228-2086
Website: https://fo12.dswd.gov.ph

DSWD Region 12 Crisis Intervention Section Offices

Sarangani Province & General Santos City
Office Address: Unihub Building, Pendatun Avenue, General Santos City

South Cotabato Province
Office address: Sumpay Building, Maranon Village, Brgy. Zone 3, Koronadal City

South Cotabato-Upper Valley Areas
Office Address: Zone 1 , Barangay Libertad, Surallah

Sultan Kudarat Province
Office Adress: Abe Building, Bonifacio St. Pobalcion, Tacurong City

Cotabato City
Office Address: San Isidro St. RH-10, Cotabato City

Province of Cotabato
Office Address: JMD Building, Estinal, Brgy. Sudapin, Kidapawan City

DSWD Region NCR Field Office
Contact Person: Monina Josefa H. Romualdez, Regional Director
Tel: (02) 8-733-00-10 to 14
Website: https://ncr.dswd.gov.ph
Office Address: 389 San Rafael Street corner Legara St., Sampaloc, Manila

Protective Service Division
Contact Person: Ms. Rowela F. Hizon, Officer in Charge
Tel. No: 310-1725 loc 104

Crisis Intervention Section
Contact Person: Mr. Edwin S. Morata, Officer-in-Charge/
Social Welfare Officer III
Tel. No: 735-5413, 493-7907

Lingap sa Masa
Contact Person: Ms. Krishna Mae Salazar, Officer-in-charge/
Social Welfare Officer III
Tel. No: 735-5413, 493-7907 loc 118

Office of the Regional Director
Contact Person: Vicente Gregorio B. Tomas, Regional Director
Tel: 733-00-10 to 18
Website: https://ncr.dswd.gov.ph

DSWD Region CARAGA Field Office
Contact Person: Mari-flor D. Libang, Regional Director
Tel: (085) 8-342-5619
Website: https://caraga.dswd.gov.ph

DSWD Region CARAGA SWAD Satellite

Crisis Intervention Section-DSWD Field Office Caraga
Office Address: R. Palma St. Brgy. Dagohoy, Butuan City,
Agusan del Norte
Contact Person: Ana T. Semacio, SWO III
Tel: (0950-390-7617: Mobile: 0963908-0902

Crisis Intervention Section-DSWD Field Office
Agusan Del SurDistrict 1 and 2
Office Address: St. Francis Realty Building, P-4, Brgy.
Hubag, San Francisco, ADS
Contact Person: SWAD TL Michael John B. Andohuyan, SWO II
Tel: (0950-390-7617: Mobile: 0970-900-2888

Crisis Intervention Section-DSWD Field Office Surigao Del Norte
District 1
Office Address: Governor's extension Office, Barangay 12 Dapa, SDN
District 2
Office Address: Navaro St., Brgy. Taft, Surigao City, SDN
Dinagat Islands
Office Address: P-2 Brgy.San Juan, San Jose, Province of Dinagat Islands
Contact Person: SWAD TL Arlene M. Ontua, SWO II
Mobile: 0909-482-6552

Crisis Intervention Section-DSWD Field Office Surigao Del Sur
District 1
Office Address: New Elderly Building Capitol Hills, Brgy. Telaje, Tandag
City SDS
District 2
Office Address: Old ESWM Building, P-2 Sampaguita Brgy. Poblacion,
Tagbina , SDS
Contact Person: SWAD TL Juderiz O. Neri, SWO III
Mobile: 0948-922-5984

DSWD Region CAR Field Office
Contact Person: Leo L. Quintilla, Regional Director
Tel: (074)446-5961
Website: https://car.dwwd.gov.ph

DSWD Region CAR SWAD Satellites

PAT Abra
Office Address: Torrijos St., Zone 6, Bangued, Abra
Contact Person: Carmencita L. Chaluyen, SWO II
Email Address: clchaluyen@dswd.gov.ph

PAT Apayao

Office Address: Preciouse Sarah Residence, San Isidro Sur, Luna , Apayao
Contact Person: Gretchen P. Garcia, SWO II
Email Address:swadapayao@dswd.gov.ph

PAT Benguet

Office Address: RSCC Building, Wagal, La Trinidad, Benguet
Contact Person: MAnuaela S. Ortiz, SWO II
Email Address:msortiz@dswd.gov.ph

PAT Ifugao

Office Address: 2F BAB Commercial Bldg. Yakal St. Poblacion East,
LAgawe, Ifugao
Contact Person: Imenlda N. Tuguinay, SWO II
Email Address: intuguinay@dswd.gov.ph

PAT Kalinga

Office Address: 2F Golda's House Balinag St., Purok 3 Bulanao, Tabuk City
Contact Person: Lorna C. Lumioan, SWO II
Email Address: iclumioan@dswd.gov.ph

PAT Mt. Province

Office Address: 3F Tudlong's Building, Kalonglong, Samoki, Bontoc
Contact Person: Jackielyn O. Guitangan, SWO II
Email Address: joguitangan@dswd.gov.ph

Angeles Bahay Bata Center, Domestic Violence Spiritual

The Angeles Bahay Bata Center is an institution in Central Luzon.
Address: Barangay Cuayan, Angeles City 2009, Pampanga,
Contact No: (045) 436-5955
http://www.bahaybata.org/intro.htm

Apalit Municipal Police Station

Emergency Legal Assistance Health Substance Abuse Domestic Violence
Address: Brgy. San Juan, Apalit, 2016 Pampanga
Contact No: +63 998 598 5449
https://www.facebook.com/PampangaApalit/posts/1...

Babyanne's Mansion A Home for Children Inc.

Homeless Shelters ,Domestic Violence, Youth Shelters, Childcare Education, Counseling Clothing, Meals, Health, Mental Health ,Physical Health, Legal Assistance

Address: 569 P. Cruz St. Barangay Tarcan, Baliuag, 3006 Bulacan

Contact No: (044) 619-4818

https://babyannesmansion.wordpress.com/

Bahay ni San Jose Tarlac

Homeless Shelters, Domestic Violence Youth Shelters ,Child Care, Physical Health Substance Abuse Counseling, Education, Legal

We Welcome

1. Orphaned Children

2. Abandoned and neglected Children

3. Differently Abled Children.

Address: Brgy. San Jose, Tarlac City, Philippines

Contact No: +63 915 571 7869

https://bahaynisanjosetarlac.weebly.com/index.html

Bahay ni San Jose Orphanage Nueva Ecija

Homeless Shelters , Youth Shelters Domestic Violence, Childcare, Education ,Clothing, Meals, Legal Assistance, Spiritual Health, Mental Health, Physical Health ,Substance Abuse

We Welcome:

1. Orphaned Children

2. Abandoned and neglected Children

3. Differently Abled Children.

Address: Barangay Papaya, San Antonio, Nueva Ecija

Contact No: (044) 975-0119

https://bahaynisanjosetarlac.weebly.com/index.html

Bahay Sibol Home of Hope

Childcare ,Homeless Shelters Domestic Violence ,Youth Shelters, Education, Counseling, Clothing, Health Mental, Physical Health, Legal Assistance, Meals, Spiritual Health

Address: Dulong Bayan Rd, San Jose del Monte City, Bulacan

Contact No: 0929 564 6972

https://www.facebook.com/BahaySibol

Baliwag Municipal Police Station

Emergency Legal Assistance, Health Substance Abuse ,Homeless Shelters
Domestic Violence
Address: Doña Remedios Trinidad Hwy, Pulilan, 3006 Bulacan
Contact No: (044) 766-2328; 09338765386
https://www.facebook.com/baliwag.policestation/

Bethany House Orphanage

Homeless Shelters Domestic Violence, Youth Shelters, Childcare, Legal
Assistance ,Education, Counseling, Clothing, Meals, Spiritual Health
,Mental Health, Physical Health
Address: Tabe, Guiguinto, Bulacan 3015 Guiguinto
Contact No: +63 44 306 8012
https://www.facebook.com/p/Bethany-House-Sto-Ni%C3%B1o-
Orphanage-Guiguinto-100082227954572/

Bulacan Drugs Rehabilitation Foundation, Inc.

Homeless Shelters, Domestic Violence Health Substance Abuse, Mental
Health, Physical Health, Counseling
Address: San Nicolas, Bulacan
Contact No: 0922-861-1316
https://www.facebook.com/askbdrfi/

Casa Miani Sto. Niño

Homeless Shelters, Domestic Violence Youth Shelters, Childcare,
Education, Health, Mental Health, Physical Health, Substance Abuse Legal
Assistance, Meals, Spiritual Heath
Address: Sto. Nino, Lubao 2005 Pampanga
Contact No: (045) 433-0045
http://casamianistonino.blogspot.com/p/about-us

International Children's Care (ICC)

Childcare Homeless Shelters, Domestic Violence Youth Shelters, Education, Clothing, Meals, Spiritual Health, Mental Health, Physical Health, Legal Assistance.

"To assist orphaned and abandoned Children to have a meaningful and fulfilling life.

Address: Floridablanca, Pampanga
Contact No: 0906-561-8001
http://gpsonlinetv.com/websiteicc/

King's FilAm Home, Inc.

Childcare, Homeless Shelters, Domestic Violence Youth Shelters, Education, Health, Mental Health, Physical Health ,Clothing, Meals, Spiritual Health

Address:16 Coral St. Gordon Heights, Olongapo City Philippines 2200
Contact No: +63 920 963 8413
https://www.facebook.com/KingsFilAmHome/

King's Garden Children's Home

Homeless Shelters, Domestic Violence Emergency Shelters, Overnight Shelters, Childcare, Education, Health, Mental Health, Physical Health, Clothing, Meals

Address: Palonatin Road Upper Sabatan, Orion, Bataan
Contact No: (047) 244-6025/ 0998 302 7564 / +63 919 004 9835
http://kingsgardenchildrenshome.org/

Lubao Police Station

Emergency Legal Assistance, Health Substance Abuse, Domestic Violence
Address: San Nicolas, 1st Lubao, Pampanga
Contact No: +63 998 598 5457

SOS Children's Village Bataan
Childcare, Homeless Shelters, Youth Shelters Domestic Violence, Education, Clothing, Health, Mental Health, Physical Health, Substance Abuse, Meals, Legal Assistance
Address: Golden Heights Subdivision, Brgy. Mt. View, Mariveles, Bataan, 2105, Philippines
(047) 807-0764/ +63 283738767
http://www.sosphilippines.org/

Subic Bay Children's Home
Childcare, Homeless Shelters, Youth Shelters Domestic Violence, Emergency Shelters, Counseling, Education, Clothing, Health, Mental Health, Physical Health, Substance Abuse Legal Assistance, Meals, Spiritual Health
Address: 61 PUROK 5 NEW CABALAN OLONGAPO CITY
Contact No: (049) 356-6054/ +63 998 558-9113
https://www.sbchome.org/

Ang Bahay Parola ABP
Adress:96 Alconville Subdivision,Landayan,San Pedro,Laguna
Contact no: (046)847-4102/ 09213003077
https://angbahayparola.weebly.com/contact-us.html

Chosen Children Village Foundation Inc.
Address:49 Gen. Emilio Aguinaldo Highway Lalan 2, Silang Cavite 418 Philippines
Contact No: (046) 413-5503 / 0919-999-8915
https://chosenchildrenfoundation.com/contact-us/

Dar Amanah Foundation
Address: Barangay Hoyo, Silang, Cavite Philippines
Contact No.: +63 917 870 8027
https://www.daramachildrensvillage.org/index
www.daramachild

Destiny Promise Home for Children
Address: Dolores, Taytay, Rizal 1900 Philippines
Contact No.:0912-503-3870
Website: https://destiny promise.com/

Gabay sa Landas Gala
Address: 241Brgy.San Pedro Angono, Rizal, Philippines
Contact no: (042)570-5066
Facebook Page: Gabay sa Landas Foundation Inc. | Facebook

Haven for the Elderly
Address: Camp Mateo Capinpin,Rizal
Contact no.: 0929-552-2632
Facebook Page: https://www.facebook.com/DswdHavenForTheElderly/

Lifechild Asia Foundation
Address: Brgy. Hukay Silang, Cavite Philippines
Contact No: (260)701-2423
Email Address: info@lifechild.org
Facebook Page: https://www.facebook.com/lifechildaf

Little Angels Home Inc Address: Bonifacio Drive, Silang Junction
Address: Tagaytay City, Philippines
Contact No: Sor Pauline: Cell No. +63 917 597 0637, Sor Monica: Cell No. +63 917 832 8023, Sor Gladys : Cell No. +63 905 776 8114
Email add: lahi_hrc@yahoo.com / belle_suliva77@yahoo.com
Website: https://lahif.jimdofree.com/

Madre de Amor Hospice Foundation
Address: 9957 Amethyst Street, Los Banos Subdivision
College Laguna, 4031 Philippines
Contact No: +63 (918)915-7490
Telefax: +63 (49) 536-0644
Website: Home - Madre de Amor Hospice Foundation

Mary Mother of Mercy Home For The Elderly
Address: 47 Magsaysay Rd. San Antonio, San Pedro,4023
Laguna (049)869-1529
https://calabarzon.graceslist.org/directory/listing/mary-mother-of-mercy-home-for-the-elderly

Meritxell Children's World Foundation, Inc
Address: 24 Peach St. SSS Village Barangay Concepcion Dos 1811,
Marikina City Metro Manila
Contact No: (+632) 997-1479
Website: Meritxell Children's World Foundation Inc. (meritxell children's foundation.org)
Email address: meritxellchildrenshome@gmail.com

Norfil Foundation, Inc
Address: Banay-banay 11,San Jose,4227
Contact No: +63 283723577
https://www.norfil.org/portfolio/norfil-building/

Open Heart Foundation Worldwide, Inc
Address:14 Peace Street East Fairview Subdivision, Brgy. Fairview,
Quezon City
Email add://openheartfoundation.org.ph/
Contact No: +63 (02) 3520326

RED CROSS Zambales
Address: Beside Barangay Hall of Palanginan, Iba, Philippines
Contact No: +63 998 994 7865

Municipality of Iba
Address: National Highway, Iba,2201
Contact No: (047)811-1260

VIOLENCE AGAINST WOMEN AND CHILDREN (VAWS HOTLINES)
Inter-Agency Council on Violence Against Women and Their Children
Secretariat
iacvawc@pcw.gov.ph
8735-1654 loc.123, 124
0917-867-1907
0945-455-8121

ABS-CBN FOUNDATION, INCORPORATED
Gina Lopez Building, Quezon City, Philippines
+63 234152272

BETHLEHEM HOUSE OF BREAD
Little Baguio, Brgy. Poblacion, Baliwag, Bulacan
Telephone No: (044) 766-4977
Cell Phone No:0915-4070838

CHILDREN'S BIBLE MINISTRIES PHILS, INC.
formerly PHILIPPINE CHILDREN'S BIBLE CRUSADE, (HEBRON INCORPORATED)
Address 525 Cagayan Valley Road, San Rafael, Philippines
Contact No: +63 44 816 6710

CHILDREN's HOME OF THE IMMACULATE HEART OF MARY
Address: Sta. Maria Village, Balibago, Angeles City
Contact No: (045) 322-7532

HELPING HANDS HEALING HEARTS MINISTRIES, INC.
Address: 159 Milfores Street, Amparo Heights, Camp 7, Baguio City
Contact No: 074 422 3745
website@helpinghandsministries.com

INTERNATIONAL CHILDREN'S ADVOCATE, INC.
Address: (Ninos Pag-asa Center) Zone 13, Mulawin Lane, Old Cabalan, Olongapo City
Contact No: (047) 224-1286/ +63 928 503 8349
Email address: ninospagasacenter@gmail.com

JIREH CHILDREN'S HOME, INC.
Address: Magsaysay, Castillejos, Zambales
Telephone No: (047) 623-2410
Cell Phone No: (0927) 404-2213
Email address: office@pfmonline.org

MARY IMMACULATE CHILDREN'S CENTER
Address: Lourdes Grotto, San Jose del Monte, Bulacan
Telephone No: (044) 691-0759; 691-2301 to 02
Fax No: (044) 691-4326
Email address: micc@yahoo.com

NAZARETH HOME FOR STREET CHILDREN FDN, INC.
Address: 9012 Claro Santos St., Bonga Menor, Bustos, Bulacan
Tel. #: (044) 791-2520/619-1370 Fax#: (044) 662-1460 Mobile Cel. #:
(0922) 8011964

PEOPLE'S RECOVERY EMPOWERMENT AND DEVELOPMENT
ASSISTANCE (PREDA) FOUNDATION, INC.
Address: Upper Kalaklan, 2200 Olongapo City
Telephone No: (044) 222-4964/222- 5373/223-9628, (047) 223-9629 to
30 Fax No: (044) 222-96-28
Cell Phone No: 0917-5324453/0917-7932274
Email address: predair@info.com.ph

REHOBOTH CHILDREN'S HOME INC.
Address: 43 Barangay Sta. Maria, Camiling, Tarlac
Telephone No. (045) 609 4967
Cellphone No: (0999) 6860468
e-mail address: reho2009_phil@yahoo.com

STA. MARINA OMURA HOME, INC.
Address: Purok III, Pantok Manggahan, Sta. Arcadia, Cabanatuan, Nueva
Ecija PO Box 175, San Juan Accfa, Cabanatuan City,
Cell Phone No. 0950-136-6560

TAHANAN MAPAGKALINGA NI MADRE RITA, INC.

Address: Topaz St., Rosaryville subd., Phase II, Barangay Sta Cruz,
Guiginto, Bulacan
Telefax: (044) 794-33-30
NCR Office: La Consolacion Convent, 273 Santolan Road, San Juan
Tel. #: 725-2727
Fax #: 721-5445

CHILD'S FAITH FOUNDATION, INC.

Address: B12, Lot. 33 Graceville Subd., Barangay Muzon, SJDM Bulacan
Cell Phone No: (0916) 738-0814

EDUCATIONAL RESEARCH AND DEVELOPMENT ASSISTANCE (ERDA) FOUNDATION, INC.

Address: 66 Linao St. Sta Mesa Heights, Quezon City
Cell Phone No: 09287324327

MOTHER IGNACIA NATIONAL SOCIAL APOSTOLATE CENTER, INC.

Address: 214 N. Domingo St. barangay Kaunlaran , Quezon City,
Philippines
Cell No: (0919) 840-5154

NORWEGIAN MISSIONARY ALLIANCE CENTER PLARIDEL

Address: 169 Ignacio St., Sta. Ines, Plaridel, Bulacan
Telephone No: (044) 795-0381
Norma Center Pulilan - Dampol 2nd, Pulilan, Bulacan
Telephone No: (044) 676-0071

BAHAY PANGARAP WOMEN'S CENTER FOUNDATION, INC.

Address: 649 Mercado St., Tabe, Guiguinto, Bulacan
Telephone No: (044) 690-4376

AWECA FOUNDATION, INCORPORATED

Address: Unit "S", S & L Bldg., Essel Park, Telabastagan, San Fernando,
2000 Pampanga
Telephone No: (045) 888-6715
Email Address: info@awecafoundation.org.ph

SAN LORENZO RUIZ CHARITY (SJDMC), INC.

Address: Phase 1, Pleasant Hills Subdivision, City of San Jose del Monte, Bulacan

Tel. No. (044)769-0568

Email address: sircharity@yahoo.com

SOCIAL ACTION CENTER OF PAMPANGA (SACOP)

Address: (formerly: Grassroots Organization Volunteers, Inc.) Government Center, Maimpis, San Fernando, 2000 Pampanga

Phone: +63 45 455-3790, 455-4049, 455-3740

Fax: 045 649 6136 loc 107

Email Address: sacpampanga@yahoo.com

Website: www.sacop.org.ph

SOCIAL ACTION CENTER OF ZAMBALES, INC.

Address: #5 12th St. cor. Galagher, East Tapinac, Olongapo City, Zambales

Telephone No: (047) 222-2050/ +6347 232 9174

Email address: saczambales@yahoo.com

ANG ARKO NG PILIPINAS, INC.

Address: 116 Camia St., Bayanihan Village, Cainta Rizal

Mobile: +63 918 371 7592

Email address: arko_phil@yahoo.com/larchepunla@yahoo.com.ph

ASIAN HOPE MISSIONARY OUTREACH OF THE PHIL.,

INC. "Rehoboth Children's Home"

Address: Masalat Rd., Barangay Sampaloc, Tanay, Rizal

Telefax No: 401-4493

Mobile: 0975119 0810

Email Address: Ailyn@rsm.com.ph

ASIAN STUDENT CHRISTIAN FOUNDATION, INC.

Address: Office: #24 Pariñas St., Project 8, Quezon City

Telephone No: 275024124

Fax No: 926-45-72

Facility: Kasiglahan Village, Brgy. San Jose, Rodriguez, Rizal

Email address: mango@ascf.ph/ascsmango@yahoo.com

BEACON OF HOPE FOUNDATION-PI, INC.

Address: Barangay Sapa, Naic, Cavite
Telephone No: (046) 686-3710
Cellphone No: 0919-5419989
Email address: beacon.of.hope.orphanage@gmail.com

CASA DEI BAMBINI SAN GUISEPPE, INC.
(ST. JOSEPH CHILDREN'S HOME)

Address:181 Aguinaldo Highway, Lalaan 1, Silang, Cavite
Telephone No: (046) 411-0784
Fax No: (046) 414-1229
Cellphone No: 09171068542
Email address: cdbsilang@gmail.com

CHRISTIAN MISSION SERVICE PHILIPPINES, INC.

Address: Brgy. Calabcob, San Roque, Naic, Cavite
Telephone No: (046) 856-0237

COTTOLENGO FILIPINO BAHAY PARA SA MAY KAPANSANAN - BLESSED LUIGI ORIONE

Address: Gloria Vista Subdivision, San Rafael, Rodriquez, Rizal
Telephone No: 942-3013/14
Email address: cottolengofdp@yahoo.com.ph

FELICISIMO-AURORA BAHAY KALINGA, INC (formerly PHILIPPINE INTERNATIONAL GOLDEN HARVEST FOUNDATION, INCORPORATED)

Address: Sitio Ulahan, Barangay Santiago, Baras, Rizal
Mailing Address: c/o Edgar R. Santiago 506 Marinez St. Morong Rizal
Tel No. 02 870 7028
Cellphone No: 0917-8126210

FAITH, HOPE AND LOVE KIDS RANCH, INC.

Address: Sitio Marilag, Brgy. Montecillo, Sariaya, Quezon
Cellphone No: 0920-2449832/0919-8058793

GRACE CHRISTIAN MISSION, INC.
Address: Sitio Old Boso-Boso, Barangay San Jose, Antipolo City
Telephone No: +63 273427249
Cellphone No: 0920-6914736

GRANADA EDUCATIONAL FOUNDATION, INC. - BAHAY SAN RAFAEL HOME FOR SPECIAL CHIL- DREN
Address: San Ricardo Pampuri Center, 026 Barangay Salaban,
Amadeo, Cavite
Telephone No: (046) 413-1737/483-
Email address: juandedios4410@yahoo.com

HELP INTERNATIONAL, CHRISTIAN MISSIONARY COMMUNITY INCORPORATED
Address: 495 New York St., Brookside Hills subd., Cainta, Rizal
Telephone No. +63 (0) 2 7 52 72 35
Email address: citymission@helpphilippines.org/ helpkids@skyinet.net

INTERNATIONAL MINISTRIES, INC. (The Little Children's Home)
Address: No. 06 Liwayway St., Blooming Hills Subdivision, Kaytikling,
Taytay, Rizal
Telephone No: 658-4706/ 658-4503/413- 8053
Email address: deborahannegustafson@gmail.com

HOPE WORLDWIDE PHILIPPINES, INCORPORATED
Address: Coastal Road, Brgy. Dela Paz, Biñan, Laguna
(+63)949.359.7176
aimee.gonzaga@hopewwph.org

JARDIN DE MARIA (SOMASCAN MISSIONARY SISTERS) FOUNDATION, INC.
Address: Mater Orphanorum Ph 5 Bahayang Pag-asa Subd., Molino V,
Bacoor, Cavite
Telephone no.: (046) 477-0090
Fax no.: (046) 872-0990

LITTLE ANGELS HOMES, INCORPORATED
Address: Bonifacio Drive, Silang Junction, North Tagaytay City
Telephone No: (046) 413-8058
Cellphone no.: 0920-8636028/0916-4777649 / +63 908 887 9956

LOVE 146, INCORPORATED
Address: Sampalok St., corner Ilang-ilang St. Sitio Sampalukan Barangay.
Masaya, Bay, Laguna
Telephone No.: 309-8271

MAMA'S HOPE HAVEN OF NORWAY, INC.
Address: 25 D. Manalo Rd Pag-asa St. General Trias Cavite
PO Box 31359, Imus Post Office, Imus, Cavite
Telephone No.: (046) 4312681
Telefax No.: (046) 434-0784
Cellphone No.: (0918) 869-8117
mamashopehavenofnorway@yahoo.com.ph

MINISTRIES WITHOUT BORDERS PHILIPPINES, INC.
Address: Arnaldo Highway, Purok 5, Barangay Santiago,
General Trias, Cavite
Cellphone No: (0916) 213-1726
Email Address: mwbpi@yahoo.com

MISSION TO THE WORLD PHILIPPINES FOUNDATION, INC.
(Ang Bahay Parola Street Children Center)
Address: Zavalla Compound, Tatlong Hari St., Market Area,
Santa Rosa, Philippines
Cellphone no.: +63 917 129 6878

MOTHER CATERINA RONCALLI SHELTER HOME, INC.
Address:214 Banay-banay, Amadeo, Cavite
Telephone No: (046) 506-3422
Cellphone no.: 0917-8942886/ 0917- 5063422/ +63 927 003 8627

MOTHER TERESA SPINELLI'S TREASURE

Address: Cabangaan Road, Barangay Iruhin West, Tagaytay City
Telephone No.: (046) 483-3945/413-9216
Fax No.: (046) 483-3946
Cellphone No: 0921-5538484
Email address: scarmenborg@yahoo.com

NEW FAITH FAMILY CHILDREN'S FOUNDATION, INC.

Address: Lot 3 B2 #35 Sitio Dilain, Valleygolf Rd., Barangay San Juan,
Cainta, Rizal
Cellphone no: +63 947 432 2340

OBLATE SISTERS OF THE MOST HOLY REDEEMER,
INCORPORATED – ST. MARY'SHOUSE

Address: Barangay San Jose, National Road, Tagaytay City
Telephone No: (046) 413-1284

SAINT ANTHONY BOY'S VILLAGE FOUNDATION, INC.

Address: Km 52 Aguinaldo Highway, Barangay Lalaan, Silang Cavite
Telephone No: (046) 414-1015/ 046 414 2039

SENDEN HOME FDN, INC. - RESIDENTIAL CARE AND
TRAINING CENTER

Address:354 Quarry Road, Pantok Binangonan, Rizal
Telephone No: 563-7271
Mobile: +63 286522861
Fax No: 562-8886
Email address: senden@tri-isys.com

SR. MARIA BERTILLA VANGELISTA HOME FOR CHILDREN

Address: Barangay San Sebastian, Mataas na Kahoy, Batangas
Telephone No: (043) 703-2127 / 774-5039 / 043 757 2382

SOUTHEAST ASIA MEDICAL AND RELIEF INSTITUTE FOR TRAINING ASIAN, NON -GOVERNMENT SERVICES, INC. (SAMARITANS, INC.)

Address: Lot 19-22 Blk 224 Metrogate Silang Estate, Silang Cavite 4118
Telephone No: 806-8716
Cellphone No: 0917-8420626/0917-8588949
Email address: samaritansplace_27@yahoo.com

THE LAMB'S HOME CHRISTIAN FOUNDATION INC.

Address: P.O. Box 2030 Don Enrique Rd. 1870 Antipolo City Sitio Old
Boso-boso, Barangay San Jose, Antipolo, Rizal
Telephone No: 393-8345
Cellphone No: 0917 851 4598

THE REDEEMER'S HOME FOUNDATION, INC.

Address: No. 441 Emerald Lane Street, Cristimar Village, Barangay San
Roque, Antipolo City
Telephone no: (632) 697-0960
Email address: redeemershome1997@yahoo.com

BATONG SANDIGAN DEVELOPMENT FOUNDATION, INC.

Address: Blk. 74 Lot 6, Phase 2, Paliparan 3, Dasmariñas, Cavite
Telephone No: (046) 506-2559
Celphone no: +63 948 212 0668

CHILDREN'S HELPER PROJECT INC.

Address: M. Santos St., Sta. Cruz, Cavite
Telephone No: (046) 431-3038
Email address: chp_cavite@yahoo.com

CHRISTIAN ACTION FOR RECONCILIATION AND EVANGELISM (C.A.R.E.) PHILIPPINES

Address: Sitio Tanza II, Barangay San Jose, Antipolo City
Telephone No: 02) 8297-4224
Cellphone no: 09082424172
Email address: mabuhayfilipinos@gmail.com

LIPA ARCHDIOCESAN SOCIAL ACTION COMMISSION, (LASAC) INCORPORATED

Address: LAFORCE Building, JP Laurel Hi-way, Marawoy, Lipa City, Philippines
Telefax No: +63 43 757 6182
Email address:nfo@lasaclipa.org

NORWEGIAN MISSIONARY ALLIANCE – CENTER DASMARIÑAS

Address: Private Lot Barangay Fatima 1 DDBK, Cavite
Telephone No: (046) 416-2067

OPEN HEART FOUNDATION WORLDWIDE INCORPORATED

Address: Lot L. Unit 3, 2nd floor, Pasao de Carmona, Barangay Maduya, Carmona, Cavite
Telefax no: (046) 414 9742
Email address: opnheart@info.com.ph

PANGARAP FOUNDATION

Block 47 Phase 2, Site Paliparan, Dasmariñas, Cavite
Telephone No: (046) 506-0727
Email address: pangarapfoundation@yahoo.com

SISTERS OF ST. PAUL OF CHARTES (SPC) VIGIL HOUSE, INC.

Address: 22 Km. Manaila East Road Barangay Dolores, Taytay, Rizal
Telephone No.02- 660-9736
Cellphone No: 0926-6730024

VISAYAN FORUM FOUNDATION, INC.
BAHAY SILUNGAN SA DAUNGAN

Address: Port of Matnog, National Highway, Matnog
Telephone No:(056) 198-4931

ADVENTIST DEVELOPMENT AND RELIEFAGENCY (ADRA)

Address: J. P. Rizal, Barangay Sabutan, Silang Cavite ,
P.O. Box 254118 Silang, Cavite
Telephone No: (046) 414-2464/414-0146
Fax No: (049) 414-1492

ADVENTIST DEVELOPMENT AND RELIEF AGENCY (ADRA) FOUNDATION
Address: South-Central Luzon Conference of SDA 24 San Rafael, 4000 San Pablo City, Laguna
Telephone No: (049) 562-0803
Telefax No: (049) 800-0966

SACRED HEART COLLEGE (Hermana Fausta Development Center)
Address: Enriquez Street corner Guinto St., Lucena
Telephone No: (042) 710-6826

REGION 6 (WESTERN VISAYAS)

Bacolod Rescue Emergency Group and Communication

Bacolod Disaster Risk and Reduction Office (DRRMO)
Telephone No: (034) 432-3879
Mobile:0930 243 4706

Bacolod Emergency 911 Hotline
Telephone No: (034) 432-3871 to 73

Red Cross – Bacolod Chapter
Telephone No. (034) 434-8541

VICTORIAS CITY RESCUE OFFICE
Telephone No: 09216224397 / 09155210316

VICTORIAS Philippine National Police
Telephone No: 09985987454 / 09399647454

EB Magalona Disaster Risk and Reduction Office (DRRMO)
Telephone No: 09491231923 / 09278833731

Silay City Disaster Risk and Reduction Office (DRRMO)
Telephone No: 0918-489-6175

Talisay City Disaster Risk and Reduction Office (DRRMO)
Telephone No: 0917 811-4078 / 0969-453-6321

Bacolod City Police Office
Telephone No: (034) 432-1865

Negros Rescue Federation
Telephone No: (034) 433-6563 / 435-0636

Bacolod Women and Children Protection
Telephone No: (034) 434-8659

Guimaras Police Provincial Office
Telephone No: +63 998 598 6180

Buanavista MDDRMO
Cellphone No: 0917-501-0085 /0946-407-2714

Jordan Guimaras, MDRRMO
Cellphone No: +63 923 415 1503

Nueva Valencia MDRRMO
Cellphone No: 0963 298 9914

San Lorenzo MDRRMO
Cellphone No: +63 950 423 5772

ILOILO(REGIONAL CENTER)
OCD/RDRRMC: (033)333-2333
PDRRMC: (033)330-7860

DDSWD Iloilo
Telephone No: (033) 330-7860
Cellphone No: +639395751814

Negros Occidental City Hall Department of Social Welfare and Development
Address: PAC Compound, Gatuslao St. Bacolod 6100 Negros Occidental
Cellphone No: 0939-453-3499

Provincial Social Welfare and Development Office-Negros Occidental
Telephone No: (034)454-3077
Email Address: pswdoneg2020@gmail.com

DSWD DIRECTORY OF OFFICIALS: PHILIPPINES

DSWD (Office of the Regional Director)
Telephone No: (033)330-7860 loc.no.16001
Email address: fo6@dswd.gov.ph

REGION 7 (CENTRAL VISAYAS)

DSWD (FIELD OFFICE 7(DSWD FO7)
Address: M.J. Cuenco Avenue Corner General Maxilom Avenue Barangay Carreta Cebu City,6000
Telephone No: (032)233-8785/ (032)412 9908

Dangpanan (KADASIG COMMUNITY CENTER)
Address: Katipunan St. Tisa, Labangon Cebu
Telephone No: (032)253-4867/ (032) 2731473

KALIHUKAN SA KALUOY, INC
Address: Spring Village, Lot 12-C Zone 6, Sitio Riverside Dumlog Talisay City Cebu
Telephone No: (032) 236-0035

Policy and Plans Division-DSWD Central Visayas
Address: DSWD FIELD OFFICE M.J Cuenco, Avenue, Corner General Maxilum Ave. Ext. Cebu City, 6000 Cebu
Telephone No: (032)261-8107

Institutional Development Dinska - DSWD CENTRAL VISAYAS
Address: DSWD Field Office, MJ. Cuenco Avenue, Corner General Maxilom Ave Ext. Cebu City, 6000 Cebu
Telephone No: (032) 232 1192

DSWD LAPU-LAPU
Address: 8x88+J77, Lapu-lapu City, Cebu
Cellphone No: 0927 644 724

DSWD-HOME FOR GIRLS AND WOMEN
Address: Labangon Bliss, Cebu City
Telephone No: (032) 2660491

National Center for Mental Health (NCMH)
Crisis Hotline: 1553, 0917-899-8727,(02), 7-989-8727

Philippines Mental Health Association
(CEBU CHAPTER VISAYAS REGION 7)
Address: 3rd floor VR Apartments, Sikatuna St.
Cellphone No: 0917-655-0023
Email address: http//www.pmha.org.ph

DSWD REGION VII CENTRAL VISAYAS

Department of Social Welfare and Development (DSWD)
Location 1: 206 Miguel Parras St. Tagbilaran City, 6300 Bohol
Telephone No: (038) 4114991
Location 2: 2nd Floor Old Capitol Building, Pres. Carlos P. Garcia Avenue, Bohol
Telephone No: (038)501-8014
Location 3: CSDWD Building, Calceta Street, Tagbilaran City, 6300 Bohol
Telephone No: (038) 4114991

Provincial Social Welfare and Development Office
Address: 16 Tamblot Circumferential Road Tagbilaran City, 6300 Bohol, Philippines
Phone No:(038) 501 8014

Bohol Sunshine Home Foundation Inc.
Address: Cabauan District, Tagbilaran, Bohol
Telephone No: (038) 500-1028

City Social Welfare and Development Office
City Government of Dumaguete
Address: Rizal Boulevard, Dumaguete, Negros Oriental
Telephone No: (035) 225-0637

Provincial Office-Siquijor-Provincial Director (Director 111)
Address: Caipilan, Siquijor City, 6225
Telephone No: (035) 377-2304

City Social Welfare and Development Office-
City Government of Dumaguete
Address: Rizal Boulevard, Dumaguete, Negros Oriental
Telephone No: (035) 422-8117

SWAD Negros Oriental Office
Address: 40 Hibbard Ave, Dumaguete, 6200 Negros Oriental
Telephone No: (035)420-9555

DSWD VALENCIA
Address: Jose Peping Romero Dr. Valencia, Negros Oriental
Telephone No: (035) 423-8453

CSWD Department of Social Welfare and Development
Child Protection Unit
Address: 8836+Q7H, Dumaguete, Negros Oriental

Dumaguete City Hall
Address: Colon St. Dumaguete, 6200 Negros Oriental
Telephone No: (035) 255-3775

Department of the Interior and Local Government
Address: Kagawasan Avenue, Lunsod ng Dumaguete 6200
Lalawigan ng Negros Oriental
Telephone No: (035) 225-4441

Philippine Red Gross-Negros Oriental Chapter
Address: Surban St. Dumaguete Negros Oriental, Dumaguete,
Negros Oriental
Telephone No: (035)522-2815

City Social Welfare and Development Office Bayawan
Address: Bollos Street, Bayawan City, 6221 Negros Oriental
Telephone No: (035) 531-0018

Department of Labor and Development Negros Oriental Field Office
Address: Claytown, St. Therese of the Child Jesus St. Dumaguete,
Negros Oriental
Telephone No: (035) 422-9741

Negros Oriental Provincial Capitol
Address: Kagawasan Avenue, Lunsod ng Dumaguete,
Lalawigan ng Negros Oriental
Telephone No: (035) 225-1111

Philippine Red Cross
Address: Bishop Epifanio Surban St. Dumaguete Negros Oriental
Telephone No. +63 35 228 2835

Institutional Development Division-DSWD Central Visayas
Address: DSWD Field Office, M. J. Cuenco Avenue, Corner
General Maxilom Ave. Ext. Cebu City,
Telephone No: (032) 232-1192

Office of Assistant Regional Director for Administration-DSWD CENTRAL VISAYAS
Address: DSWD Field Office, M.J.Cuenco Avenue, Corner Gen. Maxilom Avenue Extension, Barangay Carreta,Cebu City
Telephone No: (032) 233-8785

Department Of Social Welfare and Development Regional Rehabilitation for Youth -Cebu
Address: Candabong, Argao, 6021
Telephone No: (032) 485-8524

Department of Social Welfare and Development Pinamungahan Cebu
Address: 7HCM+4P4, Pinamungahan, Cebu
Telephone No: 4689153

Department Of Social Welfare and Development
Address: Oslob Municipal Hall, Natalio Bacalso Avenue, Oslob, 6025
Telephone No: (032) 481-9054

DISASTER RESPONSE AND MANAGEMENT DIVISION
Telephone No: (033) 330-7860
Email address: drmd.fo6.dswd.gov.ph

HOME FOR GIRLS
Telephone No: (033) 522-8941
Email address: hfg.fo6@dswd.gov.ph

REGION 8 EASTERN VISAYAS

DSWD Tacloban
Address: Magsaysay Blvd, Downtown, Tacloban City
Telephone No: (053) 321 2040

DSWD Field Office Region

Address: Magsaysay Blvd, Downtown, Tacloban City, Leyte
Telephone No: (053) 321-2040

HOME FOR GIRLS-DSWD FIELD OFFICE V111

Address: DSWD, Magsaysay Boulevard, Downtown, Tacloban City,
6500 Leyte, Philippines
Telephone No: +63-53-233-3145

ILOCOS REGION

Helping Hands, Healing Heart Ministries Phillippines, Inc.

Address: Amparo Camp Heights 7 Baguio City, 2600 Philippines
Telephone No: (078) 927-5631
Email Address: http://helpinghandministries.com

Home of Peace and Immaculate Heart of Mary

Address: Judge Jose de Venecia Extension, Lucao District,
Dagupan City, 2400 Philippines
Telephone No: (075)522-1904
Facebook Page: https//www.face- book.com/The-Immaculate-Heart-O

Kalinga ng Ama Shelter for Children, Inc.

Address: Beverly Hills, Bonuan Gueset Dagupan City, 2400 Philippines
Telephone No: (075) 518-3465
Email address: https://www.facebook.com/Kalingashelter/

LAMA Ministries

Address: Baragay Pugo, Bauang San Fernando City La Union
Telephone No: (072) 705-1045
Website: https://www.lamaministries.org/

Safe Harbor International Philippines S.H.I.P
Address: 23 Dahlia Street, Polo Field, Navy Base, Baguio
Telephone No: (078)909-9400
Facebook Page: https://www.facebook.com/S.H.I.P Foundation

Sefton Village Children's Home, Inc.
Address: National Highway, Sefton Village, Divisoria Santiago
City, 311 Isabela
Telephone No: (078) 682-3785
Facebook Page: https//www.facebook.com/SeftonVillage

**Biliran-Naval City Department of Social Welfare and Development
RO8 Biliran Field Office**
Located in: Biliran, Provincial Hospital Address: Castin, Naval
Telephone No: 0956-887-0207

**Violence Against Women of Children (VAWC) Department of
Social Welfare and Development**
Hotlines: (02) 8931-8101 to 07

Department of Social Welfare and Development NCR
Address: Ugnayan, Pag-asa, Crisis Intervention Center
Hotlines:
(02)8734-8639
(02)8734-8654
(02)8734-8626 to 27

NBI VIOLENCE AGAINST WOMEN and CHILDREN - DESK (VAWCD)
Hotlines:
(02) 8523-8231 to 38
(02)8525-6028

Philippine Commission on Women (PCW)
Fax number: (02)8736-5249
(02)8736-7712
(02)8736-4449

National Center for Mental Health (NCMH)
Crisis hotlines: Trunkline;
0917-899-USAP (8727)
989-USAP (8727)
(02)8523-9001 to 10 local 201

Department of Social Welfare and Development
Text Hotline: (+63) 918-912-2813
Trunkline: (+632) 931-81-01
Disaster Response Unit: (+632) 856-3665, 852-8081

MINDANAO REGION

REGION 9 (Zamboanga Peninsula Zamboanga del Norte-Dipolog City)

Department of Social Welfare and Development -Home for girls, Dipolog
Adress: Balay Dangpanan para sa Kabataan, Sta. Isabel Dipolog City
Telephone No: (065) 212-6265

City Social Welfare and Development Office
Address: Zamboanga del Norte, Provincial Capital, Dipolog City, 7100 Philippines
Telephone No: (065) 212-4566

Department of Social Welfare and Development Office
Address: Zamboanga del Norte, Provincial Capital, Dipolog City, 7100 Philippines
Telephone No: (065) 212-4566

Department of Social Welfare and Development REGION IX
Telephone No: (062) 991-6030
Email address: f09@dswd.gov.ph
Website: Q-http;//www.f09.dswd.gov.ph

Department of Social Welfare and Development Iligan Palao
Address: 66JX+VPQ, Iligan City, Lanao Del Norte
Telephone No: (063)222-0578

Municipal Social Welfare and Development Office Sibutad, ZDN
Address: Sibutad, Zamboanga Del Norte
Telephone No: 0906-875-0339

Lanao del Norte Provincial Capital
Address: Linamen-Zamboanga Road, Tubod, Lanao Del Norte
Telephone No: (063) 341-5174

REGION 10

MISAMIS ORIENTAL-CAGAYAN DE ORO CITY

**Department of Social Welfare and Development (DSWD)-
Reception and Study Center For Children (CDO)**
Address: Macanhan, Carmen Cagayan De Oro, 9 000 Misamis Oriental
Telephone No: (08822) 728429

**Department Of Social Welfare and Development
(FIELD OFFICE CARAGA)**
Address: 8600 R. Palma St. Butuan City 8600 Agusan Del Norte
Telephone No: (085) 303-8620
hotline.focrg@dswd.gov.ph

**Misamis Occidental - Oroquieta City Department of Interior
Labor and Government**
Address: Provincial Engineering Office, Capitol Compound, Capitol Dr.
Oroquieta City, 7207 Misamis Occidental
Telephone No: (088) 531-1007

WOMEN'S MULTI-PURPOSE COOPERATIVE
Address: Department Of Social Services of Development
(Department of Social Welfare and Development, Ozamis City,
7200 Misamis Occidental)
Cellphone No: 0907-840-9010

Department of Social Welfare and Development Carmen, Cagayan
Address: Masterson Avenue, Upper Carmen, Cagayan de
Oro City, 9000 Philippines
Telephone No: (088) 858-8134

REGION 11(DAVAO REGION)

Department of Social Welfare and Development Field Office XI
Address: 36 D Suazo St. Población District, Davao City, Davao Del Sur
Telephone No:(082) 227 1964

Home for the Girls and Women Department of Social Welfare and Development
Address: Jail Rd. Talomo, Davao City, 8000 Davao Del Sur
Telephone No: (082) 244-0576

Department of Social Welfare and Development Municipal Operation
Address: Zone3, Habitat Building, Barangay, Santa Cruz,
Davao City, 8000 Davao Del Sur
Telephone No: (082) 272-1187

Department of Social Welfare and Development XI Reception and Study Center for Children (RSCC)
Address: SPMC Compound Bajada, Friendship St. Bajada
Davao City, Davao Del Sur
Telephone No: (082) 221-2873

City Social Welfare and Development Office
Address: Pichan St. Poblacion District, Davao City, 8000 Davao Del Sur
Telephone No: (082) 225-0417

Provincial Social Welfare and Development Office-
Provincial Government of Davao Del Norte
Address: Provincial Capital, Davao Del Norte, Capitol Road,
Tagum 818 Davao Del Norte
Telephone No: (084) 217-3810

Tagum Home For the Aged
Address: CQPX+V59, Tagum, Davao del Norte
Telephone No: (084)216-0738

ABOUT THE AUTHOR

April Key is the brave, courageous, silent yet attentive little girl who now became the woman that she trained to become.

She holds a Bachelor's degree in Hospitality and Tourism. She keeps a blog, Rodes On The Road and The Keys Journey to Life.

April was awarded an Honoris Causa 'Doctor of Literature' by Gawad Ophir IV for Literature and the Arts. Along with this, she was also recognized as the 'Most Outstanding Writer of the Philippines, Asia, and the Pacific', following by her International Certifications for 'Peace Education', 'Research', 'Educational Strategies and Approaches', 'Leadership', and 'Literature, Language, and Linguistics'. She's also a John Maxwell certified speaker and is working with her Informed Trauma Coach certification. In order for her to be able to help other family and especially young children.

April had a strong faith in God since she was very young, and she continues to witness God's miracles in her life to this day.

GLOSSARY

Ate - a Filipino term for big sister

Kuya - a Filipino term for big brother

Tita - a Filipino term for an aunt

Tito - a Filipino term for an uncle

Mama/Nanay - a Filipino term for mother

Papa/Tatay - a Filipino term for father

Lolo - a Filipino term for grandpa

Lola - a Filipino term for grandma

Inday - a Visayan term, refers to female family members. Some use it as a nickname for people who are dear to them

Dodong - the male counterpart of Inday

Maldita - a woman with an attitude, or is mean, a snob, aloof, cruel, sharp-tongued, rude, bitchy, or self-centered; sometimes it is used to refer to a person who is also good but will fight back if needed

Maldito - is the male form of maldita

Barangay Captain - also known as the Barangay Chairman, he or she is the highest elected official in the Barangay or the smallest administrative unit in the Philippines.

Barangay - the smallest administrative unit in the Philippines; it is the Filipino term for a village, district or ward

Flores De Mayo - Flores, from the Spanish flores or flowers, also known as Flowers of May, Flores de Maria (Flowers of Mary), or alay (offering); it may refer to the whole Flower Festival celebrated in May in honor of the Virgin Mary

Bahay Kubo/Nipa Hut - The bahay kubo or nipa hut is a type of stilt house indigenous to the cultures of the Philippines; it is also known as payag or kamalig in other languages of the Philippines; it also often serves as an icon of Philippine culture

Sari-Sari Store - a portion of one's residential property that is used for selling dry goods and/or groceries

Carinderia - started in the early 1800s, it refers to a food stall with a small seating area where patrons can order food that is cooked and displayed in the same place and sold at an affordable price

Puto Balanghoy - grated cassava roots

Dalunggan - an ear-shaped Filipino cookie with a dark pink line spiralling around it

Bahug-Bahug - a sweet, creamy Filipino bread pudding

Ice Candy - a Filipino term for a kind of cold refreshment that's put inside a plastic and frozen; the most common form is frozen juices or fruit shakes; similar to a popsicle, it is sometimes available in sari-sari stores

INDEX